A Daybook for October

In Yellow Springs, Ohio

A Memoir in Nature

**and a Handbook for the Month of October,
Being a Personal Narrative and Synthesis of
Common Events in Nature
between 1981 and 2023
in Southwestern Ohio, with Applications
for the Lower Midwest and Middle Atlantic
Region, Containing Weather Guidelines
and a Variety of Natural Calendars,
Reflections by the Author
and Seasonal Quotations
from Ancient and Modern Writers**

By

Bill Felker

A Daybook for the Year in Yellow Springs, Ohio
Volume 10: October

Cover Image from a Watercolor by Libby Rudolf

Copyright 2023 by Bill Felker

Published by The Green Thrush Press
P.O. Box 431, Yellow Springs, Ohio

Printed in the United States of America
Charleston, SC

ISBN-13:978-1722765408
ISBN-10:1722765402

For Rachel, Josh, Julian and Lewis

For Rachel, Josh, Julian and Lewis

No one suspects the days to be gods.

Ralph Waldo Emerson

Introduction

Here are no stories told you of what is to be seen at the other end of the world, but of things at home, in your own Native Countrey, at your own doors, easily examinable with little travel, less cost, and very little hazard. This book doth not shew you a Telescope, but a Mirror, it goes not about to put a delightful cheat upon you, with objects at a great distance, but shews you yourselves.

Joshua Childrey, 1660

The Daybook Format

The format of my notes in this daybook owes more than a little to the almanacs I wrote for the *Yellow Springs News* between 1984 and 2017. The quotations, daily statistics, the weather outlooks, the seasonal calendar, and the daybook journal were and still are part of my regular routine of collecting and organizing impressions about the place in which I live.

Setting: The principal habitat described here is that of Glen Helen, a preserve of woods and glades that lies on the eastern border of the village of Yellow Springs in southwestern Ohio. At its northern edge, the Glen joins with John Bryan State Park to form a corridor about ten miles long, and half a mile wide, along the Little Miami River. The north section of the Glen Helen /John Bryan complex is hilly and heavily wooded, and is the best location for spring wildflowers. The southern portion, "South Glen" as it is usually called, is a combination of open fields, wetlands, and wooded flatlands. Here I found many flowers and grasses of summer and fall. Together, the two Glens and John Bryan Park provide a remarkable cross section of the fauna and flora of the eastern United States.

Other habitats in the daybook journal include my yard with its several small gardens; the village of Yellow Springs itself, a town of 4,000 at the far eastern border of the Dayton suburbs; the Caesar Creek Reservoir, twenty miles south of Yellow Springs and created by the Corps of Engineers in 1976. My trips away from that environment were principally northeast to Chicago, Madison, Wisconsin and northern Minnesota, east to Washington and New York, southeast to the Carolinas and Florida, southwest to

Arkansas, Louisiana, and Texas, and occasionally through the Southwest to California and the Northwest, two excursions to Belize in Central America, several to Italy.

Quotations: The passages from ancient and modern writers (and sometimes from my alter egos) which accompany each day's notations are lessons from my readings, as well as from distant seminary and university training, here put to work in service of the reconstruction of my sense of time and space. They are a collection of reminders, hopes, and promises for me that I find implicit in the seasons. They have also become a kind of a cosmological scrapbook for me, as well as the philosophical underpinning of this narrative.

Astronomical Data: The *Daybook* includes approximate dates for astronomical events, such as star positions, meteor showers, solstice, equinox, perihelion (the Sun's position closest to earth), and aphelion (the Sun's position farthest from Earth).

I have included the sunrise and sunset for Yellow Springs as a general guide to the progression of the year in this location, but those statistics also reflect trends that are world wide, if more rapid in some places and slower in others.

Even though the day's length is almost never exactly the same from one town to the next, a minute gained or lost in Yellow Springs is often a minute lost or gained elsewhere, and the Yellow Springs numbers can be used as a simple way of watching the lengthening or shortening of the days, and, therefore, of watching the turn of the planet. For those who wish to keep track of the Sun themselves in their own location, abundant sources are now available for this information in local and national media.

Average Temperatures: Average temperatures in Yellow Springs are also part of each day's entry. Since the rise and fall of temperatures in other parts of the North America, even though they may start from colder or warmer readings, keep pace with the temperatures here, the highs and lows in Yellow Springs are, like solar statistics, helpful indicators of the steady progress of the year throughout most of the states along the 40th Parallel (except in the mountains). The daybook journal entries can be cross-referenced with the list of monthly average temperatures between 1981 and 2017 in order to compare the daily inventories with the month's weather in a given year.

Weather: My daily, weekly and monthly weather summaries have been distilled from over thirty years of observations. They are descriptions of the local weather history I have kept in order to track the gradual change in temperatures, precipitation and cloud cover through the year I have also used them in order to try to identify particular characteristics of each day. They are not meant to be predictions.

Although my interest in the Yellow Springs microclimate at first seemed too narrow to be of use to those who lived outside the area, I began to modify it to meet the needs of a number of regional and national farm publications for which I started writing in the mid 1980s. And so, while the summaries are based on my records in southwestern Ohio, they can be and have been used, with interpretation and interpolation, throughout the Lower Midwest , the Middle Atlantic States and the East.

The Natural Calendar: In this section, I note the progress of foliage and floral changes, farm and garden practices, migration times for common birds, and peak periods of insect activity. Some of these notes are second hand; I'm a sky watcher, but not an astronomer, and I rely on the government's astronomical data and a few other references for much of my information about the stars and the Sun. I am also a complete amateur at bird watching, and most of the migration dates used in the seasonal calendar come from published sources. And even though I keep close track of the farm year, the percentages listed for planting and harvesting are interpretations of averages supplied by the state's weekly crop reports.

Daybook Entries: The journal entries in the daybook section provide the raw material from which I wrote the Natural Calendar digests. All the times used here are Eastern Standard Time.

The daybook section is a collection of observations made from the window of my car and from my walks in Glen Helen, in parks and wildlife areas within a few miles of my home, and on occasional trips. It is a record that anyone with a few guidebooks could make, and it includes just a small number of the natural markers that anyone might discover.

When I began to take notes about the world around me, I found that there were few descriptions of actual events in nature available for southwestern Ohio. There was no roadmap for the course of the year. My daily observations, as narrow and incomplete as they were, were especially significant to me since I had found no other narrative of the days, no other depiction of what was actually occurring around me. In time, the world came into focus with each particle I named. I saw concretely that time and space were the sum of their parts.

As my notes for each day accumulated, I could see the wide variation of events that occurred from year to year; at the same time, I saw a unity in this syncopation from which I could identify numerous sub-seasons and with which I could understand better the kind of habitat in which I was living and, consequently, myself. When I paged through the journal entries for each day, I was drawn back to the space in which they were made. I browsed and imagined, returned to the journey.

Journal Essays: At the end of many of the daybook entries, I have included brief essays from my almanac column in the *Yellow Springs News*.

Companions: Many friends, acquaintances and family members have contributed their observations to the daybook, and their participation has taught me that my private seasons are also community seasons, and that all of our experiences together help to lay the foundation for a rich, local consciousness of natural history.

The Month of October
October Averages: 1981 through 2023
Normal October Average Temperature: 53.9

Year	Average
1981	52.1
1982	55.4
1983	54.1
1984	58.8
1985	57.4
1986	55.3
1987	48.5
1988	47.1
1989	54.1
1990	53.4
1991	56.7
1992	52.2
1993	51.6
1994	56.2
1995	56.1
1996	54.6
1997	54.0
1998	55.6
1999	54.6
2000	57.1
2001	54.8
2002	51.5
2003	52.4
2004	53.8
2005	54.5
2006	50,6
2007	60.0
2008	53.9
2009	50.9
2010	56.5
2011	53.4
2012	52.4
2013	55.5
2014	54.6
2015	55.8
2016	59.3
2017	57.0
2018	54.9
2019	58.4
2020	54.8
2021	62.4
2022	54.9
2023	57.0

October 1st
The 274th Day of the Year

Hail, old October, bright and chill,
First freedman from the summer sun!

Thomas Constable

Sunrise/set: 6:31/6:18
Day's Length: 11 hours 45 minutes
Average High/Low: 72/50
Average Temperature: 61
Record High: 93 – 1897, 94 – 2019
Record Low: 31 – 1895

The Daily Weather

The first day of October brings highs above 80 on 25 percent of the years, brings 70s on 40 percent of the years (it is the last time this season that the combined possibility for 70s, 80s and 90s reaches so high), 60s on 25 percent, 50s on 10 percent. Skies are completely overcast and rain occurs 40 percent of the days. Lows are in the mild 50s or 60s more than half the time, and frost comes only once in a decade.

The Weather in the Week Ahead

Light frost strikes ten to 20 percent of all the nights this week, with October 3rd most likely to bring a damaging freeze in the 20s (a five percent chance of that). Highs in the 80s occur on approximately ten percent of the days, and 70s can be expected 30 percent of the time. Moderate 60s dominate 50 percent of the afternoons, while colder 40s and 50s come 15 to 20 percent of the time.

The likelihood for colder weather almost always increases after the 4th - after which day the chances of highs only in the 50s swells from an average of 15 percent to 30 percent. Rain falls about one day in three. The driest days are the 3rd, the 6th and the 7th, and the wettest days are October 1st and the 4th. Skies are clear to partly cloudy 70 percent of the time. The sunniest days are typically the 3rd, and the 6th, when clouds are almost completely absent.

The October Outlook

The average number of major cold waves increases to seven this month in the Lower Midwest. There are typically only four to five in September, just three or four in August. These fronts bring an occasional day when the thermometer reads only in the 30s; three or four days stay in the 40s; at least a week of afternoons are in the 50s, another seven in the 60s, another seven in the 70s, and two to four in the 80s. Normal highs drop fourteen to fifteen degrees, slipping from the lower 70s into the upper 50s. Average lows move from about 50 all the way down to the upper 30s.

The warmest October days, those with at least a 30 percent chance of highs above 70 degrees, are the 1st (typically the warmest day in October), 2nd, 3rd, 4th, 8th, 9th, 10th, 15th, 16th, and 31st.

The coldest days, those with at least a 50 percent chance of highs below 60 degrees, are the 20th, 22nd, 25th, 27th, 28th, and 29th.

Frost occurs at least twice in a southern Ohio October; and it usually strikes six nights in the next 30 (and it occurs one night out of every two in the coldest years). The early mornings on which frost is most likely to occur are those of the 13th, 16th, 19th, 20th, 25th, 26th, 27th, and 29th.

October is the peak of the dry season in the Lower Midwest. Less precipitation falls at this time of year than at any other, and the skies offer more sun than clouds. There are typically 11 completely clear days in October, eight partly cloudy, and 12 mostly cloudy or fully overcast.

The driest October days, those with only a 15 percent chance of rain, are the 26th, 28th, and 29th. The sunniest October days, those with at least a 75 percent chance of sun are the 2nd, 3rd, 5th, 6th, 7th, 8th, 10th, 13th, 14th, 15th, 28th and 29th. October's sunniest day of all is the 15th.

The rainiest October days, those with at least a 35 percent chance of precipitation, are the 1st, 4th, 10th, 12th (the wettest day of the month), 13th, 16th, 17th, 22nd, and 23rd. Light snow falls between the 12th and the 31st two years in ten.

Frostwatch

The following chart shows the chances that frost will often have occurred by the date indicated. Calculations are based on typical frequency of freezing temperatures at average elevations along the 40th Parallel during the month of October. The data can be adjusted roughly by adding five percent for each 100 miles north or south that Parallel. Local frost histories, of course, offer much greater detail.

Date	Chance of Light Frost	Chance of Killing Frost
October 1:	80 percent	10 percent
October 5:	85 percent	15 percent
October 10:	90 percent	20 percent
October 15:	95 percent	30 percent
October 20:	98 percent	40 percent
October 25:	100 percent	50 percent
October 30:		75 percent

Key to the Nation's Weather

The normal October temperature at average elevations along the 40th Parallel, the average of the high of 65 and the low of 46, is 55 degrees. Using the following chart based on weather statistics from around the country, you can calculate the approximate temperatures in other locations.

For example, with the base of 55 you can estimate normal temperatures in Minneapolis by subtracting 5 degrees from the base average. Or add 8 degrees to find out the likely conditions in Atlanta during the month.

Fairbanks AK	-28
Cheyenne WY	-10
Portland, ME	-5
Minneapolis MN	-5
Des Moines IA	-2
Seattle, WA	-2
AVERAGE ALONG THE 40TH PARALLEL:	**55**
St. Louis MO	+4

Washington DC   +4
Atlanta GA   +8
New Orleans LA   +16
Miami FL   +22

Autumncount

Between the first threat of frost and the first breath of winter, approximately 18 major weather systems cross the United States. Four of those systems arrived in September; October brings at least seven more:

October 2: This front is typically a strong and consistent one, and it usually brings freezing nights to the North. The two mornings following this front often bring a damaging freeze along the Canadian border.

October 4: A secondary front often comes through around the 4th of October, signaling further progress in the advent of autumn. Planting, harvest and hiking are favored for a day or two after the passage of this system.

October 7: This front, the final one of the subseason of "Early Fall," is often weaker than the weather systems of October 2nd and 4th, but frost is still to be expected in the Northeast, upper Midwest, the Plains and the Rockies. The weather following this front is typically dry and stable, but the advance of the October 13th high increases the chances of precipitation on the 10th through the 12th. Snow is not uncommon at higher elevations on those dates, and the 12th brings the first chance of flurries to the Ohio Valley. In 2015, this front pushed Hurricane Joaquin to the northeast, sparing the northern coast from wind, but drenching South Carolina with once-in-a-millennium rainfall.

October 13: This cold front almost always accompanies a chillier and more dramatic subseason of autumn known as "Middle Fall." This high-pressure system can be expected to bring rain or snow and nights in the upper 20s in the North, upper 30s in the South.

October 17: Chances of freezing temperatures continue to grow as the October fronts advance. Lows in the 20s or 30s are most likely to occur on the mornings of the 19th and 20th, with the latter date carrying the highest chances of a freeze so far this season.

October 23: This system almost always produces rain or snow. After it passes through, however, the 26th, the 28th, and the 29th are often some of the best days of the month for harvest. But the mornings most likely to bring a killing frost during the month's final week are the 25th and the 26th. Both have a 35 percent chance of a low only in the 20s along the 40th Parallel, the first time this season the odds have risen so high.

October 27: The high-pressure system that arrives near this date often preempts the October 30 front, chills Halloween and brings down the foliage of the most brittle maples.

October 30: When this cold front moves is late, it brings mild south winds under which to finish harvest. Between today and the arrival of early winter, there should be up to 20 days of relatively benign, dry days for fertilizing, harvesting, wood cutting, planting spring crops, raking leaves, transplanting and digging in spring bulbs.

An Approximate Sequence of Leaf Turn and Leaf Drop in Early, Middle and Late Autumn

August 10: Black walnut trees have started to shed, and black walnuts begin to fall in large numbers. Leaves often begin to yellow on cottonwoods, locusts, box elders, spicebush and crabapples.

August 20: Orange patches have appeared on a few Judas maples. Many locusts are brown from leaf miners. Buckeyes can be half yellow. The earliest ash trees blush.

August 30: Some catalpa and black walnut trees have lost most of their leaves.

September 5: Cottonwoods fade more dramatically as goldenrod and the soybean fields turn gold.

September 10: Silver olive foliage has streaks of ocher.

September 20: Ashes start their autumn transformation, some becoming maroon, others gold. (After the die-off of the early 21st century, ash-turn is no longer a marker for autumn in many locations.)

September 25: Black walnut trees are completely bare. Crab apples and hackberries are thinning. Color spreads across the red maples. Blush appears on the sweet gums. Box elders are shedding.

October 1: Enough leaves have fallen from the canopy to reveal the deep red of the Virginia creeper on branches and fences. Amber hickories blend with the ashes. White birch leaves show gilded edges.

October 5: Orange maples, yellow sumacs, hickories, redbuds and red oaks have now joined the ashes and cottonwoods to give a full sense of autumn to the landscape. The burning bush is deep scarlet. Beeches are flushed for their November change. The late fields of goldenrod, the dry corn, and the rusting soybeans complete the fall scenario.

October 10: Peak leafturn is starting to occur in woodlots where maples, ashes, buckeyes, wild cherry and locusts predominate. Most Osage are yellow now, a few ginkgoes starting. Cottonwoods and the rest of the box elders lose their leaves, and more holes open in the tree line. Fencerows are shedding their Virginia creeper. Grape vines hold on yellow-green.

October 15: Witch hazel, the last of the flowering shrubs, opens. Rains often take down the ashes and redbuds by this date, ending Early Fall. Full Middle Fall begins, bringing in the remaining maples for approximately a week.

October 20: White oaks are crimson, and the end of soybean harvest and the browning of goldenrod finally subdue the glowing September fields.

October 25: Silver maples are champagne gold, and the sugar and red maples are down or are shedding quickly. Tulip trees are almost gone. Some ginkgoes are green, others fully gold and losing foliage. Light frosts accelerate the passage of Middle Fall.

October 30: Osage, sweet gum, ginkgo, and white mulberry continue to keep their leaves. Beeches are half turned. Maples collapse in storms. Some sycamores are totally undone; others are only thinning as the mottled land enters Late Fall.

November 5: The pear trees are red brown. Sweet gums are coming down. Ginkgoes and white mulberries reach their brightest, and then disintegrate.

November 10: Rose of Sharon shrubs are half bare. Honeysuckles weaken, berries becoming more prominent. Across the countryside, the woodlot canopies are dark and empty.

October Phenology

When Halloween crops have come to town, then the dark-eyed juncos return to bird feeders.

When streaks of scarlet appear in the oaks and shades of pink in the dogwood trees, then cut gourds, winter squash and pumpkins for winter storage. Harvest grapes, too.

When the fruits of the ginkgo tree turn pink, then next year's skunk cabbage protrudes in the swamp and the knuckles of next year's rhubarb show in the garden.

When the burning bush is completely red, then snow becomes a possibility.

When beggartick seeds stick to your pants legs, then check horses for horse-bot eggs.

When the winged seeds of Japanese knotweed fall, then great flocks of blackbirds move across the land.

When leaves reach peak color, then farmers plant winter wheat, and mating season begins for the white-tailed deer.

When ash leaves fall, then divide peonies, lilies, and iris.

When red maple leaves are down, then plant crocus, daffodils, tulips, snowdrops, and aconites before November turns the weather much chillier.

When the pointers of the Big Dipper are aligned north and south at 10:00 p.m., then hosta seedpods split open in rainy weather, revealing their black contents. That is the time to dig dahlias and gladioli for winter.

When the barn swallows leave the barn for the South, begin the sugar beet harvest and look for frost within two weeks.

When the soft heads of cattails start to break apart, then complete autumn pruning of trees and shrubs.

When the first killing frost takes the peppers and tomatoes, then dig up the onions, remove the mum tops, cut flowers and herbs for drying.

When the second bloom of forsythia bushes occurs, then about 14 mild, dry days for outdoor work remain before winter.

The Natural Calendar

Deep in Early Fall the first slate-gray junco arrives in the Lower Midwest for winter. Goldenrod is seeding now, pods of the eastern burning bush are open, hawthorn berries redden, wild grapes are purple, and the tree line that seemed so deep in summer just days ago is suddenly poised to break into its final color of the year.

When juncos arrive, streaks of scarlet appear on the oaks, shades of pink on the dogwoods. The ashes all show red or gold; the catalpas and the cottonwoods blanch. Shagbark hickories, tulip trees, sassafras, elms, locusts and sweet gums change to full yellow, merge with the swelling orange of the maples to create a variegated archway into Middle Fall.

When the first junco appears, the terns and meadowlarks, yellow-rumped warblers and purple martins migrate. Hawks wait on fences and high wires, looking for prey. Titmice chirp, and sometimes cardinals sing. Robins give their short migration clucks.

Cabbage butterflies become more reckless in their search for nectar. Aphids disappear in the chilly nights. daddy longlegs disappear from the undergrowth, and spiders of all kinds move indoors. Damselflies are rare along the rivers now, and darners have left their suburban ponds.

Daybook

1982: End of the raspberry season this year, only a few berries left for nibbling.

1983: Raspberries still coming in strong. Some tomatoes still ripening, should last at least through the middle of the month, and well into November indoors on the kitchen sill. Crickets still sing. Some Japanese honeysuckle still blooming.

1986: Cardinal sings at 6:19 a.m.

1987: First light frost of the year.

1989: I work outside, surrounded by sparrow and cardinal song, crickets, robin migration messages, crows. The blue dayflowers have now faded from time and disease. Peony stalks half decayed.

1990: The ash tree outside my window has lost almost all of its leaves. Grackles in the ginkgo, the sky bright, air crisp.

1991: Aster *novii belgii* completely gone now. And sudden advent of early color in the tree line. Some maples already turned, brilliant patches of orange here and there. Violet, red, deep purple poison ivy and Virginia creeper outline the changes. My ginkgo is full of acorn size fruit. Locusts and ash are well along in their transformation. More and more box elder, cherry, apple, and mulberry weathering.

1992: Starlings in the trees every afternoon. I watch the drying of goldenrod until it blends with the dead Bermuda grass, foxtail, smooth brome, orchard grass. The black walnut trees are bare. One blue lobelia, one tall bellflower, some red clover, scattered white snakeroot along Jacoby Branch. Yellowing of the wild grape leaves, yellow milkweed, yellow elms, yellow shagbark hickory, yellow spicebush, a locust yellow around its red thorns, nettles bleached with age, the last huge silver spider webs hanging in the black wingstem shining in the early morning sun, timothy all fallen from its stalk, the sound of October crows.
Crickets jumping in the warm grass; no daddy longlegs hunting, but red and blue dragonflies are still out by the swamp. Leaves on the path, sycamore, sassafras, dogwood, ash. More woolly bears every day. Small flocks of robins migrating.
From one woods to the next, summer to fall. One patch fully green, no signs of change. Down river a mile, another season, dark, thinning. First gold mulberry leaf. Cottonwood almost gone, staghorn sumac, too. First junco seen today. High rivers early this year, and pussy willows sprouting new leaves in the heat. Fresh mint replaces cress and forget-me-nots in the marsh streams. Asters die back. Thyme-leaved speedwell goes to seed. Buzzards are in their roost by the bend of the river. Hundreds of blackbirds upstream feeding in the fallen leaves, bathing in the pebbles and sand uncovered by last month's drought.

1995: Leafturn has been late this year, just like it was in 1988, the year of our most recent drought. Even the earliest trees, the buckeyes, box elders, locusts and ashes, stayed green until the end of September. Then this weekend those early varieties began to change, and a few of the maples started in, too. Along the roadsides, purple New England asters and the tall goldenrod are still in full bloom, adding to the new autumn landscape.

1996: The Japanese beetles seem to be completing their departure this week. Taking their place, cucumber beetles hide in the roses. The mornings bring occasional robins passing through, and once in a while a cardinal will call. Cricket song has replaced cicada song. Yellow jackets becoming more numerous, cabbage butterflies tamer or more reckless in the search for nectar and favorable sites to lay their eggs. Aphids are disappearing in the colder nights. The autumn crocus has completed its season. Most of the domestic asters started from seed in March and blooming late into September have died back. The first goldenrod has just started to rust. Soybean leaves are finally yellowing, and a few cornfields are turning brown.

1999: Cardinals sing on and off all morning.

2001: First milkweed pods seen open today as I was driving south to Washington Court House.

2003: Light frost on the roof and on the car windshields this morning. My ash tree at school is about two-thirds down, and leaf-turn on the ashes in the parking lot is well underway. One full-color maple in Wilmington. At home, pussy willow and red quince leaves have been gone for a week or so, fell with the black walnut foliage.

2004: At South Glen, the river is low after the dry September, and the undergrowth is tattered. Some of the wingstem seeds have turned brown, and the wood nettle foliage is blanching from age. One lobelia and one black-eyed Susan have decaying blossoms. All the goldenrod is rusting. Only the small heart-leafed asters, Short's asters, and small white asters are still strong. Geese flew over about 10:15; kingfishers were chattering up and down the river throughout my walk. Mike said they might be migrating. At home in the north garden, the New England asters are almost completely done blooming for the year. My depression strong today as the moon wanes.

2005: A vole caught under the sink last night; the invasion continues (two mice in the last two weeks of September). A very small camel cricket jumped into the toilet this morning!

2008: One monarch surprised in the New England asters late this afternoon, the only one I've seen in weeks. Jeanie told me that the cats killed a giant vole in the greenhouse while I was gone on the 27th.

2009: A definite freeze reported by Jerry Rohrs in Archbold this morning. Here at home, there is an increase in black walnuts accumulating on the sidewalk and in the alley. More than half of Mateo's black walnuts have come down in just a few days. Serviceberry trees are shedding. Hops flowers are brown, some knotweed still full, and a small praying mantis, maybe an inch and a half long, in the stonecrop. Crows and cardinals at 6:13 a.m.

2010: No monarchs or swallowtails, only a couple of skippers, in spite of mild and sunny weather. The pussy willow catkins in the bush along the front sidewalk are pushing out as though it were early March.

2011: Cold settling in across the Miami Valley, clouds, wind. When I walked Bella this morning, I thought I heard a faint buzzing of tree or ground crickets, but the rustling of leaves was the dominant sound. Along Xenia Avenue, the ash trees a full yellow gold. On the sidewalk near the corner of Limestone Street, thousands of maple seeds have joined the black walnuts. Only a couple of mournful field cricket chirps when I walked Bella tonight, temperature in the upper 40s.

2012: Full ash color now building suddenly. Dawn Shovar sent the following: "Just wanted to let you know that a sampling of persimmon seeds in the Montezuma, Mitchell, and Turkey Run State Park areas of Indiana all show spoons this year. Guess we all will be shoveling snow! Last year, I could not find any knives, forks or spoons in any of them. In talking about that, my husband said, 'Well, we didn't have a winter last year.' Guess those old trees knew ahead of time!"

2013: Crows late again this morning: 6:39. The way to Wilmington is gradually turning toward early full color – could be there in a week. The ashes, walnuts and locusts are leading, and many maples have joined in. Tonight: katydids, field crickets, melodious tree frogs, and the high static of thrips.

2014: Moya's maple (so much taller than last year) has a deep red-orange patch of color on its top east side, and the Danielsons' maple is suddenly outstripping Mrs. Timberlake's, which was the first to start. Peggy's burning bush and Lil's are half red. Two forsythia flowers noticed next to the sidewalk on High Street. Ashes at the college and in the neighborhood, full rich brown, not shedding yet. All the Mills Lawn black walnuts are bare. At the Mill Dam, distant robin peeping, all the wingstem of September gone, all the snakeroot and wood nettle gone to seed, only Short's asters and the small white asters *(Aster vimineus/ Symphyotrichum lateriflorum)* in bloom. I took a few water willow plants from the large clump growing in the shallows below the dam. Annie called tonight: She said the foliage throughout her drive to from the ocean at Newburyport to Vermont was the most brilliant and dramatic she had ever seen.

2015: Drew Monkman notes that ospreys have begun migration south from east-central Ontario. The first major hurricane of the season, Joaquin, approaches the southeastern United States – as a storm cell causes severe storms over Sardinia.

2016: Light wind, bright sun, mild: The New England asters, late goldenrod, the rose bush, the sedums, the zinnias and many tithonias hold on, attracting bees, one, about half a dozen cabbage whites, one silver-spotted skipper. At the northwest corner of the porch, the white autumn crocus is still blooming, some stalks toppling over. As I walked down High Street at sunrise, a long flock of blackbirds clucked above me heading northeast, stretching from one end of town to the other.

2017: An identical day to last year, but with a breeze and without the blackbirds (but robins peeping in the honeysuckles). I see the painted ladies and cabbage whites. I wait for a monarch and a skipper. Instead, more painted ladies arrive, four or five at one time in the afternoon, maybe a new hatch. From Spoleto, Italy, Neysa sends a photo of hillside of golden autumn croci in full bloom.

2018: No painted ladies this year, but at least two monarchs playing in the tithonias, one Eastern black swallowtail (the first in a very long time) in the zinnias, one small checkerspot, one silver-spotted skipper and a few cabbage whites exploring. Two canna lilies brought in from the garden for the fall. The dahlias, New England asters, zinnias and tithonias keep the garden bright even as the viburnum blushes more, the Japanese knotweed goes to seed and the whole feel of the yard becomes rustier, more tinted with ocher.

2019: Record heat of 94 degrees. Cabbage whites, several silver-spotted skippers and one small checkerspot in the garden today, but no hummingbird or monarch or painted lady seen when I walked about. Male goldfinches have lost their summer color. At Ellis Pond, I found fallen pecans, the first I have seen on the ground since we lived in North Carolina.

2020: Chilly in the 50s today, and breezy with light showers. No butterflies. Jill and I walked into the Glass Farm wetland, past the great fields solid with small white asters (*Aster pilosus* or *Aster dumosus)* intruded occasionally by tall goldenrod.

2021: Cloudless and mild in the 70s. At Jill's this morning, a hummingbird came to check her south plantings. Then after lunch at home, another hummingbird. explored the canna lilies and the New England asters. Three or four cabbage white butterflies through the day, many honeybees and smaller bumblebees in the asters. Several maples fully turned in the neighborhood, but High Street remains green.

2023: Pearl's Fen with Jill: Red-winged blackbirds heard and seen.

What appeared to be a flock of finches fed in the goldenrod. Blue jays calling, robins clucking. Woodpeckers chattering, a Downy and Red-Bellied. Like I described after my walk with Jeff in 2021, the fen is in decay, plants fallen over in disarray as in photos of an ancient battlefield. One Meadow Beauty found in bloom, and many late small white asters, New England asters and purple-stemmed violet asters, a variety of potentilla, tall goldenrod. Although I have always missed the pivot time of flowering in the fen, the change must occur quickly in the last ten days or so of September. One monarch butterfly. The fields throughout the county: corn and soybeans look ready to harvest. In the yard, I am noticing a paling in the dense hedge of hops, honeysuckle and climbing false buckwheat. Time count for canna lilies: 15. Crickets, tree frogs and katydids strong as the round moon rises.

Now, too, the first of October, or later, the elms are at the height of their autumnal beauty, great brownish-yellow masses, warm from their September oven, hanging over the highway. Their leaves are perfectly ripe. I wonder if there is any answering ripeness in the lives of the men who live beneath them.

Henry David Thoreau

October 2nd
The 275th Day of the Year

'T is the noon of autumn's glow,
When a soft and purple mist,
Like a vaporous amethyst,
Or an air-dissolved star,
Mingling light and fragrance, far
From the curved horizon's bound
To the point of heaven's profound,
Fills the overflowing sky.

Percy Bysshe Shelley

Sunrise/set: 6:32/6:16
Day's Length: 11 hours 44 minutes
Average High/Low: 71/49
Average Temperature: 60
Record High: 90 – 1900, 94 – 2019
Record Low: 28 – 1908

The Daily Weather

The 2nd of October warms to the lower 80s twenty-five percent of the afternoons and to the 70s fifteen percent, a significant decline from yesterday's possibilities. Highs get into the 60s fifty percent of the time and into the 50s ten percent of the time. Sky conditions are usually less cloudy than on the 1st: 80 percent of the days are partly sunny. Rain occurs one day in three. Half the nighttime lows fall below 60 degrees, but frost is rare on this date.

Natural Calendar

As the canopy thins, hemlock, ragwort, yarrow, waterleaf, violets, wild ginger and sweet Cicely grow back. Mums are often at their brightest, and the slowest raspberries ripen. Sometimes, forsythia and lilacs come into bloom again. Pussy willows that have lost their foliage to leafminers sometimes make new leaves. But the tall sedums begin to relinquish their petals, and autumn crocuses die back. Asters are winding down. August's jumpseeds have almost all jumped. Touch-me-nots are popping, thimble plants unraveling.

The toothed leaves of beggarticks darken overnight. Buckeye fruits, hickory nuts, pecans and black walnuts have fallen. Three-seeded mercury has lost its seeds.

The Stars

Before midnight, the Northern Cross, Cygnus the Swan, is setting in the west, accompanied by Aquila and Lyra. The Great Square lies below the Milky Way. In the east, winter's Orion has risen behind Taurus and the Pleiades. In the northern sky, the Dig Dipper hugs the horizon. Deep in the southwest, Fomalhaut hovers above the tree line. An hour before sunrise, all the winter constellations are in place, Orion due south, brilliant Sirius and Procyon in the southeast. In the south-southwest, red Aldebaran and the Pleiades follow the Great Square.

Daybook

1983: Another quart of raspberries today: the patch is peaking. At South Glen, asters still full bloom, jumpseeds jumping, wood nettle yellowing, a final great blue lobelia found, a couple of touch-me-nots, some white snakeroot, one tall bell flower with four violet blossoms, some red clover, wild ginger more prominent now as the summer foliage dies back. Goldenrod has rusted. Bright red creeper has appeared in a yellow Osage tree. Elaborate spider webs hang between the black wingstems, catching the sunlight. Grape leaves are yellow and brown, milkweed dusky, decayed. Dozens of white caterpillars, timothy fallen from its stem, all kinds of birds chanting and chattering, crows in the distance, crickets jumping in front of me in the grass.

1984: Covered Bridge: Feathery hemlock coming back, two feet high, beggartick leaves purple. No daddy longlegs seen today: it's the end of Early Fall for sure. Crickets strong, grasshoppers hopping. Leaf color stable, hasn't changed much in the past two weeks. Some white snakeroot fading. Waterleaf has new leaves. Jump seeds are almost all gone. Sassafras yellowing and reddening. Bur marigolds done blooming. Most Jerusalem artichokes finished along the roadsides. One catchweed blossom found, a fragment of second spring.

1985: Leaf change accelerating rapidly. Ash, hickory, tulip trees, sweet gum, sycamore, cottonwood in the center of their color.

1986: Cardinal sings at 6:09 a.m., then silence.

1988: South Glen: asters still full, goldenrod holding. Fall violets in bloom along the path. Some decline of the zigzag goldenrod. Migrating robins hardly seen at all this year. A few ironweed still blooming, most to seed. Wingstem now completely gone. Rudbeckia speciosa still golden but tattered.

1989: The major turning and falling has begun. This afternoon, I was surrounded by sparrow song, robin migration song, crows calling, cardinal calling, grackles clucking in the trees behind the house, the sky clear, air crisp (Thoreau associates grackles with fall, saying they come back in the autumn after mating in the north). Sycamore hole: only one small sunfish. They take the bobber way down but stay off the hook, pulling just the end of the worm. At Wilberforce the locusts are gold, and the reds show more now on the ashes. The hedgerows are bright scarlet. All the leaves are gone from the fragile ash by my window. The full turning and falling has begun through the countryside. Katydids and crickets loud tonight. Uncle Bill says that lows are in the 20s now in northern Minnesota, nights staying at least ten degrees below Ohio temperatures, sometimes 15 to 20 degrees.

1991: Sycamore Hole: The river is down and filling up with leaves. Wind has been rising this afternoon, pulling off foliage from box elders and sycamores, red creepers, some elm and hickory. Not a bite at the fishing hole, no chubs or shiners stealing bait. No birds. Finally a black-capped chickadee high in a bare box elder, a long "chrrrrr", singing upside down, then off across the river.

     Throughout town, today is the beginning of peak color, the maples going early, dovetailing with the height of the ash and dogwood. It will be a quick and brilliant fall, all the colors so sharp and clear, reds, pinks, violets, browns, all blended together into new colors without names, flushed, excited, vibrant. Starlings fill the trees at the dairy at sundown, chattering, loud.

1992: Ashes deeply flushed now, accelerated by the last two light frosts. Hawthorn berries noticed red at Wilberforce.

1993: At South Glen, zigzag goldenrod is still open, and most asters, scattered white snakeroot. North from Jacoby, most tall goldenrod has rusted, and the August wingstem is turning black, the ironweed seeds becoming brown and soft. Swamp bidens is lanky and old now. Burning bush all blushing in town, maybe a quarter turned. Darners seen still hunting, but the damsel flies are gone along the river. Long "V" of geese flies over at 6:40 p.m.

1995: Jeanie reports a "city of spiders" discovered by her kindergarten class. I've been noticing more spiders all fall. Did I fail to see them before? (of course)

1998: Cardinals at 8:00 and 9:45 this morning. Peaches have been done about a week out at the orchard.

1999: To Oakwood this afternoon, riding through the peak of the first tier of color.

2000: At my parking place in Springfield: white birch has a fringe of yellow. Ash fully gold and shedding. Some bright red in the sweet gums. Burning bush full scarlet.

2002: Dove heard at 8:15 a.m. Grackles fill the back trees from 9:30 through the rest of the morning. Spicebush swallowtail in the zinnias at 10:00 a.m. Katydids are still strong in the warm evening.

2003: Heavy frost this morning damages the tomatoes and the elephant ears. One woolly-bear caterpillar and a few cabbage butterflies seen today, but no monarchs, no painted ladies. Goldenrod deteriorating quickly.

2004: To Archbold and back this morning: Early full leafturn of the first tier of trees from Yellow Springs into northern Ohio. Many ashes are deep maroon or gold, some shedding. Hickories are a deep yellow, many maples bright orange, cottonwoods turned or fallen. A flock of robins and blackbirds seen above Grand Lake.

Most of the goldenrod has rusted. One patch of chicory seen, many roadsides full of New England asters (even though ours have stopped blooming at home). The milkweed leaves and pods were yellow, but few plants had open pods. Maybe half the soybean fields I saw had been cut, but far less of the corn.

2006: Ash and cottonwoods in full color in and around Yellow Springs. Sudden decline of virgin's bower. New England asters hold at their peak. One monarch seen today. One dragonfly zoomed across the yard in front of me.

2007: Walking in the alley this morning, I heard distant clucking and whistling of starlings – a few birds seen in the barest trees. At Wilberforce, my ash tree is completely down. Other ashes near the parking lot are mostly turned, but mottled this year. The small locusts are full yellow, and one maple has shed between the Administration Building and Wesley Hall. The heat of this past September continues into the new month, high in the low 80s again today. Ruby Nicholson reports seeing a hummingbird today (September 25th is their average departure date, October 16, 1925 the latest recorded by the Dayton Audubon Society). This evening, katydids and crickets were loud.

2008: At 7:00 a.m. in the alley, a few grackles in the trees at Limestone. Jeanie said that a large flock of grackles were cackling in the back trees this afternoon. Coming home from Wilmington, I saw a number of cottonwoods bare.

2009: I have been reading George Lakoff and Mark Johnson's, *Philosophy in the Flesh,* noted this statement: "A fixed duration of time is a bounded region on a path along which an observer moves. In short, a duration of time is, in this metaphor, conceptualized as a container."

The canopy of leaves appeared solid throughout the hot summer, its entire nature dense and uniform, its shade thick and deep. Within a few days, that canopy will shatter. If I accept the philosophers' time as a container, autumn is a jug into which and during which all the leaves come down and all the last flowers fall. In such a scenario, October is not so much a part of an astronomical sequence as it is a bounded region in which we live.

Everything from the whole year past goes into the jug of October. Events and objects get mixed up in the tumble. The smooth wall of June is torn apart. The best sense of what we are in this place dissolves. All of the long green horizon crumbles.

Any meaning that an observer might have associated with the middle of the year is recast. The change of appearance is the change of essence. The undoing of the trees and flowers tips the full glass of summer to empty, pours out old and familiar landmarks and gauges and pointers all at once.

Untied from the orderly queue of Earth's relationship to the Sun, the contents of October's jug have no geography recognizable from August. Nothing looks the way it used to look. The inner space contains pathways but no direction or destination. Nothing linear matters because there is no place to go until the container is filled with leaves and snow then overflows and tumbles, empties and is free for spring.

2010: Crows at 6:11 this morning, clear skies, then clouding up and rain in the afternoon. I worked at the store all day; Jeanie said the birds fed heavily, sparrows and songbirds, and a flock of blackbirds and starlings settled into the back trees at about 4:00.

2011: Crows at 6:13 this morning, red-tailed hawk crying above High Street when I walked Bella this morning. Light frost on the truck windshield from an overnight low in the middle 30s, but no damage to the plants. Tonight, only a few mournful cricket sounds: intermittent, slurred trills.

2012: Full color gathering all along the highways. An orb-weaver stays in its web on the east bedroom window.

2013: The garden continues to be taken over by crabgrass. In the roses and honeysuckles, climbing false buckwheat *(Polygonum scandens)* still flowers. At Ellis Pond, very little change in the past few days, darkened ashes holding steady, no sign of new color on the oaks or sugar maples. When I came home from Annie's last night at 8:45, I found a large praying mantis on the front screen door. Crickets and katydids were calling all around me. Ed Oxley reports hundreds of daddy longlegs in the woodpile, also several toads. Maybe the daddy longlegs are the same as the "city of spiders" discovered by Jeanie's students this day in 1995.

2014: Geese flew over as I walked Bella this morning about 7:45. At the corner of Dayton and High Streets, the first milkweed pod is starting to split. In the yard and around the neighborhood, black walnut trees are mostly bare, and muddy-looking hackberry leaves are scattered on the lawns. In spite of a high in the middle 80s today, only a couple of butterflies seen: a cabbage white and a painted lady (*Cynthia*). At John Bryan Park, drifts of pink smartweed losing its seeds.

2015: Venice, Italy with Neysa and Ivano: The dusky landscape of Late Summer into Early Fall continues from the Veneto countryside. In some corners, horseweed and Joe Pye weed (*Eupatorium*) all to seed, small white asters, many larger violet asters (similar to Short's asters) full, sycamore foliage rusted and partially down in the promenade off Via Garibaldi toward the sea. Most curious to me was a second full bloom of yucca in various places, the remnants of the earlier bloom beside the new flowers.

2016: Cool and sunny: Three monarchs at one time in the north zinnias, a couple of silver-spotted skippers and cabbage whites, a small fritillary. Jill's cottonwood has shed almost all its leaves. The black walnuts in town hold almost all their leaves. This afternoon, I planted a butterfly bush in the dooryard garden, cut back some of the honeysuckle, grape vine and crab apple to give it more sun.

2017: At least eight painted ladies and two silver-spotted skippers in the zinnias throughout the morning and afternoon. Most black walnut leaves are down now, and the walnuts just keep falling, making it hard sometimes to walk on the sidewalks because of all the nuts. Rick found more glow worms this morning: "A few out there at four this morning, trying to get down between rocks in patio. Wonder if the glow seen above the ground was a glowworm on a log or vegetation. When hunting, try the gravel area along High Street."

2018: Three monarchs sailing around the north garden this morning! Milkweed beetles have disappeared. Milkweed pods still not open.

2019: Intense heat and sun. Cabbage whites, painted ladies and monarchs in the zinnias and tithonias. Now the New England asters have begun to darken, their purple browning. Katydids began to call about 6:45 this evening.

2020: A chilly morning in the 40s, a high this afternoon only 58, despite the sun.

2021: Only bees and cabbage white butterflies in the garden. The viburnum at the north side of the house is solid rusty, dusky maroon now, many burning bush shrubs partially red. At the Springfield Museum of Art, the decorative locusts are golden and shedding, reminding me of the trees at Wilberforce in the '80s. On High Street, the maple that T. K. (who committed suicide so many years ago) planted is the first to turn.

2023: Time count of canna lilies: 17 in bloom today, the plants continuing to produce at a little less than half their July level. Two cabbage whites visiting the garden.

If we are ever going to dwell in the house of the Lord, I believe, we do so now. If any house is divinely made, it is this one here, this great whirling mansion of planets and stars.

Scott Russell Sanders

October 3rd
The 276th Day of the Year

'I'm just going out to check the ewes,'
I said, but then I found
October dancing on the hill,
her robust fullness gowned
in scarlets, golds, and brassy browns,
seducing with her hat of blue,
her perfume heady, humming tunes,
giving nuts and apples too.

Pat Elliott

Sunrise/set: 6:37/6:17
Day's Length: 11 hours 40 minutes
Average High/Low: 71/49
Average Temperature: 60
Record High: 93 – 1900, 91 – 2019
Record Low: 29 – 1888

Weather

For the first time since May 9th there is a 25 percent chance of a high only in the 50s. On the other hand, 30 percent of the days rise to the 60s, thirty percent to the 70s, and 15 percent to the 80s. The sky is clear to partly cloudy 90 percent of the time, and rain occurs just one day in four. Morning lows in the 20s become slightly more frequent after this date, and lows below 50 degrees now occur 60 percent of the time.

The Natural Calendar

Wind comes in ahead of the first real October cold, pulling off foliage from box elders, buckeyes and sycamores, hickory and chinquapin oaks leaves. Sparrow song, robin migration song, crows calling, sporadic cardinals, cackling grackles and whistling starlings mark the days.

From one woods to the next, the season moves from summer to fall and back again. One woodlot can be fully green, no signs of change. Then down the path a mile, there is a whole other season of the canopy.. The full turning and falling has begun. The locusts are gold, and maroon shows more now on the ashes. Maples are blushing. The black walnut trees are bare.

In the undergrowth, zigzag goldenrod is still open, most white and violet asters, and some scattered white snakeroot. But the ironweed seeds are becoming brown and soft. Drying tall goldenrod blends with the dead Bermuda grass, foxtail, timothy, smooth brome, and orchard grass. Nettles are bleached with age. The last huge silver orb-weaver spider webs hang in the brittle wingstem, shine in the early morning sun.

Daybook

1982: Milkweed bursting its seedpods along the way to Wilberforce. Almost all trees have some color change now. Some maples are bright red and orange. Greenhouse tomato season begins: four picked.

1983: White snakeroot and goldenrod deteriorating, Queen Anne's lace finished in most fields. Only the asters are still in bloom. More milkweed bursting.

1985: It appears that garlic mustard is sprouting along the back shrubs in the rain. (Note – a plant biologist from Wright State University has told me that garlic mustard only sprouts in early spring, around April 1st.) Starlings seem to be more abundant. These days Lisa reports her trees full of birds, but she hasn't seen any yellow jackets yet this year.

1987: First phase of early peak leaf color began today, the best time for the ash and locusts. Goldenrod gone in many places. Beggarticks and amaranth going to seed.

1988: Major turning time for ashes in Wilberforce, and all the small locusts in the parking area are yellow.

1989: Yellow hibiscus flowers in the greenhouse have been opening regularly for about a week, coming out at dawn, closing at sunset. Six weeks until paperwhites. Seven to amaryllis.

1991: Sun rising deep red through the rain.

1992: Geese fly over at 7:30 a.m. The squirrel in the back locust trees keeps up his steady whine through the morning. Zinnias about three-fourths gone, deteriorating more quickly now. All the rest of the carrots pulled, still fresh and tasty. The pepper plants are full of peppers, finally, after six months of procrastination. Tomatoes continue to come in. A small bowl of raspberries picked this morning. Small white asters declining throughout the yard.

1995: After a week of sun, there is a soft rain this morning. All my ambition of the past month has disappeared. I want to stay inside and hibernate. Cardinals have been singing on and off since breakfast. Yesterday, robins passed through the back yard, clucking their migration or flocking message.

2000: Chicory still blue along the highways. Goldenrod has passed its prime. Ironweed seed heads puff up. Box elder leaves falling more. Stonecrop flowers have gone to seed. Early Fall is closing. Maple color accelerates. Some ashes on Xenia Avenue are completely gold. Oaks touched with yellow

2001: In just the last day, the tree line has developed color. The ashes have reached full turn, the cottonwoods have darkened, and enough locusts and maples have joined in to bring the whole landscape close to the edge of Middle Fall. Enough other leaves have come down to reveal most of the scarlet creepers. Red and gold sumac and poison ivy are more prominent. The soybean fields contribute to the effect instead of standing out, separate from the green wood line like they did a week ago. In Columbus, my white oak has more bleached out sections. The upper part of my red maple is half turned.

2003: South Glen after a light freeze: I walked through the sun and the melting frost, the sound like that of a gentle rain. One catbird seen in an Osage tree. Scattered maples are now full orange. One small cherry tree completely red. Jeanie reports seeing two crows at the Antioch School campus today – the first time this autumn. Violet autumn crocus still bloom in front of the house across the street.

2004: Heavy frost on the truck windshield this morning, but the plants suffered no damage in the garden: the zinnias and elephant ears were untouched. Starlings fill the back trees, cackling and fluttering throughout the morning.

2006: Bindweed white and blue, full New England asters and small-flowered asters. Moyas's maple a third turned, Danielsons' has started. Large ash at the corner full ochre. Virginia creeper red. Mateo's goldenrod rusting. Burning bush a third turned. Wilberforce ashes full and shedding. Full decline of virgin's bower. My ash at school almost gone. One ginkgo ochering. Chicory strong. Horseweed to seed. Cosmos still bright. Some second growth of purple coneflower. Sundrops full. Ochre grape leaves. Cottonwoods full gold into Dayton. Peonies cut back, foliage decayed. Phlox cut back. Cardinal at 6:15 a.m.

2007: The New England asters are starting to decline now, as are the Jerusalem artichokes. Virgin's bower has been done for at least a week. The late yellow coneflowers hold on. The Sun rose red through the clouds; the front garden with its red stonecrops and coleus glowed red. A cardinal heard about 6:40 this morning; starlings were whistling and chirping as I walked the alley (Starling Whistling Season beginning at the end of September).

2009: Three monarchs in the butterfly bushes this morning, serviceberry leaves coming down on Dayton Street, Jerusalem artichokes suddenly almost gone (at the full of the Jerusalem Artichoke Moon).

2010: Crows at 6:18 this morning, gusty cold wind, clouds. No starlings heard in town this week.

2011: Crows loud and close this morning between 6:15 and 6:45. No crickets heard on my walk with Bella at 9:00. Mostly sunny skies and milder temperatures in the 60s brought three monarchs, a small fritillary, two sulphurs and a handful of cabbage whites to the zinnias - the first monarchs in more than a week. Tonight, temperature at 65 degrees, katydids were the dominant insects calling (for the first time in quite a while); no chirping field crickets heard, many intermittent calls of ground or tree crickets, near Gerard's (whose katydid was silent) house, and in the field next to the big solar house, "castanet-like" calls of the castanet cricket.

2012: Full leaf color throughout the area as ashes peak and maples come in strong. A huge flock of starlings and grackles over the alley at 8:15 this morning. Tonight, temperature at about 60, there was the soft, intermittent chirring of crickets and tree frogs, the rasping of one katydid near Dayton Street.

2013: Peak leaf color is just a few days away along the road south to Wilmington. The serviceberry trees in front of Don's house are turning orange and shedding quickly.

2014: A cross-line wave moth on the porch, pale beige with a darker brown line across its wings, two "eye" like marks, quite small toward the edge of both wings, a *Tetracis*.

2016: At 6:45 this morning, robins peeping in the honeysuckles off High Street. Crows calling north of town. Partly cloudy and mild throughout the day, only a handful of cabbage whites, a couple of skippers. Honeysuckle berries continue to fall all over the sidewalk and the car.

2017: Sun and warm: At least six painted lady butterflies in zinnias through the day. On a drive to Columbus, all the tree lines were green, soybean and cornfields brown. In the middle of the city, a murmuration of starlings circled and circled high above the skyscrapers and then suddenly swooped down, seeming to fall, hurtling into some decorative crab apple trees nearby.

2018: Heavy morning fog. I picked the first greenhouse tomatoes for sandwiches last night – like in 1982. Only one monarch noticed in the garden today. And a small checkerspot.

2019: Another day in the 90s. Many painted ladies and cabbage whites, a few monarchs in the garden. One burning bush along Park Place has turned half dusky red. A few black walnut trees are almost bare, but the definitive leafturn has not begun yet.. One limb of Jeannie's redbud tree seems to have died, its leaves wrinkled and gray and falling. No hummingbirds seen since September 30th. This evening, the katydids began to call at 6:45, and a flock of geese flew over at 6:50.

2021: Pearl's Fen with Jeff in warm, light rain: The goldenrod is leaning and sagging. The red-stemmed purple asters are withering. The white snakeroot is shriveling. The tall ragworts, so thick and strong a month ago, have fallen over, the edges of their leaves blackened. The violet Joe Pye plants have turned gray like the thistles. The Jerusalem artichokes have faded into the goldenrod, no longer flagships of the fen. Blackbirds or grackles in the bare trees. Jeff mentioned he heard doves calling last week.

2022: Cool and sun: Cabbage whites play in the full New England asters. Small bumblebees in the flowers. Mateo's black walnut tree keeps its foliage. Slow gilding of the village trees, and a few Judas maples. A patch of thin-leafed coneflowers still holds its petals in the alley, but most coneflowers in town are gone.

2023: The great blue heron, tall as my chest, was at the pond again this morning, 7:30. So he came back to finish off the smaller koi. The netting I put on over the water yesterday will hopefully disrupt his upcoming visits. In the garden, canna blossoms hold at 17. The cup plant foliage on one of the plants is browning now, the others holding. Crickets and katydids boisterous after dark. Lori told me, with no little excitement that the last of the eight monarch butterflies she had in her back yard milkweed had taken wing today.

There are forces in the woods, forces in the world, that lay claim to you, that lay a hand on your shoulder so gently that you do not even feel it: not at first. All of the smallest elements – the direction of a breeze one day, a single sentence that a friend might speak to you, a raven flying across the meadow and circling back again – lay claim to you, eventually, with a cumulative power.

Rick Bass

***October 4th**
The 277th Day of the Year

*Breeze riffles leaves.
Rain fills the earthen cup.
The rain's refrain-surcease of pain.
Rain plays its down cards
Faces up.
Fall fans its hand –
Red kings and queens –
Bare sceptre boughs
And blowing cloaks of leaves
Wind-tossed,
Whose earthy plus will ermine
With white-rimed fringe of frost.
Cold wind blows out the wind
God's mouth
And courtier birds bestir their plumes
And fly their muted mantlets South
To laze and drink from rills
In marshes rank, whilst here the sunny
Blaze will bank neath ashen clouds
And sink behind the hearth of hills,
Now autumn chooses brighter garb.
The rain-wrought stream plucks gushing harp.
Moss hangs in tatters from a tree,
Green velvet peeled—
Soft mushrooms spring from rotted bark.
Brown-spotted leaves bestrew the ground,
The fall-besotted poet wanders
Midst the pageant frayed.
Pale asters trail
Like breeze-stirred windmill blades—
A lilting sight -- white rayed, quintains
For the lance of spear-straight light.
A lone bird turns Fall's water wheel
With plaintive chant;
The crumbling halls with stream song ring.
And after russet-raftered Fall,*

And Winter's white veiled bride
Have glammed and flung their icy fling,
We'll gambol in the greening glades
Like wide-eyed foolish knaves
Of Spring.

Robert Paschell

Sunrise/set: 6:34/6:13
Day's Length: 11 hours 39 minutes
Average High/Low: 71/48
Average Temperature: 60
Record High: 91 – 1900
Record Low: 28 – 1901

The Daily Weather

Highs in the 80s come 15 percent of the time, in the 70s twenty-five percent, in the 60s forty percent, in the 50s fifteen percent. And for the first time since May 9th, an afternoon only in the 40s becomes possible. Rain occurs 50 percent of all the days, the second highest percentage of the month. Frost strikes one morning in four, the highest odds until the 13th. A little more than half the lows reach below 50 degrees.

Natural Calendar

This time of Early Fall, brings Full Leaf Color Season to the ashes. It opens Junco Season at local birdfeeders, Sprucegrowth Season on the spruce trees and Asian Ladybeetle Invasion Season throughout the country. This week finishes Purple Martin Season, Autumn Crocus Season, Swamp Marigold and Beggarticks Seasons, Autumn Sedum Season, Virgin's Bower Season, Jumpseed Season (all the seeds having jumped to the ground), Touch-me-not Season, Cicada Season and (if the weather is cold) Daddy Longlegs Season.

Daybook

1983: Today in the rain, the ash outside my office window lost almost half its leaves. The Osage at home is yellowing. The maple in front of the house is half red.

1984: Grinnell Swamp: Fall is holding back, green staying. But most white snakeroot and goldenrod are breaking down. All bur marigolds and touch-me-nots are gone. Zigzag goldenrod and asters are still full, but more of the zigzag is fading. A few maples are full yellow. Smartweed is still bright pink. Canadian thistles and ragwort are growing back.

1987: Jacoby Swamp: All goldenrod brown here. Shagbark hickory, tulip tree, sweet gum full deep yellow. Small flocks of migrating robins. So many trees bare: black walnut, cottonwood, poplar, wild cherry. Scarlet patches on the oaks. Panicled dogwood red and falling. Sassafras is old, rusted, blackberry leaves purple. Sumac bright red.

1990: Many of the young cottonwoods have lost their leaves. Some patches of peak color of ashes, hickory and maples. Crickets are still loud, katydids still calling.

1991: Peak leaf color began yesterday, coinciding with a number of opossums killed on the highway overnight. Is there a connection between the possums and the leaves? Why wouldn't there be a connection?

1992: Crows vociferous before dawn. Cardinal sings at 6:50 a.m. Box elder leaves almost cover the grass in the far backyard. A few raspberries hold.

1994: Ash and locust are full color at Wilberforce. Hawthorn berries are suddenly red in the park across from my office. Violet stonecrop and mums at the best of their bloom in the east and south gardens.

1995: Yesterday afternoon coming home from work in the rain, I saw a large flock of blackbirds feeding in the fields along Wilberforce-Clifton Road. This morning at the triangle park, the silver maple along my walk had a bruise of pale yellow. West of the maples, crab apples were starting to lose their leaves. In the countryside, some cottonwoods and locusts were almost bare, ashes still full early color. At Wilberforce, the red-leaved crab apple trees had dropped much of their foliage. On the way to school, buzzards were circling and swooping around the road kills. I saw another large hawk.

1998: Crows loud at 6:27 a.m., sky dark and cloudy. Goldenrod and New England asters are still in bloom near Cincinnati. Peak color for some ash and hickory. More hawks and road kills seen.

1999: My usual autumn energy is failing me now. Is the surge only a late August and early September phenomenon? Does October bring too much nostalgia? Does it bring frustration instead of restlessness, sadness instead of anticipation?

2001: Constant "chrrrr" of a wren in the apple tree this morning. This afternoon, I discovered the skunk's lair on the north side of the house, the entry neatly paved in pebbles. Indoors, the Christmas cacti are budding.

2002: Russian sage, New England asters, catmint, and a few butterfly bush flowers hold along the north stone wall. Mums are still bright. Many zinnias have been killed by mildew, but others provide patches of deep color to the aging garden. The yellow rose and Queen Anne's lace are still blossoming. The new purple clematis has six big, sleek flowers. At South Glen, goldenrod has rusted, and most of the jumpseeds are gone. Buckeye and black walnut leaves are down, ashes, maples, and ashes just starting. Katydids still call out at night.

2003: This morning at 6:50, I heard a crow, the first early morning crow of the year. A Nashville warbler with its distinctive eye ring seen in the forsythia bushes in front of the house late this morning. It was on the way to Nashville from Ontario.

2006: Ironwood tree is bare at the park, one ash shedding quickly.

2008: The purple crocus are almost done in the alley. Starlings, grackles and blackbirds swarmed and sang in the back trees for about two hours at midday, and then they were gone. The American beech is starting to turn in the park, and red maples are blushing a deeper red. Some sugar maples have patches of orange around town, and the first bittersweet berry has opened along High Street.

2009: Orb-weaver seen at Peggy's. Two monarchs in the butterfly bushes. Crows at 6:20, cardinal at 6:30 this morning.

2010: No orb-weavers seen so far this year. Crows at 6:17 this cool and rainy morning, no cardinals heard for several days. And the squirrels are not raiding the bird feeders this fall. Has there been a predator here, or some change in habitat?

2011: North to Mohican State Park, full color ashes, early maples to early peak near Mohican, reds and yellow and bright oranges in the valleys and hills. Soy fields brown to pale yellow (the late plantings). Crows at the campground until about 6:00 p.m.. Totally quiet at 6:00. At 6:30, full pulsing grating of what must be tree crickets, occasional windows of katydids. Black walnuts all over the ground, falling every few minutes.

2012: Serviceberry trees finally shedding. A cardinal sang throughout much of my walk with Bella this morning at 8:30, and there was a steady chirping of robins. From Madison, Wisconsin, Tat writes: "Leaves are brilliant yellows and reds -- the color is simply spectacular." At Ellis Pond, the bur oak was yellowing and one grove of ashes was more than half down. The yellow poplar continues to show patches of gold, and the sugar maple leaves are stained and blotchy. Watercress rises above the stream, so much taller than just a few weeks ago, October lush. Throughout the county, the soybean harvest is underway. The gibbous moon rose red at 10:00 o'clock this mild evening, crickets loud and steady.

2013: Several cabbage whites playing, mating in the zinnias. And a monarch came by in the afternoon, the first I have seen in what seems like weeks. At Ellis, the sassafras tree has turned a rusty orange. The pawpaw tree has large green fruits. The black maple is turning and shedding rapidly. Across the street, the Danielsons' maple is maybe a fourth turned, began to color in the last week of September. Lil's burning bush is half bright red.

2014: A cold morning walk in the 40s. (Janie said she thought she felt sleet for a few minutes when she went outside.) Bittersweet berries are a dusky orange in the alley. Pale honeysuckle leaves scattered on the front sidewalk, pulled down by the rain and wind. Odd that I think of the honeysuckles as being impervious to Early Fall, but it is not so.

2016: North Glen at 8:00 this morning with Emily: The murder of crows here was excited, flying back and forth. Then a vast flock of grackles passed through and above the trees, some of them settling high for the small acorns of the Chinquapin oak. They stayed for maybe ten minutes, and the acorns rained down around us, some half eaten. I saw two that were on the ground were sprouting. One blue jay and one downy woodpecker heard, some tree crickets, some field crickets. All of the touch-me-nots had lost their foliage, a few pods left to pop. A number of violet asters in bloom (the heart leaf and arrow leaf, both with leaf stems), and a few zigzag goldenrods. Bittersweet berries by the parking lot were dusky orange. Emily, taken with paw paws, searched for their fruit in the river grove and came back with five. Her first paw paws ever, she said, and she devoured two right away.

2017: Cutting zinnias in the north garden, surrounded by half a dozen or more painted ladies. They were unafraid, and they worked beside me as I thinned the spent blossoms. One silver-spotted skipper visited, one dark fold wing skipper, too. By the porch, the white autumn crocus is flopping now. Spiderworts transplanted, phlox and daffodils trenched in.

2018: Warm 71 degrees this morning, overcast. By the north corner of the porch, the leaves of the white autumn crocus have collapsed and withered. Even without sun: one monarch browsing in the tithonias. The Danielsons' maple leads the maples on High Street, small patches of golden brown among the green. Moya's maple, however (and unlike previous years), shows no change at all.

2019: After a week of afternoons in the high 80s and low-to-middle 90s, the October 2-4 cold front arrived, bringing lows into the 40s for the first time this fall. A formation of geese flew over the house at around 8:00 this morning. Monarchs, cabbage whites and painted ladies visited the zinnias, tithonias and cannas throughout the cool, sunny day. I found the last flower stem of the white autumn crocus overgrown and squelched by the spreading hostas. News reports tell of severe drought throughout the South, heavy rains in the North.

2020: Cloudy, rainy, 50s: Geese this morning over the south end of town. This afternoon at Ellis, I saw that the jewel weed, so ubiquitous through September, was gone, and the last nodding *Bidens cernua* was fading, the end of the flowering for the year, except for the smartweed, along the water. In the north garden, the viburnum is rich maroon, complements the zinnias, marigolds and New England asters across from it. Except for T. K.'s maple, the High Street trees near my house hold late summer green. As the wind came up, I placed netting over the pond to catch the coming leaves.

2021: Cloudy, soft, mild. Only a couple of cabbage white butterflies in the garden today. Gradual foliage turning, the river birch all pale now, isolated maples reddening, dusky ochre in the city tree line, more leaves on the sidewalk, a few large Osage fruits on the ground. I saw the first open milkweed pod at the corner of Dayton and High Streets.

2022: More sun and deep blue sky and cool temperatures: I sit in the backyard and watch the bees and the cabbage white butterflies in the still rich New England asters. Peggy's yard is overgrown with small white asters. The foliage in town and on the way to Xenia is turning quickly, more maples orange, oaks reddening. At Clifton Gorge, bright zig-zag goldenrod, small white asters and pale violet arrow-leaved asters in full flower along the path, the late afternoon light gilding all the trees.

2023: Full sun and wrm in the 80s, time. count at 19 canna blossoms. Moya's maple is blushing, T.K.'s maple with just a slight tint, my hackberry tree trickling leaves into the north garden. Beggartick leaves area cloudy violet now. Three cabbage whites play seen visiting one zinnia or aster after another. Along the freeway, only very light weathering of the tree line. At the radio station, the Canadian thistles were dry and brittle, all the down matted and sticky.

Paying attention provides the gift of noticing, and the gift of connecting. It provides the gift of seeing a little bit of ourselves in others, and of realizing that we're not so awfully alone. It allows us to let go of the burden of so much of what we habitually carry with us, and receive the gift of the present moment.

Sharon Salzberg

October 5th
The 278th Day of the Year

Greatly shining,
The Autumn moon floats in the thin sky....

Amy Lowell

Sunrise/set: 6:36/6:11
Day's Length: 11 hours 35 minutes
Average High/Low: 70/48
Average Temperature: 59
Record High: 93 – 1900
Record Low: 28 – 1901

The Daily Weather

There is a 15 percent chance of highs in the 80s today, and 15 percent for 70s. Sixties occur 30 percent of the afternoons, fifties 40 percent (the first time the chances of 50s have been so high since May 3rd). The sky is clear to mostly sunny 80 percent of the years, with rain coming one year in three. Frost occurs 15 percent of the mornings, and lows fall to the 30s thirty-five percent of the nights, the first time that percentage has been so high during the second half of the year.

Natural Calendar

In mild Octobers and Novembers, catchweed blooms. Cardinals and Carolina wrens briefly renew their songs. Cabbage butterflies reappear. Parsnips, violets, chickweed, celandine, dandelions, clover, sow thistles, and even forsythia blossom. The grass continues to grow on paths and in pastures, glowing in the low sun. Winter wheat creates patches of bright green in the countryside. New hepatica leaves are dark and strong along rocky paths. The tips of many spruce trees put on pale, fresh growth. Throughout the swamps, skunk cabbage comes up again. Ragwort and hemlock and watercress grow back. In the garden, red knuckles of rhubarb sometimes push to the surface.

Daybook

1982: South Glen: Touch-me-nots have lost their seeds. Catalpas are pale, dropping foliage. A few thin leaves of the locust are spinning down. Some animal or bird making a loud, hollow, continuous chirping sound, like the beating on a hollow pole. Maybe a titmouse. Clearweed is soft yellow green. A small garter snake seen hunting among the leaves that were floating in the river.

1984: Tree coloring intensifies. Maples in front of the house are two-thirds turned.

1986: Buck Creek: Some velvetleaf and jimsonweed still flower among the asters. Sweet clover grows back with the dock and cinquefoil, yarrow, and henbit. Last night, katydids were still calling. Crickets sing all day and night. Butterflies are everywhere. All the oaks and hickories here are green. It still seems like Late Summer in the woods.

1989: Caesar Creek, fishing: Panfish nibble steadily along the shore line, but only one small bass, six inches, and a five-inch sunfish are the afternoon's catch. The leaves are in full early turn now. More bare branches: all black walnuts, and some poplar and cottonwood gone. Sneezeweed found in full bloom along the west bank of the river. All the other flowers faded except the asters. Beggarticks going to seed here. The water low, the colors reflected more prominently, sharper contrasts, the crisp air accentuating the distinctions. At home, some katydids and most crickets survive several nights of light to medium frost.

1990: Thimble plants unraveling, white snakeroot tufted and old. Heart-leafed asters are still in their prime. Zigzag goldenrod fading.

1992: The maple in front of the house a third gold and losing leaves quickly. Very early leaf-turn throughout town; this is a pivot time.

1995: Barometer low at 29.55 this morning. Steady rain, gusts of warm wind. My body feels lethargic, all it wants is to sit by the fire and watch the summer come down around it.

1997: Giant, the green frog that lives at the pond, croaks before dawn. Crows wake up at 6:15 a.m. The koi are active in the hot afternoons, working the shallow water in the early morning. Just a few days ago, frost on the roof, they lay at the bottom, ignoring the food I threw in. New England asters in the yard suddenly start to die back. The violet autumn crocus flowers across the street are falling over.

1998: Water lilies are diminishing now. Blue jay at 8:55 a.m. Cardinal at 9:19 a.m.

1999: Autumn crocus have been gone for more than a week. A spider in the bathtub this morning, running from the frost.

2000: In the rain, huge golden ash trees shed most of their leaves at school today. In town, the mountain ash is thinning, its orange berries becoming more prominent. Yellow poplar starting. The small-leaved maples that have turned so deep red are losing leaves quickly. Hickory is golden. Tiny gold warblers seen in my spruce. South to Wilmington, parallel disintegration, and sugar maples moving in to compensate for the ashes.

2001: Susi's Osage is suddenly turning gold. The maples at the corner of High Street and Dayton Street are bright red. The ginkgo at the corner of Xenia Avenue and High has started to turn. Last night, the temperature stayed in the 60s, and the katydids were loud and fast, lots of crickets too.

2003: A few painted lady *(Cynthia)* butterflies and a few cabbage butterflies in the tattered zinnias today. No monarchs seen since the end of September. Mrs. Lawson's maple is starting to turn. Many ashes are red or gold, with a large percentage of maples coming in beside them. Most cottonwoods have come down, and all the black walnuts.

2004: A skunk has been digging in the yard for several days now; this morning at about 4:00 a.m., Bella ran out and attacked it, got severely sprayed. Skunk odor in the back yard all day (and in the house!). After the abrupt leafturn of the last two weeks, a period of stability seems to be occurring, caused, perhaps by the clear and cool weather of the past week. My mood climbs slightly as the moon moves into its fourth quarter.

2005: An early blizzard has stymied Wyoming and the Dakotas.

2006: Fall moving rapidly now, all the ashes full (almost all down at Wilberforce), jumpseeds all jumped, Lil's tree coming in, Danielsons' at least a third turned, all the tall pink sedum are done, the red Autumn Joy holding. Mateo's elm and red mulberry suddenly decay. Box elder at the northeast corner of the yard is bare. Two very large starling flocks seen. A few areas full color, others deep green. My ash at school gone. Full maples at Wilberforce, ashes two-thirds down, locusts full and thinning. Large mallows have yellow leaves. Black snakeroot flowers fading quickly. The first Christmas cactus flower opens in the greenhouse.

2007: At South Glen, the river is about two feet low from the dry autumn. One tall bellflower seen, many asters, some fading zigzag goldenrod, rusting tall goldenrod by the place where the old barn stood. A pileated woodpecker heard, and crows. All the foliage dry and turning, the sycamores especially brown, falling, and many Osage.

2008: Two robins chasing each other in the alley this morning. Giant wheel bug visited the lawn chairs this afternoon.

2009: Beggartick foliage is a rich purple now, Mateo's goldenrod is rusting, Lil's burning bush half red, Don's maple half golden, one question mark butterfly as I walked down High Street.

2010: Crows at 6:15 a.m. I stopped at the Covered Bridge this morning. Cool and partly cloudy, the ground wet, the river low, sandbars high at Yellow Springs Creek and the Little Miami: Late goldenrod fills the field here; by the path - pink smartweed (some with "lady's thumb" marks, some without); skeletons of wingstem, seed heads bristly, old ironweed, seed heads soft but not gray yet; some white snakeroot, a lone tall lobelia, a few heart-leafed asters, many small white asters, some with short leaves, some with long; a white fuzzy caterpillar about an inch and a half long on a brown stem of foxtail grass; crows, robins, a pileated woodpecker and downy woodpeckers heard; a great blue heron flew off ahead of me, buzzards circling over the old mill. The canopy here is mostly green and intact, mainly sycamore leaves on the path, patches of yellow maple leaves appearing as I drove back toward town. A cardinal called when I got out of my truck at 10:20. Near the back porch, the white fall crocus still holds, raggedy, by the wisteria. At noon, the temperature about 60 degrees, one giant swallowtail came to the butterfly bushes. A few cabbage butterflies were around at the same time.

2011: Mohican State Park in northeastern Ohio: Crows heard at 6:19. Chipmunks chipping throughout the day (not cardinals like we thought at first). When we walked the North Ridge Trail, we heard katydids in the woods from time to time, and intermittent trills of crickets, took photos of many different fungi. Many white caterpillars with black markings on their backs, crawling across the roads and through the leaves: caterpillars of the hickory tussock moth.

2012: The national news reports two feet of snow in parts of northern Minnesota today. Here, robins peeping throughout my walk this morning, peak leaf color spreading so quickly. The Danielsons' maple is half turned now, and the upper branches of Lil's burning bush are bright scarlet. The ashes on the way to Cedarville are in full color, dominating the roadways. The viburnum on the north side of the house is full burnished red and shedding. At Ellis Pond, 4:00 p.m., clouds dark purple, wind from the northwest, ash leaves glittering as they fall to the water, bur oaks coming down, some sugar maples, more and more momentum accentuated by the arrival of the cold front. Here, the Korean lilac, violet dun. I saw Eric Wolf today: He said that when he gave names to plants, people were turned off by the threat of the words themselves. I told him that I used names as a way of touching them.

2013: New England asters *(Aster novae-angliae)* and small white asters *(Aster vimineus)* suddenly decline in the yard. Sweet gums at the south edges of town quite dark orange and maroon.

2014: Sycamores at the Mill Dam habitat are half turned. Many maples down near the college. Sycamore fruits on the ground there. In this cold day, no butterflies noticed. A red-tailed hawked screamed above me as I walked Bella around the campus. A small sweet gum there has a large patch of red and pale yellow. No cardinals noticed in the yard for quite a while. Did a cat get them? Flurries reported at the Dayton airport.

2015: Record, once-in-a-millennium rainfall along the South Carolina coast, up to two feet in some areas, flooding widespread.

2016: Hurricane Matthew, Category 4, batters the Caribbean and then moves toward eastern Florida, expected to proceed up the Carolina coast. In Yellow Springs, the Sun is shining and the day is warm. But only a couple of cabbage whites, a silver-spotted skipper and a small fritillary joined the honeybees in the still full-blooming zinnias and New England asters. Katydids still strong in the evening.

2017: Rain today and projected into the middle of the month. A new hurricane is forming off the coast of Central America, on track to strike the Gulf region of the United States.

2018: Clouds and mild: one fat rabbit, the first I've seen in a long time, in the yard this morning, and the two male finches at the feeder were only pale yellow, had lost their summer brilliance. When the sun came out and the air became humid and warm in the high 70s, I saw four of five monarchs at a time in the tithonias, three silver-spotted skippers and even a painted lady, the first of the autumn.

2019: Cool and crisp, 52 degrees at sunrise. Italian honeybees, a painted lady and several cabbage whites in the flower beds. No hummingbirds seen here since September 30, but Leslie reports she saw one female on October 3 at her place on Talus Drive. No robins seen or heard since they went into hiding in Late Summer, the drought maybe keeping them away. Almost all the New England asters have gone to seed; without their purple complement, the asters stand out even more.

2020: Fog this morning, now sun this afternoon, almost 60 degrees, five cabbage white butterflies appear, playing randori in the deep purple New England asters. Robins peeping in the honeysuckles. In Xenia, red maples bright red along the highway. Throughout Yellow Springs, leafturn has reached peak Early Fall color. Drifts of asters along the road in the Vale. Jeff says it's time to plant garlic in his Cedarville plot.

2021: Another soft day, fog in the morning. One monarch butterfly seen in the full-purple New England asters downtown. Two cabbage butterflies in the north garden. No robins heard for over a month. No painted lady butterflies seen all year. Sedum rusting. Geese flew over at about 5:30 this evening.

2022: Surge in leaf color: the top foliage of Moya's maple has started to turn, as has Lil's, the changes seeming dramatic for being so sudden. And I notice that the April-blooming viburnum is full deep maroon. Robin heard peeping in the honeysuckles in the afternoon. Geese flew over at about 6:00 p.m.

2023: Time count: Canna blossoms remaining at 18. Cardinal at 6:13 this morning. Carolina wren at 6:30. A bird with a single note called a few times, maybe like a blue jay waking up. Light rain began in the morning, prelude to the cold forecast for the week ahead.

First Snows
Since I came to Yellow Springs, I have recorded the dates for many of the earliest snows between 1982 and 2023.

October 5, 2014: A few snow flurries noticed as I drove to Dayton.
October 12 of 1988 and 2006: The first flurries of the season in my garden.
October 18, 2022: First flurries in the sleet.
October 19, 1989: First light snow in town.
October 23, 2013: This morning, the first snow of the winter, light and wet.
October 27, 2017: Jill sent me photos from the first snow of the year on High Street.

October 30, 1993: The first snow of the year is falling, accumulating up to four inches deep by the roadside, sticking on the newly plowed fields. By the riverbank down in South Glen: the sound of the snow dropping from branches, plopping into the water.

October 31, 2019: First snow of the year, wind gusts up to 30 miles an hour.

November 3, 1991 and 1999: First flurries of the year.

November 5, 1982: The first snow covered Yellow Springs at 5:00 a.m. with heavy, fat flakes.

November 6, 1988: First snow, one inch, as Late Fall pushes through with a sudden plunge in barometric pressure.

November 11, 1984 and 1986: First snow and first snowball made.

November 13, 2021: First snow in the night, half an inch.

November 15, 2008: The first snowfall came today covering the ground for an hour or so.

November 27, 2018: First snow of the year, accompanied by sandhill cranes.

November 29, 2011: The first snow of the year late this afternoon, the ground covered for a few hours before the wet grass soaked it up. More worms stranded from the earlier rain.

November 30, 2020: First snow, three inches

December 5, 2007: First snow of the season last night and this morning, four to five inches. The alley bamboo is full of snow, bowing and blocking half my path there.

December 18, 2023: First hard snow with wind, slight accumulation

December 19, 2009: The first snow of the year covered all the branches this morning, showing off the daffodil spears that had grown up in the warm November. On the news tonight, details about a huge storm moving toward the Northeast.

December 31,1998: The first snow of the year overnight, maybe half an inch

Let sunlight slip from overhead
and slant toward afternoon.
Let evening cool more quickly
than before, and morning warm
more slowly. Let what blooms move
from pink to russet, from lemon to

deepest gold, from baby blue to aster-purple.
Let leaves abandon green for warmer hues.
Let breezes grow cool, rains grow chill,
sleeves grow long. Let thoughts turn
once more toward the woodstove
and second quilts appear on beds.
Let nights grow longer
at the expense of days.
Let autumn come, as it must;
be not afraid. No season has
the final word, but takes its turn.

Deborah Walker

October 6th
The 279th Day of the Year

By the sixth of October the leaves generally begin to fall, in successive showers, after frost or rain; but the principal leaf-harvest, the acme of the Fall, is commonly about the sixteenth.

Henry David Thoreau

Sunrise/set: 6:36/6:10
Day's Length: 11 hours 34 minutes
Average High/Low: 70/48
Average Temperature: 59
Record High: 87 – 1946
Record Low: 27 – 1980

The Daily Weather

Completely cloudy conditions are rare today: the 6th is one of the two sunniest days of the month (the other is the 8th), bringing only one day in ten without at least some blue sky. Today's high temperature distribution: ten percent chance of 80s, fifteen percent for 70s, forty-five percent for 60s, thirty percent for 50s. Showers occur twice in a decade. Lows drop below 50 on 70 percent of the nights. And one more pivotal step to winter: for the first time in the autumn, the chance of a morning in the 20s rises to 15 percent.

Natural Calendar

Chimney swifts, wood thrushes, barn swallows and red-eyed vireos move out of the Middle Atlantic region as Early Fall comes to an end. Flocks of blackbirds and robins migrate across the country. Terns and meadowlarks, yellow-rumped warblers, yellow-bellied sapsuckers, red-bellied nuthatches and purple martins migrate through the Lower Midwest. Between now and March, shorebirds, such as dowitchers, yellowlegs and black-bellied plovers, feed in the salt marshes of southern Georgia.

Daybook

1983: Wild lettuce is brown throughout. The ash by my window lost all its leaves today. The rest of the trees around it are green.

The first yellow mulberry leaf seen today. Osage is turning behind the woodshed. Some forsythia is red.

1984: Middle Fall arrives, trees suddenly deepening. A long flock of migrating blackbirds seen near Springfield.

1985: North along the railroad tracks: dozens of robins. Most wild cherry leaves and some dogwood gone. Three meadowlarks flying together. First yellow-rumped warblers seen. First junco of the year. Eastern burning bush: some pods opening, berries showing. White snakeroot mostly gone. Wild black cherry thinning, elms yellow brown and thinning, red poison ivy, black walnut trees totally bare, a few naked catalpas, goldenrod nine-tenths gone, geese loud and active at Ellis pond, some maples full color. Bouncing bets still flowering. Cottonwood, some yellow, some almost gone. Sassafras just starting to be orange. Staghorn leaves are gone, wild lettuce stark, black.

1986: It's Middle Fall for sure: beggarticks stuck to my pants today. New leaves sprouting on the pussy willow that had dropped most of its leaves last month. In the woods, zigzag goldenrod is about gone.

1987: Three-seeded mercury has lost its seeds, pods empty, a bright burnt sienna color against its green leaves.

1990: A cardinal sang at 12:30 p.m. Cicadas sporadic, but long silences in the afternoon. At 3:50 p.m. a large flock of blackbirds flew over the yard, continuing for about ten minutes, settled in the woodlot for an hour, then moved on. This is the fourth year in a row I've seen them near this day.

  1992: To Springfield: Early full leafturn in some wood lots, locusts gold, maples orange, catalpas pale yellow, bright scarlet burning bush, touch of blood red on the oaks, pink dogwoods, violet brown ash. Starlings along the wires. Cornfields finally brown, soybeans rusting, ready to harvest. Some hickory deep solid red-orange, ashes holding late. They should blend with maples to create a spectacular peak.

1999: A cricket hunter visited the pond today, but insects are thinning out now. The red mulberry along the south hedge is just starting to turn. Many ash trees and walnuts are coming down around town. Koi still feed heavily. One late red water lily holds on in the pond. Hackberry pale yellow on the north border. False boneset still in bloom on the way to Fairborn. Along the roadsides, four or five groundhogs killed, their activity or carelessness increasing as winter approaches? In the local paper: more and more sick raccoons captured by the police.

2000: In the wind and rain, the first tier of leaves is collapsing fully. As I eat lunch at school, a flock of crows moves south, prelude to the November gathering. At Clifton, the canopy has thinned. All the flowers are gone in the undergrowth except the long-leaved purple asters. Zigzag goldenrod has gone to seed like the rest of the tall goldenrod.

2003: Sunny, high in the 50s. Half a dozen painted lady (Cynthia) butterflies were in the zinnias when I went out to check the garden this afternoon. My ash at school is about three-fourths gone, the remaining leaves a mottled yellow. Along the freeways, the small wild dogwood and sumac are a dusky red beside the graying goldenrod.

2005: Another vole caught in the kitchen mousetrap last night, the third so far this week. The high is again expected to be in the 80s today, the last day in an exceptional spell of warm weather. The ash below my old window at work was all yellow this afternoon, more than two-thirds shed.

2007: Mateo's Jerusalem artichokes are done blooming; ours have only a few blossoms left. The alley coneflowers are pretty much done, and even the chicory is getting ragged. Asters are still bright, white and violet. Along the front sidewalk, almost all the jumpseeds have jumped. Eve reports that her red chestnut tree is blooming again in all this heat - all six days of October have been in the 80s, and those highs are expected to stay for another three days. I went to take a photograph of the flowers, and the tree was standing, no leaves and only a few chestnuts left, but several bright pink flowers were open, along with clusters of new foliage. This warm evening, katydids and crickets called from Tony's field and the back woods.

2008: A few cabbage butterflies and one yellow sulphur.

2009: Clear before dawn with huge white full moon setting. Cardinal at 6:16, crows at 6:25. New small-flowered coneflowers have started up in the alley. Serviceberry trees more than half down. Korean lilac leaves have blushed roseate. The viburnum is deep red orange. Five flowers found on the back witch hazel. The toad lily still has three flowers by the red-leaved redbud.

2010: Cool and sunny again today, crows very late – maybe 6:25 this morning. Then at 8:15, a giant flock of grackles stopped in the Stafford Street trees along Limestone Street, moving on after a few minutes. At the South Glen, a few cabbage butterflies and silver-spotted skippers, tattered wood nettle, huge, aging pokeweed plants with their berries half gone. One swamp bidens seen. At John Bryan State Park, early leafturn with some bright maples.

2011: Highs in the 80s today and a similar forecast for tomorrow. One monarch at Mohican State Park, then home in the garden, one more, plus a sulphur and two cabbage whites. Goldenrod full and also rusting in the fields, New England asters still full bloom throughout the 130-mile trip. No fields harvested all along our trip home, corn and soybeans still waiting to mature, browning but not ready. Walking Bella tonight at 7:00 p.m., I listened to katydids all along Dayton and High Streets, and intense high-pitched crickets, steady screams, and some intermittent metallic-like castanet calls, and a few chirps of field crickets, the volume and intensity much greater than the last two nights at Mohican State Park.

2014: The large grove of ashes at the west end of Ellis is a rich burnt sienna and holds most of its leaves. The grove closest to the parking lot is golden brown and more than half shed. The small red maple is down, and most of the small dogwoods are red. The beggartick foliage is violet, and the heads have gone to seed – as they have at home. Only one cabbage white seen on this cool, windy, mostly cloudy day.

2015: Umbria, Italy: The landscape has changed considerably since I arrived on September 28th. The yellow-gold of many cottonwoods, hickories, sumacs, buckeyes, poplars and black walnut trees has spread and deepened, and the sense of Early Fall has become much stronger.

2016: Mild and shining sun: A few cabbage whites, a small fritillary or skipper, two yellow sulphurs and, for the first time in quite a while, a red admiral in the north zinnias. New England asters still at full bloom. The red Knockout rose in the northwest side of the garden pulls the eye deep into the yard. At the northwest corner of the back porch, the center stalks of the white autumn crocus are still straight and tall, the side stalks flopping., Tithonias have definitely declined, their season ended now. Lil's burning bush with splotches of red, her maple slightly weathered. Mateo's black walnut tree still has half its foliage.

2017: Leafturn in town is happening quickly now, the solid pale greens of last week suddenly becoming rusted and gilded. In the garden, the New England asters are closing as the leaves change color. Painted lady butterflies still in the zinnias this morning: there were four at least. Against the north side of the house, Virginia creeper leaves are burgundy, matching the shedding viburnum, against the dark barn red of the siding. As I worked in the cool and cloudy afternoon, a hummingbird came close by me to the zinnias and the feeder. Jill noticed glow worms by the front sidewalk when we got home from seeing a play.

2018: This morning as I walked through the yard, I saw at least three monarchs in the tithonias, several cabbage whites, a small checkerspot and a painted lady once again.

2019: From upstate New York, Dennis Brown reports the first frost and 28 degrees. Here in Yellow Springs, rainy, sun and clouds and cool.

2020: A perfect Early Fall afternoon, the sun bright on the zinnias, the New England asters and the orange tithonias. Six cabbage whites and the first painted lady of the year playing in the flowers. A few prairie dock blossoms remain at the West South College Street corner, the latest I remember them blooming. At Ellis Pond, one ragged sulphur butterfly fluttered across my path into the cornfield. Geese flew over near sundown.

2021: Maggie sends a photo of a silver-spotted skipper from Madison, Wisconsin, but only two cabbage whites here. The weather holds warm and humid. Honeysuckle berries have begun their autumn fall, covering the car and sidewalk with red and orange.

2022: Robin peeping in the honeysuckles. New England asters still full. Tree of heaven along the north garden is rusting. At the south wall: a travelling yellow-bellied sapsucker was tapping in search of insects, like on the 16th in 1995. One or two cabbage whites and many bees in the asters.

2023: Time count: Canna blossoms at 15 today. Now the hops leaves are ochre and its fruit clusters rusting. Wild grape foliage has become pale, turning the hedge to autumn. Blue jays quiet, robins and geese rare, painted lady butterflies absent this fall. One dove feeding in the back yard. Jill noted that honeysuckle berries were covering the sidewalk near the front of the house. Some beggartick plants have lost their leaves. The Paulownia tree has begun to shed, and it seems to have buds now for spring? And silver maple trees have shed their winged seeds that have covered the sidewalks.

Thus times do shift; each thing his turn does hold;
New things succeed as former things grow old.

Robert Herrick

*We wondered
if everything were as fragile
as the brittle love vines
holding to the nettle
below Mill Dam,
this seventh of October,
fog coming south
down river in the rain.*

Leon Quel

Sunrise/set: 6:37/6:08
Day's Length: 11 hours 31 minutes
Average High/Low: 69/47
Average Temperature: 58
Record High: 89 – 2007
Record Low: 26 – 1899

The Daily Weather

Overcast skies come 30 percent of October 7ths, but rain continues at yesterday's light 20 percent. Eighty-degree afternoons are observed 5 percent of the time, 70s twenty percent, 60s thirty percent, 50s forty percent, and 40s five percent. Only 10 percent of the morning lows are above 60 degrees; only 20 percent are even above 50. Frost strikes one day in five.

The Natural Calendar

The Japanese beetles and aphids disappear in the cool, shortening days. Taking their place, cucumber beetles hide in the late roses. Cricket song has completely replaced cicada song. Yellow jackets become more numerous, cabbage butterflies tamer and more reckless in the search for nectar and favorable sites to lay their eggs. Insect numbers decline, and spider webs start to disappear from the woods. Woolly-bear caterpillars, however, multiply, sometimes swarm across the roads on sunny afternoons.

1983: Grinnell Swamp: Jumpseed and clearweed foliage is yellowing. Red-bodied dragonflies still seen. Hobblebush leaves becoming pale, wood nettle almost white now, avens a golden green. Only a couple of touch-me-not flowers left. New sweet rocket basal foliage is almost a foot long. Sedum and ginger are growing back. Aging clearweed is creamy white. The high canopy still intact. Bees still working, even in this cool late afternoon. Aphids still mating on the dead wingstem. Beggarticks still soft. No cobwebs found this afternoon: another step into Middle Fall.

1985: A few Osage leaves turn and fall.

1987: Colors deepen quickly after two frosts, the entire spectrum of underbrush, shrubs, small and tall trees changing together. Robins very common, flickers and meadow larks, too. Flocks of birds pass overhead. Opossums and groundhogs are still being run over on the back roads. The maple in front of house is about half thinned. Lil's maple is still green, Mrs. Lawson's only turning lightly.

1991: First frost reaches the lawn but not the garden this morning. At Wilberforce, the parking lot locusts are down. At home, the earliest maples are bare before the scarlet ashes. Full leaf color continues.

1992: South Glen: Sycamore leaves crunching on the path. Streaks of full leaf color across the tree line: sycamores, yellow Osage and paling box elder along the river. A few bees in the last of the goldenrod. Drooping, blanching wood nettle. Two autumn violets on the path. Two dragonflies cross the field in front of me. Ironweed tufted, foliage black like the wingstem. Still some asters left, although the *lateriflora* seem almost gone. Near Sycamore Hole, the long-leafed white asters seem the strongest; some heart-leafed also full. At Wilberforce, ashes reach peak yellow and red, some falling.

1995: Rapid change in the leaves now. A few of the crabapple trees have lost most of their foliage, a dense crop of orange berries on the earliest; the reds are coming, too. The upper leaves of the witch hazels on Dayton Street are yellow. Most redbuds have become pale yellow. Yellow poplars show deep slashes of color, cottonwoods weakening. Some ashes hold at their peak. New England asters passing their zenith in the south garden. As I weeded in the sun this afternoon, I saw the spring-autumn glow coming into the grass, the whole tint of the world shifting.

1997: Full late color on the locusts. Half of the catalpas are yellow, dogwood full red. Peak of the first tier of leaves. Full yellow redbuds. Early maples. Late ashes, full red burning bush.

1999: The maple in front of the house is half turned, maybe a fourth fallen.

2000: First light frost of the year on the roof this morning. Crows at 7:39 a.m.

2001: First cardinal (the only cardinal) at 6:14 a.m. Goldenrod done at Susi's, and her tomatoes have been cut back. First frost this morning, light damage to the elephant ears.

2003: One monarch butterfly seen at Washington Court House this morning at 11:10. Woolly-bear caterpillars common on the road. Many locusts and ashes are now full color, maples joining them in many wood lots. The landscape slowly turns an ochre-green. This afternoon, Asian lady beetles were swarming at Washington Court House and also in Yellow Springs. The autumn crocuses are still standing across the street.

2007: One cardinal song at 6:20 a.m., crows a little earlier. As we sat reading the Sunday paper, starlings whistled in the back trees. Sparrows and doves came in spurts to the bird feeder, and a red-bellied nuthatch flew back and forth for seeds. A female goldfinch came to the finch feeder, but the finches have been few and far between for the past month. No butterflies at all this morning, only a few cabbage whites in the afternoon. Along Dayton Street, the serviceberry trees hold half their yellow and brown leaves. Patches of bright gold have appeared on the white mulberry and the Osage in the back yard.

2008: The landscape lies on a plateau of full Early Fall, little change seen in the past week. About a dozen, maybe a few more, apples hold in the alley. Euonymus berries fully formed, white. The berries of the panicled dogwood are disappearing, red stems sticking out. Don's tall black walnut tree is down to about a fourth of its leaves. No bird song heard today. As rain moves toward the Miami Valley, crickets and katydids are calling in the mild, humid evening.

2009: Blustery, cold this morning. First the moon, just past full, was so white before sunrise, and the sky was clear, Venus in the east. Then the clouds blew in, and now the weather is gray and raw. In the alley, more black walnuts came down last night in the wind. Great ragweed flower stalks have been stripped bare. All of Don's late hostas have stopped blooming now, and, in the North Garden, the New England asters are about three-fourths gone to seed, but the violet arrow-leaved asters and the small whites are still strong. Euonymus berries are white, some privet berries are blue, bittersweet berries darkening. But Peggy's virgin's bower remains at peak bloom. At the back door, a yellow jacket is huddled against the screen.

2010: Crows at 6:23 this morning, cool and clear. The witch hazel by the south window has small round buds, two premature flowers.

2011: Another day in the low 80s but few butterflies (one skipper, multiple cabbage whites). Crows at 6:20 this morning, cardinal "chits" about five minutes later. The Danielsons' maple turned suddenly a dirty gold a few days ago, Lil's maple only tinged with color, her burning bush almost all red. The land all around is in early full stage. The north garden remains full of color, mums and zinnias and marigolds. Our viburnum is full dusky red, the Korean lilac a mottled violet. Ashes full gold and red and shedding along the back road to the mall. Asters of all kinds remain dominant. Tonight, katydids were everywhere, intermittent tree crickets filling the neighborhood, a few field crickets, too.

2012: A cold and raw day: I went out to Ellis Pond and looked at leafturn, the bur oaks continuing to yellow and shed, sweet gums holding their deep maroon-red leaves, no change in the scarlet oaks – just a few leaves turned, most of the ashes down, leaves dry and crunching underfoot, a flock of geese in the pond (the two white ducks leading them around the water), and along the dry creek bed near the hickory tree, a deep green cornucopia of Second Spring foliage: fresh, tall watercress, wide dock, parsnips, garlic mustard, sweet Cicely.

2013: A small orb-weaver put its web under the front porch light, caught lots of insects last night. At the bird feeder, I saw a gold finch that had been molting, its once bright colors mottled. In the alley, bittersweet berries are a pale orange now, have darkened quite a bit over the past week. At the Ellis Pond arboretum, the ash grove is rusty brown and shedding rapidly; the buckeye and horse chestnut are bare; the Kentucky coffee tree and the persimmon are yellow and losing leaves; no color on the oaks yet; huge red berries on the flowering dogwood; the European beech leaves are deep purple-maroon. One monarch seen flying south when I crossed Dayton Street.

2015: Judy wrote this evening before her trip to Greece: "The geese are flying. I saw three flocks yesterday and heard honking today. The ducks are gathering on the pond, and I'm sorry I'll miss the huge flocks that stopped by last year to grab a quick bite and rest on the shallow waters before continuing on." I replied that since the Italian countryside was turning just a little behind Ohio's, maybe the leaves in Greece would not be so far behind Indiana's.

2016: Stymied by a bad cold, I sit and look at the north garden full of sun. The viburnum has suddenly started to show red shading. I pay attention to how the hops and the climbing false buckwheat and the honeysuckle and the Japanese knotweed and the trees of heaven have encroached on the old garden area. The invading growth demonstrates to me what happens without Jeanie here to give her own vision to this space, to contrast with my own tendency to let things spread in order to see what will happen. At the height of the New England asters, the honeybees and the small bumblebees are almost the only insects seeking pollen. Then a cabbage butterfly or two, then one fold-wing skipper, one sulphur.

Then three monarchs come and visit one zinnia after another, transforming the afternoon, reassuring me.

2017: A soft and humid morning in the middle 60s. Hurricane Nate coming up from Merida in the Yucatan toward New Orleans, expected to bring rain to Ohio in four or five days. One painted lady at 9:00 a.m., and Jonatha reported seeing a monarch. Warming through the afternoon. I took time to transplant phlox to the southwest corner of the porch (cutting them back to their roots in order to foil the beetles that destroyed them this year) and to weed the failed daisy patch.

2019: Occasional maples turning about town, all very slow so far. The viburnum is flushed some, like Lil's burning bush across the street. Too cold for butterflies today.

2020: Another perfect day, sun and cool, only cabbage whites in the garden. Stopped at South Glen, wandered the overgrown paths, corridors of withered wingstem and wood nettle, only a few small white asters in bloom.

2022: The mild stability of Early Fall dissipates as the barometer begins its autumnal rises and falls. Frost is forecast for tonight. The landscape, both in town and in the country, is early full color now. Moya's maple doubled its color overnight. T.K.'s maple full gold, Lil's turning early. The locusts near the hospital in Xenia are all turned pale yellow, shedding.

Like Altair and Vega,
We ride the night sky alone,
Reflecting only the light
Which shines on us
From other burning stars.
Be still. Stay a moment
Just as you are.

Sam Hamill

October 8th
The 281st Day of the Year

The woods is shining this morning.
Red, gold and green, the leaves
lie on the ground or fall,
hang full of light in the air still.

Wendell Berry

Sunrise/set: 6:38/6:07
Day's Length: 11 hours 29 minutes
Average High/Low: 69/47
Average Temperature: 58
Record High: 88 – 2007
Record Low: 23 – 1889

Weather

Chances of rain continue at a low 20 percent today. Chances of completely overcast condition are also just 20 percent. The high temperature distribution is as follows: 80s fifteen percent of the time, 70s thirty percent, 60s thirty percent, and 50s twenty-five percent. Frost comes one day in five.

The Weather in the Week Ahead

While some days this week are often warm (the 8th of October bringing a 40 percent chance of highs above 70 degrees), others are typically cooler. October 11th, 12th, and 13th are the days most likely to see highs in the 40s or 50s. The coldest morning so far in the season usually comes on October 13th, when the chances of a low in the 20s are 20 percent for the first time since spring.

The first part of the week is usually dry (with only a 20 percent chance of precipitation on the 8th), but precipitation often increases thereafter, with the 10th bringing a 40 percent chance of rain, and the 12th a 50 percent chance. The 12th is also the first day that snow has a five to ten percent chance of falling.

The Natural Calendar

Middle Fall approaches the land along the 40th Parallel, and leafturn surges. The last monarchs depart for Mexico as the high canopy thins and the burning bush turns scarlet. The ashes, redbuds and hickories shed quickly. Many catalpas are down, beans left swinging in the wind. Ginkgo fruits, which will be on the ground by late November, are turning pink. Box elders, poplars, elms, red mulberries and sycamores are mottled.

Daybook

1982: Stopped at upper North Glen. Purple berries noticed on the brown Solomon's seal.

1985: Mill habitat: Hundreds of migrating blackbirds along the river, bathing, feeding in the fallen leaves and in the pebble beaches laid bare by the autumn drought. Maybe 30 or 40 buzzards circling above me, 28 counted on the sycamore roost, a couple with wings spread toward the sun. Shagbark hickory is yellow and thinning. River very low. Undergrowth benign, glowing like it does in April. Most asters declining. Zigzag mostly gone. Large cluster of red berries at the end of a fallen jack-in-the-pulpit. Only smartweed seems fresh. School of carp seen. Strong basal sweet rocket leaves, some a foot long. Some dogwood almost bare. In the yard, maples at high color and thinning, at the corner of Dayton and High: full gold. After just two light frosts, crickets so quiet, only a few sluggish ones calling in the yard.

1989: The speed and violence of the season increasing. Red mulberry, buckeye and some red-leafed crab apple leaves about gone. Ashes and locusts at Wilberforce still full color. All the buckeye fruits have fallen. Some black walnuts brought in today to dry; the nuts are coming down, but many are still left. Starlings in the back trees cackling. Now the July planted zinnias are full bloom in the greenhouse, and tomatoes blooming inside too, and yellow hibiscus and more geraniums. Aloe will blossom any day. Outside at night, no katydids, and crickets are slow in the cold.

1990: Leaves rapidly moving to peak, maples suddenly brilliant, the early side of the best color, but no real frost yet.

1991: The first tier of leaves is in the middle of falling now, the early maples, the box elders, ashes, red mulberries, locusts.

1992: To Springfield: At the freeway, a flock of blackbirds migrating southeast. A flock with no beginning and no end, flying out of the center of the city on one side of the horizon all across the sky into the countryside on the other side. I stopped at Sycamore Hole on the way home from work: leaf showers, clatter of sycamore leaves.

1994: All but a handful of New England asters have gone to seed in the south garden. Just the zinnias and violet mums left there, and a few spiderworts. Along the house and into the back yard, the impatiens are still as bright as in summer. In the garden, marigolds have overrun the cabbages and tomatoes.

1996: As frost time comes closer, I bring in the tomato plants I seeded in July, and I set up the greenhouse for winter.

The bugs and I will fight there until the new year. It will be a fair fight up until then, but they will begin to win as January ends, their ability to breed outlasting my ability to keep up with them, or my hope of overcoming them.

I could, I suppose, eliminate the insects with strong and efficient poisons, but they are part of a psychological system as well as an ecological system I set in place each year.

Throughout the fall and early winter, I can pretend I am lost in a seasonal wilderness, suspended in time. I have escaped the lush expectations of summer. I can hide and rest. I don't need to produce. I can build energy. I can wait and plan.

In this hermetic endeavor, the tomatoes, the whiteflies, mites and aphids are my allies and my guides. I don't need the tomatoes for my survival. Their fruit is a gratuitous response to my awareness. And so the bugs are not really a threat. In fact, they keep me on my toes. They are a gauge of my interest and the quality of my hibernation. As long as I hold them in check, I know the trajectory of winter is on the rise.

Once the insects get the upper hand, however, I know my resolve is weakening. I know I am getting restless for spring. And the tomatoes, of course, know, too. By the first of March, bugs or no bugs, they will become tired and pale. The season will fall apart, the balance of winter will be tipped, and I will grope to find a new purpose. I will be less dependable and caring. I will be looking elsewhere.

1997: Ashes have peaked in the last couple of days, now starting to shed. Leaf fall accelerating as the early maples fill with color. The foliage around the yard is weakening a little each day, letting in more of the neighbors. No monarch butterflies seen for a while. The frog in the water garden still croaks a little. No water lilies - even after a week of afternoons in the 80s. Along the south hedge, the rose of Sharon is fading, no flowers since late September.

2001: Beeches rusting now. Dogwood full red and thinning. Squirrels eating Osage, a robin at the honeysuckle berries. Bamboo in the south garden has a few yellowing leaves. Water willow turning in the pond. Along the highway to Columbus: ashes, hickory, and locusts peak, and maples begin to blend in with them. Rapid deepening now, the tree line almost everywhere at the door of Middle Fall. Goldenrod fields rusting. At my school window, the red maple's color has trickled down haphazardly through the branches. Some of the other campus maples have turned completely.

2003: Only a couple of painted ladies seen today. The tree lines are beginning to turn now, and about a third of the maples are yellow and orange in Wilmington. Peak leaf color reported across Michigan and Wisconsin. Katydids and crickets still sing in the mild evenings.

2005: Another vole caught this morning under the kitchen sink. Four in a week! This afternoon, the first fire in the wood stove, the afternoon cloudy, damp and windy, high only in the 50s. Along the freeway south, some woodlots have suddenly become full of color.

2007: Crows, grackles, starlings in the background as I walked the alley this morning. Robins whinnied and peeped their migration signals. In the yard, the New England asters are about three-fourths gone. I cut back the peonies and the heliopsis yesterday. The Jerusalem artichokes have ended their brief flowering time. The crab apple tree in the east garden is almost bare. A long flock of blackbirds flew over Limestone Street as I drove downtown to buy lunch this noon, and this afternoon, Jeanie saw another long flock fly over the house. All afternoon I could hear them chattering in the trees around us.

2008: The first rainy day in weeks. No bird song this morning, but the finches are feeding heavily.

2009: A hummingbird at the butterfly bush this afternoon at 2:00. Morning glories in the alley in rapid decline. Chocolate brown oakleaf hydrangea flowers now. Christmas cacti left outside through the summer are budding.

2010: Crows at 6:16, a little earlier than recently. Only two skippers seen today. On the drive into Beavercreek this afternoon, many maples and all the ashes were in full color, and the tree line was in early turn. In the yard, the zinnias are still fresh (a red one sent downriver with Ruth), but the Jerusalem artichokes have finished blooming, New England asters starting to decline. Goldenrod at the covered bridge is rusting now. At the nursery and the grocery store, the mum displays were dramatic, huge pots of flowers, all the buds completely open. Warm in the 70s today – tomorrow will be close to 80.

2011: Another day in the 80s, full color to the landscape all the way to the monastery in Cincinnati, all the major maples on High Street here turning deep, even the McDaniels' silver maple turning. At the St. Clare monastery, white snakeroot and small violet asters, probably the arrowhead leaf asters, common. Tonight, crickets screamed above the sound of rock band music from downtown.

2012: Very light frost this morning only touched the dahlias along the north fence, turning their leaves dark purple. A huge flock of blackbirds/grackles/starlings, flew across town from the northwest, its beginning and its ending lost in the far horizons on either side of the village. Migrating robins were peeping throughout my morning walk. Here at home, I cut back the caladiums, dug the two biggest amaryllis bulbs and put them in pots. Our crab apple tree has lost most of its leaves now.

2013: After two days of hard rain and a low of 37, maple and walnut leaves cover the Lawson's side lawn. My back yard has the hackberry leaves, and the front honeysuckles are shedding. A great number of black walnuts and many Osage fruits came down in the wind. Along Limestone and Stafford Streets, a steady whinnying of robins, one cardinal call, some chickadee and sparrow chatter. More and more gold on the town maples. The zinnias are suffering from age and the cool weather, lean toward the south and the sun. Throughout the countryside, most of the woodlots are in early color. At Ellis, the ashes are about three-fourths down, patches of yellow on the tulip trees, a few young maples shedding, one bare. Robins calling at the pond during my late afternoon walk there with Bella.

2014: Warmer in the 60s with sun today, and several painted ladies, cabbage whites and sulphurs seen. Leafturn on High Street holding steady for the last few days, a pause before the crash.

2015: A last day in Umbria, Italy. Neysa and Ivano photographing olive groves in the hills around Trevi and Campello Alto. The olives ripening, nets (for olive harvest) seen below several trees. Through the groves, I found a white-flowered cress just reaching early bloom, chicory, spent amaranth and great mullein, a parsnip-like plant in late flower, clumps of wild thyme in bloom, great patches of wild mint that spread their fragrance throughout our walk. Small checkerspot butterflies and cabbage whites played around us. Hummingbird moths flew into and around the ancient stone fencerows. Ivano pointed out the wild asparagus and a prickly plant that he called *asparagino*, which usually accompanies the asparagus in this area.

2016: Sun and cool in the low 50s this morning. Now the garden goldenrod and the New England asters have quickly turned past their peak, more spent than blooming. I sat by the zinnias but didn't even see a cabbage white butterfly; only the small bumblebees were out. Then in the afternoon, one cabbage white.

2018: The monarchs continue to play in the tithonias, four in one patch when I went out to look this afternoon.

2019: No significant leafturn yet in the village. It is still a dusky, ochre Early Fall.

2020: Another perfect day in the 70s, wood pile all stacked, one red admiral in the zinnias after lunch. Throughout the county, major early leafturn is occurring, with giant maples deep red and orange. The New England asters, the zinnias and the tall marigolds keep their color in the north garden, graced with cabbage whites and, for hours today, two silver-spotted skippers and a bright red admiral butterfly. The tall goldenrod is getting dusky now along the road to Xenia. The downtown Zelcova is half-turned rusty red; the Kentucky coffee trees are pale and thinning. Along the north hedge of my honeysuckles, the knotweed, false buckwheat and hops are yellowing and browning. At Jill's the young redbuds are splotchy pale. Under decaying hosta leaves near the back porch, I discovered the white autumn crocus that blooms this time of year when I can find it. This evening: geese flew over in the dark, at 6:00 p.m.

2022: First light frost last night, but nothing seems damaged. Throughout town and south along the highway, leaf color is approaching early peak. Chilly wind throughout the day, the full moon rising after I completed meditation and exercises in the studio. A note from Audrey: "Walking across the Antioch field yesterday, October 8, in the late afternoon, my husband and I were stunned to see, in flight, a white turkey vulture! Indelible against the blue sky. It had a white back, darker shoulders, and white flight feathers. The white bird was part of a kettle of vultures drifting eastward toward the Glen. It circled several times, catching the light."

2023: Time count: 14 canna blossoms holding on. My goldenrod and New England asters are starting to fade now. Second day in a row with high just in the 50s. No cabbage whites seen today, but Jeff reported one monarch butterfly in the field near his house in Cedarville.

One summer, I spent an inordinate amount of time sitting on the back patio just looking out into the garden. Every few days the blossoms of the shrubs and flowers changed. I filled the bird feeders every morning, and the birds rewarded my care with their presence.

Lounging on the patio, I saw more butterflies than I ever had before, watched more bees than I had ever watched before – hover bees, carpenter bees, bumblebees, bee flies, and even a few honeybees.

I loved it.

"I'm at the beach," I told my wife one day. "It's like I'm really at the beach, and all I have to do in life is watch the waves!"

"Well, yes, but not quite," she replied, reminding me I was deep in landlocked Ohio.

But I couldn't help myself. The fantasy grew stronger. I formed tides of the clouds that moved toward me from the west above the back locust trees, tides that dissolved overhead, then rose from the locust trees again. In the steady passing of the cars nearby, I heard waves breaking on my empty shore, soothing my concerns, disconnecting me from things I thought I might accomplish. The white, crescent Midwestern moon above me became the prime mover of my inland sea, cradling me, rocking me back and forth in its motherly phases.

Now in October, my brain has been so washed and lulled by the sea that I no longer have illusions that I will earn my way or discover answers. Spoiled, as well as instructed by the beach, I listen to the new surf of falling leaves telling me I have nothing left to do.

October 9th
The 282nd Day of the Year

The Frost performs its secret ministry,
Unhelped by any wind.

Samuel Taylor Coleridge

Sunrise/set: 6:39/6:05
Day's Length: 11 hours 26 minutes
Average High/Low: 68/46
Average Temperature: 57
Record High: 86 – 1939
Record Low: 30 – 1989

Weather

The 9th and the 10th are the last two days of the year on which there is an 85 percent chance of a high temperature above 60 degrees (45 percent chance of 60s, forty percent for 70s or above). A ten percent chance remains for cool 50s, five percent for an afternoon only in the 40s. The sky is partly to mostly sunny 65 percent of the days; showers occur 35 percent of the time. In spite of the mild temperatures, today is the earliest day for snow in the Dayton area. Frost comes 15 percent of the mornings, and lows drop below 50 half the time.

The Natural Calendar

As Early Fall becomes Middle Fall, the ash, locust and hickory trees reach their finest color and then shed suddenly in the cold waves that sweep more violently across the Great Plains. When those leaves come down, high mapleturn moves into the Midwest, producing some of the brightest oranges and scarlets of the season.

New England asters now come to the end of their blooming cycle and asparagus yellows in the garden. A few lance-leaf and zigzag goldenrod still hold on, but the great roadside bloom of tall goldenrod and small white asters gradually withers. Thimble plant heads break apart like milkweed pods, and jumpseed seeds disappear into the undergrowth. The brown seeds of the beggartick plants stick to stockings and pantlegs.

June's brightest star, Arcturus, sets before 9:00 p.m. The Milky Way moves overhead, and the Pleiades, followed by the Hyades and Aldebaran, have come up in the west by midnight. Orion is fully visible then and is centered in the south by 5:00 a.m.

Daybook

1982: White bindweed is still blooming in the brown soybean fields. New sow thistles are opening. Asiatic dayflowers are still in bloom, Queen Anne's lace still strong in places.

1983: Into Dayton: Full oranges and reds on the maples. Ashes yellow and gold. New England asters and bright goldenrod still common along the roadsides, a few white snakeroot noticed, even one field of bouncing bets.

1984: A long flock of blackbirds or grackles - perhaps both - seen migrating across the soybeans fields east of town along Grinnell Road.

1986: White small-flowered asters are dying back. Late thyme-leafed speedwell goes to seed. But the trees, which should be reaching peak color, are green as in early September. Three carp, one small, one medium, one large, caught on three casts at Sycamore Hole.

1987: More maples have turned, full color advancing bit by piece.

1989: Frosts intensifying, record lows to the north in Toledo, record 30 degrees here. Red mulberry shedding, black walnuts coming down more heavily. It's suddenly the middle of Middle Fall, the season surging.

1990: Through the greenhouse glass before sunrise, Orion was centered in the southern sky above the winter tomatoes; the fat, gibbous moon was setting into the Osage orange.

1992: Early peak of leaves may be beginning. The ash have come to their best colors during early maple turn, will decline now, and the maples will come to the forefront for the center of Middle Fall.

1993: To Detroit and back: Full color of the leaves in northern Ohio and southern Michigan. One gauge of the progress of autumn north was the burning bush: solid red in Detroit, only half turned in Yellow Springs. Long flocks of grackles passed over the car near Lake Erie.

1994: Peak leaf color from Yellow Springs to Columbus, the late ashes blending with the best of the maples.

1998: The end of the New England asters, all sedum. Dead nettle still full bloom, and the bright yellow tansy.

1999: Rain and mild for the street fair. I sat at my table, my hand-made books for sale, watching the people and the rain. Sometimes, the wind picked up and the rain blew in a little on the books, but mostly the day was simply damp and enclosing, comforting and benign. Katydids heard tonight before bed.

2000: Three water lilies left in the pond, pads yellowing.

2001: Strong katydids, strong tree frogs, strong chanting crickets tonight.

2003: Asian lady beetles continue to swarm at Washington Court House and in Yellow Springs. No painted ladies in the zinnias today. One monarch sighted flying through the parking lot at the mall. Peak color now across the area for ashes. Oaks and sweet gums have started. Another week will bring full Middle Fall colors.

2004: No Asian ladybeetle invasion yet. Katydids and crickets were loud in the mild night.

2005: Looking back on last year's entry about the ladybeetles, the invasion never came. I found one in the bathroom yesterday morning, but none outside. In the north garden today, one yellow rose is blooming, and the late patch of New England asters is still in full bloom. Around the yard, a few violet mallows are flowering and one very late rudbeckia, a few bindweed, one rose of Sharon.

Around town, late hostas with purple flowers are still strong.

2006: No monarchs or butterflies today even though the high reached into the upper 70s. The small ash tree just over the line in Moya's yard is full deep red. The yellow ash next to the bare black walnut tree at Mills Lawn is almost all down. No Asian lady beetles at all this year.

2007: A few starlings sitting high in Don's bare black walnut tree this morning. Sparrows boisterous in the pear trees downtown late this afternoon.

2008: Now the Jerusalem artichokes near the pond are in decline, and the Red Baron hostas are done for the year.

2009: Don's maple is much deeper orange today; Lil's and the Danielsons' began to turn overnight. The foliage of Mateo's artichokes (that didn't flower this year) is turning rose color. The dogwoods are getting veins of rich magenta. Calico asters are holding, but some white-flowered asters are starting to die back. A flock of grackles landed in the Stafford Street trees at about 10:00. A cardinal was singing and a robin clucking when I was walking Bella in the alley just before that.

2010: Crows at 6:16 this morning. No butterflies seen today, but the weather was perfect, in the 80s, full sun. Serviceberry leaves are turning a little, but they are lagging behind the maples this year. Peggy's ash tree, all gold, has started to thin out.

2011: Crows at 6:12 this morning, a single cardinal song at 6:20. High clouds moving in the first time in days, but temperatures climbing into the 80s once again. Squirrel chattering in the back trees. Redbuds in the yard with patches of bright yellow. Some of the redbuds on Stafford Street are completely changed. Across the street, the Danielsons' maple is all turned and half shed! Lil's maple has started to turn, the full peak of leaf turn overrunning the village and the whole valley. Tonight the katydids were thinner, and the whole chorus was weaker than last night. One eerie tree frog near the house, a few field crickets chirping, but far fewer intermittent ground/tree cricket calls.

2012: Full leaf color for maples, many shedding ashes just about all down at the pond, sweet gums still deep purple red, hickories weathering more. A second frost last night did considerable damage to the zinnias along the north garden. When I walked Bella before sunrise, a cardinal sang from one end of the alley to the other.

2013: At 8:30 this morning, a great flock of grackles moved across the village heading southwest, settling from time to time in the high trees.

2014: The white autumn crocus by the back porch has wilted, all flopped over under the hibiscus. The first beggarticks stuck to my clothes. I noticed that the pussy willow tree by the front sidewalk had lost all its leaves, the yellow grape leaves the only foliage on its branches. At Ellis Pond, the parking lot ash trees are completely down, the southwest ash grove, full burnt sienna and half thinned. One sweet gum in the arboretum has leaves speckled in gold and red and green and purple.

2015: The landscape from Spoleto to Rome this morning seemed to green quickly as we drove south. In the plantings of the freeway, a few late oleanders bloomed pink, white, violet. Oleanders are now in full bloom in Greece, my sister Judy wrote.

2016: The coldest morning so far this autumn, lows in the middle 40s, as the strongest high-pressure of the season comes through.

2017: Cloudy throughout the day, a few daylilies and geraniums transplanted.

2018: From Yellow Springs to Keuka Lake, New York: The countryside in southern and central Ohio was still deep Late-Summer green, the fields cut, and the remaining soybeans and corn dusky dark brown. Above and east of Cleveland, a new shading, birches and poplars thin, willows gold and lacy, wild grape leaves pale yellow cream, cottonwoods mostly pare, maples with scattered bright orange, and then into Pennsylvania and New York, a dominance of red-orange sumac and purple-red Virginia creeper.

2019: Crows called at first light, a cardinal sang at 6:20. For the second day in a row (the second day of a hard high-pressure system) and in spite of plenty of sun: only Italian honeybees, small bumblebees, hover bees/flies and cabbage whites in the garden flowers.

2020: Such bright wispy cirrus this morning before dawn, so crisp and wild. Along the north edge of my property, the numerous weedy trees-of-heaven are turning to complement the tall marigolds which lie above the purple New England asters, a wall of October color. At Pearl's Fen, white asters, woodland sunflowers and goldenrod are no longer in full bloom, but the red-stemmed violet asters are till prominent, and the occasional sneezeweed plant. A farm along Dayton-Yellow Springs road has a hedge of burning bush in full scarlet. Hurricane Delta, the 10th named system to strike the United States this season, comes ashore as a Category 3 storm on the Louisiana coast (the third strike there of the summer).

2021: To northern Kentucky: lush green hills, some light turning in the tree lines, one monarch butterfly, two cabbage whites. No flocks of birds seen.

2022: Full moon has chilled the weather and brought full leaf color.

2023: Time count: 12 canna blossoms. Still very little leafturn. Cool 50s.

This is when the piercing power and sultry heat of the Sun abate, and gods send autumn rains, and flesh of men and women feels easier.

Hesiod

October 10th
The 283rd Day of the Year

Seasons pursuing each other,
the plougher ploughs, the mower mows,
and the winter grain falls in the ground.

Walt Whitman

Sunrise/set: 6:40/6:04
Day's Length: 11 hours 24 minutes
Average High/Low: 68/46
Average Temperature: 57
Record High: 86 – 2010
Record Low: 29 – 1888

Weather

Ten percent chance of a high in the 80s today, 30 percent for 70s, forty-five percent for 60s, fifteen percent for 50s. The frequency of showers is one day in three, and totally overcast conditions occur 25 percent of the time. Seventy percent of the mornings fall below 50 degrees, and frost strikes 15 percent of the time.

The Natural Calendar

The Sun is almost halfway between equinox and winter solstice; by the time maple color peaks, the day along the 40th Parallel has lost almost four hours from its summer length, and light snow occurs one year in a decade. The chances of frost increase every morning.

Many years, long flocks of blackbirds and grackles fly over farms and villages, their passage often lasting several minutes. Sometimes they settle into the trees and join the starlings that have come together once again for winter; they and caw and cackle throughout the day. Below the Ohio Valley, mating time begins for deer beneath the steady flight of robins into the South. Katydids are still vociferous on warm evenings, and orb-weavers still weave their webs in the mildest autumns.

Daybook

1982: Crickets still sing at night. Most tall goldenrod has rusted, only scattered stalks staying bright. Geese flew over the house at 5:45 p.m. Beggartick seeds are dry today, ready to stick. New sweet clover, sorrel, chicory blooming.

1983: Geese fly over the house at 5:45 p.m.

1984: Ginkgoes yellowing quickly this fall.

1985: No more blackbirds along the river by the mill, their migration over so quickly. Peak maple leaf color begins. Staghorn sumacs bright red. Ashes falling all at once.

1986: A flock of robins was passing through the Glen by the swinging bridge. I stood and listened to their calls as they moved south, tacking from one tree to another. Foliage on the understory trees is still early September green, but most all the wildflowers are done blooming. New leaves growing on the pussy willow, and on the lower branches of the mock orange.

1987: Japanese knotweed's winged seeds have all fallen, foliage brown from the frost.

1992: Crickets still strong at night, but no katydids heard for at least a week, even though the nights have been mild. Peak color now, hickories and ashes blending with maples and oaks. Cardinal sang at 6:45 a.m. Beggarticks stuck to my pants today. One goldenrod field at the south edge of town is bright as in September, must have been cut back in July.

1993: South Glen: A few jumpseeds hang on, and many asters are still full bloom. Some zigzag goldenrod is gone now. Wingstem and ironweed plants are black, their leaves shriveled and brittle. Jeanie cut the last cosmos in the yard this afternoon, the first killing frost due tonight. Leaf color is nearing its peak.

1998: Crows at 6:10 a.m., cardinals at 6:20 and 6:50.

1999: New England asters in decline. Yard silent in the soft rainy Sunday.

2000: To Wilmington: Palomino silver maples with deeper gilding now. Ashes gone, a pause in the turning, a deepening of the other tree color, as though the remaining foliage had been sobered by the ash-fall.

2001: Mottled wild cherry leaves. Rapid reddening of dogwoods and sweet gum trees. On the way to Columbus: early full color in a majority of the woodlots. Most cottonwoods now bare. The grape vine at my window shows a slight yellowing. White clover is in full bloom in the field by my classroom at Washington Courthouse.

2002: This morning, the trees were almost as green as in mid September, only a vague ochre moving in ever so lightly. By late afternoon, I sensed that the canopy was suddenly relenting, giving in to the chemical dictates of the season. I could not tell, however, exactly which trees had caused me to change my assessment.

2003: In South Glen this morning: The woods and fields are tattered, and the canopy has thinned considerably with box elders, locusts, black walnuts, buckeyes, and some ashes down. A few white asters, Short's aster, and an untoothed, heart-leafed purple aster still in bloom, along with some late zigzag goldenrod. The river is low after a month with little rain. Along Corey Street and on the road down along the covered bridge, maples are reaching full color. At home, Mrs. Lawson's maple is full, the Danielsons' almost full.

2004: Mrs. Lawson's maple is a full, bright orange. False boneset seeds have become fluffy; beggarticks stuck to Bella this morning when she ran through the bushes. All across the county, ashes are holding red and gold and maples are coming in.

2006: Early full color throughout the countryside as maples join the ashes. One ginkgo is ochre at Wilberforce, many of the ashes already fallen there. One monarch seen heading south in Wilmington. The small pale violet cyclamen by the shed is in full bloom.

2007: Goldenrod is tufting in the alley now (rusting throughout the countryside). Sparrows loud, more starlings chirping above the alley. The cottonwoods are three-fourths down. Lil's maple and the Danielsons' are green.

2008: Maple turn suddenly accelerates: more oranges and reds in town and across the countryside. Lil's burning bush is getting deep red. The pond frog is missing – I haven't heard or seen him in a week or so.

2009: Don's maple, Lil's maple and the Danielsons' maple are all turning quickly: Don's at early full, the Danielsons' next, Lil's last.

2010: Crows at 6:16 this morning. Two skippers, two cabbage butterflies seen by noon. Record heat of 86 this afternoon.

2011: Three monarchs, a few cabbage whites and one silver-spotted skipper in the garden today as we picked the lush yellow and violet dahlias that are just now coming to their best. All the false bonesets have gone to seed, but the purple New England asters still remain full. Across the street, Don's big maple is a little behind the Danielsons' maple (which is at least half down). In the greenhouse, a few of the Christmas cacti have buds. Tonight, after a warm day in the 70s, and under a full moon shining through a mackerel sky, an intense cricket chorus: intermittent tree crickets, field crickets and ghostly tree frogs. Katydids throughout the neighborhood.

2012: No butterflies seen for many days now, and although the hummingbird food slowly disappears, it seems that the bees are the ones drinking. The yard becomes more and more tattered, dahlias yellow and violet, deep purple and white, continuing to bloom – but on frost-darkened leaves; hackberry leaves are scattered about the yard; the fish lie low on the bottom of the pond; grape leaves streak the roadside bushes and our own forsythia; false boneset is gray; heliopsis leaves have wrinkled and broken up. Drifts of New England asters are still open, and one white bindweed has blossomed near the trellis. All the hydrangea flower clusters are brittle and dun. In the alley, Mrs. Timberlake's feverfew is still in bloom, a stray fragment of her garden from years ago.

2013: Very little change in the tree line over the past week, only the ashes shedding more and more. It appears that the major color will come quite late this year. Lil's maple and Mrs. Timberlake's and Don's have not started yet. The persimmon is still gold, speckled with chocolate brown at Ellis, the dogwoods very red, but no sign of change in the oak grove. When I was there, I watched a flock of migrating birds with dark heads and necks, white breasts, and some white on their tails, marked – as far as I could see – like female slate-colored or Oregon juncos. Around them, robins peeped. One junco chased a redbreast away. In the yard, Jeanie's pink tea rose keeps a blossom. A few spiderwort plants continue to flower but the New England asters are almost done. By the porch, the white crocus shows just a little white. Today was the third day in a row with completely clear skies.

2014: Ellis Pond: The sugar maples in the maple grove have started to turn now, the ashes continuing to shed, the bald cypress rusted just in the past few days, everything picking up speed.

2015: Intense sun and cool in the 60s for Street Fair day. Bumblebees continue to work the remaining tithonias and zinnias, often spend the night among the petals. I noticed most of the jumpseeds had jumped from their stems, the remaining seeds brittle and easily brushed off. A monarch, a few skippers and cabbage white butterflies seen, but their presence was greatly diminished since late September when I left for Italy. In the yard: small white asters and the white crocus, smartweed, nasturtium, *Aster latifolia,* zinnia (with powdery mildew), tithonia, amaranth, roses, and the very last New England asters still in bloom; the maple by the beech tree full burnished gold; red dogwoods; secret maple, Lil's maple still green, ashes, locusts, walnuts gone; snakeroot gray; grape foliage rust yellow; some red creeper; honeysuckle berries fatter and redder; trumpet vine leaves yellowing, the fallen leaves still soft; brown-red viburnum and stonecrop; Lil's burning bush bright red. Robins peeping migration signals through the day. A letter from my sister, Maggie: she exclaimed about the beauty of the southern Wisconsin maples at peak color last week.

2016: Light breeze, high barometric pressure, bright sun, afternoon in the 60s. Very little leafturn so far. Lil's burning bush has only scattered patches of red. The Danielsons' maple just a little ochre. Lil's and Mrs. Timberlake's hardly any turn at all. Janet's redbud's leaves are yellowing here and there. In an hour's vigil: Honeybees and two cabbage whites in the zinnias and New England asters (the asters about three-fourths done). Only one large bumblebee noticed.

2017: No painted ladies so far – after yesterday's fog and rain. At the quarry with Jeff: only small, narrow-leafed white asters prominent, leaves – like the whole countryside – in mid early turn. Honeysuckle berries continue to fall in front of the house, making the sidewalk slippery. (Now the black walnuts and the honeysuckle berries sometimes make walking a challenge.) At the wetlands near the west edge of town, red-winged blackbirds were whistling and chirping.

      Jonatha writes about this summer's swallowtails: "I was very disappointed how few I saw. Just a couple of years ago, they were in abundance in our yard. I saw three zebras, two giants, no tigers and five black. Now two of the black could have been Spicebush as they were too far away for me to tell. This is my count for the whole summer, during which we were only away two weeks."

2018: Keuka Lake, New York: Today I became aware of the power of ash leaves here in northwestern New York. The ash borer has not reached here, and the landscape is like an Ohio landscape of about three years ago before all the trees had died, a coloring of pale violet and gold and rusty brown. Buckeye leaves are twisted and crisp, cluttering the stairway, along with the prickly buckeye hulls, to the cottage. Chicory, crown vetch a few small white asters, some violet asters with clasping, alternate leaves, a few patches of cutover goldenrod along East Bluff Road. Up above the lake, all the grape foliage was patchy yellow brown, all the fruit harvested. A roadside stand on Culver Road had quart containers of purple grapes for sale, honor-pay system.

2019: Cardinals singing back and forth this morning at first light. A soft evening in the middle 60s, maybe the last one of the year, tree frogs and tree crickets very strong, katydids weaker in the back yard, stronger out in the neighborhood.

2020: Full leaf color now along the west side of my block of High Street, Moya's maple and the Champney's male full gold. Across the street, TK's maple is shedding hard, the Danielsons' maple turned over night, and Lil's tree is shading ochre. Hurricane Delta moves up the Mississippi Valley, may bring rain tonight or tomorrow. In the zinnias, two cabbage whites and yesterday's red admiral butterfly. The air soft and fragrant, high in the middle 70s, all sorts of layers of past autumns flickering in and out of my body. I keep expecting something to happen to me – but really it is about to happen to the landscape.

2021: One monarch in the zinnias today. At the Narrows park along the Little Miami River, only patches of white, small-flowered asters and pale violet heart-leaved and Short's asters in bloom. Most of the woodland along the river had dried up, along with the the white snakeroot, wingstem and wood nettle.

2022: Cabbage whites still play in the warm sun all around the purple aster.

2023: Time count: Eleven canna blossoms. New England asters seeding quickly. Geese have not flown over for weeks, and no flocks of blackbirds or starlings. At the Glass Farm wetland, goldenrod has grayed. Several cabbage whites and the first sulphur seen this autumn

It has taken me half a lifetime of searching to realize that the likeliest path to the ultimate ground leads through my local ground. I mean the land itself, with its creeks and rivers, its weather, seasons, stone outcroppings, and all the plants and animals that share it. I cannot have a spiritual center without having a geographical one: I cannot live a grounded life without being grounded in a certain place.

Scott Russell Sanders

October 11th
The 284th Day of the Year

The seasons alter: hoary-headed frosts
Fall in the fresh lap of the crimson rose.

William Shakespeare

Sunrise/set: 6:41/6:02
Day's Length: 11 hours 21 minutes
Average High/Low: 67/45
Average Temperature: 56
Record High: 87 – 1928
Record Low: 26 – 1906

Weather

The milder temperatures of the 9th and 10th often give way on the 11th: only 15 percent of today's afternoons reach 70. Fifty-five percent are in the 60s, fifteen percent are in the 50s; and, for the first time since April 20th, there is a 15 percent chance of highs just in the 40s. Frost occurs one morning in 15. Showers fall, and clouds cover the sky one day in three. Lows drop below 50 two nights in three.

The Natural Calendar

The transition week between Early and Middle Fall is typically associated with Leafdrop Season for locusts, box elders and ashes. It is the last week of Yellow-Bellied Sapsucker Migration Season. It is close to the end of Spider Web Season as Insect Breeding Seasons end in the cold. It is Blackbird Flocking Season, early Leafturn Season for the red maples and black maples, dogwoods, sassafras and persimmons. It is Beggarticks-Stick-To-Your-Stockings Season and Second-Bloom of Watercress Season. Aster Season, Jerusalem Artichoke Season and Zigzag Goldenrod Season diminish across the woods and fields. Pink Smartweed Season continues to spread through the dooryards and alleys. In the greenhouse, precocious Christmas cacti have entered Christmas Cactus Budding Season.

1984: Grinnell Swamp: White snakeroot gone, goldenrod gone, violet asters to seed, touch-me-nots shriveling. Ash, cottonwood, box elders fallen, some oaks brown, maples and redbuds gold and delicate, sycamore coming on heavily, elms mottled, canopy maybe a third down. Hepatica dark green, swamp mint growing back, watercress, too – some even blooming. No cobwebs. Cabbage butterflies still mating. Leafcup still blooming.

1987: First days of full leaf color.

1988: Still a little time before the foliage peak. Asters still full of color, but most all the goldenrod has turned to rust, its prime a week ago. The fields are brown, all the coneflowers have faded, and most all the ironweed, the last seven days bringing the flowers to an end.

1990: Extremely rapid deterioration now. Some crab apples at Wilberforce, the deep red-leafed ones, are gone. A few ginkgo leaves have dropped. The last two weeks have opened the undergrowth, and the street is visible now on the northwest side of the yard as the honeysuckles thin out. But no frost yet, except one night on the roof.

1992: Early full color.

1993: Carol at the printers talked about how when she left the county a week ago the trees were green, and when she came back yesterday, everything had changed. The woods, she said, were in full color all along the way from Maryland.

1998: Crows at 6:16 a.m. Cardinals at 6:35 a.m. Then grackles. Wren chatters at 8:15 a.m.

2000: Redbuds half gone, staghorn speckled with autumn red, many cottonwoods down, hickory deep gold, linden lightly fringed with gold, beech yellowing, most New England asters finished.

2001: Monarch butterfly sighted as it flew southwest across a soybean field today, orange on the rust-brown plants. Along the bike path, tall bellflowers, red smartweed, the last white snakeroot, a couple of soapworts and tall coneflowers. Goldenrod ending its cycle. Tonight, one bat, katydids and crickets in the rain.

2002: Soft, cloudy morning at South Glen: Purple asters with the arrowhead leaves are still blooming. Goldenrod seeding. Hawthorn, black walnut, box elder, sycamore, cottonwood all at similar levels of decay, a gold-green-brown breakdown. Wingstem black and withered. Grasses are dry, falling over. Mottled maroon blackberry leaves. Nine puffball mushrooms found at the turn past Middle Prairie – after a temperature last night in the mid 50s and a good rain. White-throated sparrows are back to winter over here, like juncos, Mike said. Tonight, the evening is mild, katydids and crickets singing.

2003: Only a couple of painted ladies in the zinnias today, even though the sky was clear and the sun was warm. Asian lady beetles are still flying here and there. Mosquitoes less pesky today as I worked on the woodpile. When I watered the Christmas cacti, I noticed one of the plants budding.

2008: A perfect day in the 70s, clear sky, light breeze. Through the afternoon, squirrels chattered, finally drowned out as the Sun fell behind the back trees by the clucking of a flock of grackles.

2009: A lone cardinal call at 6:30, screech owl at 6:37. Ashes full. Patches of deep red in the pears, half moon overhead, grackles in the hackberry and the maple, Joe Pye weed seed heads turning almost downy.

2010: Another day in the 80s, several cabbage butterflies and skippers seen, and one polygonia. Along the highways, early full color everywhere: red sumacs, many maples orange and gold, all the ashes ochre or maroon, yellow locusts and redbuds. A deep red-rust and black woolly bear caterpillar found in the grass on the way to the shed. Crickets loud, piercing, in the warm, 65-degree evening, hazy crescent moon setting over Dayton.

2011: Mild morning, full moon setting through altocumulus clouds.

And another warm day of full color on High Street, Carl's maples dominating the southwest corner of the block, Moya's maple matching Carl's, Lil's maple maybe a fourth turned, her burning bush bright red, the Danielsons' maple nearly gone, Mateo's black walnut completely shed and the fruit down, too. Peggy's limelight hydrangea is almost all rusted. Redbuds are yellow, rose of Sharon spotty, pale yellow with only a few flowers left, the alley golden with middle-season maples, fallen leaves covering the edges of the streets, the peak here but starting to break apart. In the afternoon, the wind came up, clipping off more leaves. Just a couple of cabbage whites today, but the crickets were especially loud tonight: intermittent ones, steady callers, field chirpers, one castanet cricket, several ghostly whistlers. Katydids were louder than any other night so far this week.

2012: More frost this morning, and most of the zinnias lost their color, foliage wrinkling, graying. Along the road to Xenia and Cedarville, most of the wood lots are in full maple color, and the ashes have held at about half along Cedarville-Yellow Springs Road. In the woods at the Indian Mound, big sycamore leaves falling steadily. All the white snakeroot had gone to seed, along with much of the goldenrod, but several fields along the high canopy were still bright with tall goldenrod flowers. At Ellis Pond: nettles fresh and green, river birch yellowing, high trees full of starlings and blackbirds, walnuts and chestnuts all down, swaths of yellow green in the tree line, two dandelions, carpet of ash leaves brown as locust pods, curled and crisp, the pin oak has turned a spotted yellow brown, chinquapin oak edges creeping brown, also the shingle oak tips curling, the small scarlet oak seven-eighths shed, clunky sycamore leaves floating down around me.

Tat writes from Madison, Wisconsin: "The wind yesterday blew most of the leaves off the trees. I've enjoyed a brilliant red one in front of my school window; in the morning, it was glowing and in the afternoon, maybe less than a third or so of the leaves were left."

2013: Casey called at 9:20 a.m.: From his farm, he was watching vultures, one kettle (flock) after another, three to four dozen in each kettle.

"They're coming up out of the northwest maybe a mile or so away," he said. "They must have roosted there overnight, hundreds of them, maybe in that place where the herons nest. They rise and rise until they hit the thermal, then they settle in and ride that surge, head southeast…. Here comes another flock now from the northwest. They've got bright beaks, no neck exposed, and they have the silvery edge of the underwing."

At noon, I ate lunch on the porch in the warm sun. Hundreds of honeybees were drinking the leftover hummingbird syrup. I saw one painted lady (*Cynthia*) butterfly and one cabbage white visit the zinnias.

2015: This morning: sky clear, air sharp, Venus above Lil's tree, crows at 7:20. As I took inventory in the yard, I saw one monarch, the only one today.

2016: At the downtown plantings, New England asters are still bright and purple, but the Russian sage is completely done. The Kentucky coffee tree has turned yellow-gold. At Ellis Pond, the ash grove is dark rusty purple, the maple grove just a little lighter, no leaf fall yet. In town, just light turning, some brilliant spots in the countryside. At John Bryan Park, Jill and I walked into a large flock of grackles clucking in the high trees for quite a distance. The flowers in bloom: heart-leaved and arrowhead-leaved violet asters, a little zigzag goldenrod and a lot of blue-stemmed goldenrod *(Solidago caesia)* with green stems. Only honeybees and a cabbage white seen in the zinnias today. When I talked with John Whitmore, he said that Japanese stiltgrass was taking over his yard and the woods.

2017: To Keuka Lake in New York from Yellow Springs in the rain: leaf color went from Early Fall into full Middle Fall, beginning about an hour north of the village, deepening steadily from ochre to yellow and orange as we drove north and east. Throughout Ohio, farmers were cutting soybeans, and many fields were bare. Some of the mountainsides of western New York were solid, mottled gold. Near Keuka Lake, the vineyards blended with the trees. Along the roads, the sumac leaves were luminescent violet-red even with the sky so gray.

2018: Keuka Lake: Across the water, the hillsides are spattered with pale yellow and rust, the ash and locust turning tinting the season to early-full leafturn. In the evening, the sultry air turns cold and hard, record heat turning to a low in the 40s. In Yellow Springs, the high-pressure arrived yesterday.

2019: A major snowstorm moves across the northwest and the northern plains, the barometer dropping here in advance of the October 12-13 cold front that is forecast to bring lows in the 30s. High clouds are turning to stratus, the mild morning temperature of 60 slowly cooling, the breeze picking up. Before dawn, cardinals called, setting territories of Second Spring in the last best days of Middle Fall. Still, the village foliage is full green, and the robins still have not returned from their Late Summer retreat. A sulphur butterfly at the pond, several cabbage whites at home. This afternoon, the sparrows were boisterous for hours in the honeysuckles.

2020: Overcast with fog and mild, the fringe of Hurricane Delta crows at 6:30 this morning. The Danielsons' maple turned full gold in the night, Lil's gaining color, the whole neighborhood transforming and collapsing around me. At Ellis Pond, the ashes are shedding quickly, and the maples there and the tree line in all directions has reached full early color. The same to the south of town, the most dramatic rapid change I can remember. Along the highway, sweet gums with a variety of violet and purple, red and gold leaves. Two sulphurs seen at the pond today, only one cabbage whites in the garden.

2021: Above-average temperatures have persisted throughout the month. The New England asters in the sunniest location have gone to seed; the more shaded plantings are still bright purple. My tall goldenrod has faded. The zinnias, castor beans and salvia keep the garden in color, suggesting options for next year's October. The corn harvest has begun in the county now, fields dry and ready to cut.

2022: Sun and breeze and 70s and cabbage whites. Moya's maple and the secret maple southwest of my property are rich gold this morning, and Lil's maple is leading the High-Street maples into their best color. Some tree of heaven foliage is pale yellow. Downtown, the Kentucky coffee trees are gold and shedding; the zelcovas are burnt-sienna brown. Peak leaf turn is in progress. New England asters are still dominant in the north garden, even though they have begun to fade. Beggartick seed heads crumble between my fingers.

2023: Morning temperature dropped to 37. Time count: Ten canna blossoms. Geese heard south of town, far off in the late afternoon.

If time is an ocean, the present is not less important than other moments, which stretch away on all sides, any more than a single water molecule in an ocean is less important than the others. In a sense each living moment is the whole of time – an eternal present because it can't be set apart from all the other moments.

David Rains Wallace

October 12th
The 285th Day of the Year

Vermillion Maples,
afternoons troubled by gangs
of Yellow Jackets.

John Blakelock

Sunrise/set: 6:42/6:01
Day's Length: 11 hours 19 minutes
Average High/Low: 67/45
Average Temperature: 56
Record High: 85 – 1928
Record Low: 26 – 1908

Weather

Today and the 21st are the two October days most likely to bring clouds – completely overcast conditions occurring half the time. Rain is also likely – showers or all-day drizzle occurring six days in ten. And the first flurries of the Ohio season sometimes fall on this date. Highs warm to the 80s five percent of the days, to the 70s fifteen percent, to the 60s thirty percent, 50s forty percent, and 40s ten percent.

The Natural Calendar

Most of the commercial grapes and apples have been picked by now. Half of the winter wheat is normally in the ground, and a fourth of it has sprouted. Most of the soybeans are mature, and many bean and cornfields have been cut clean. Farmers often apply nitrogen, phosphate and potash now in order to decrease their springtime workload.

Daybook

1983: More and more ash leaves fall along Grinnell. Rain and wind deepen the sense of autumn.

1984: Radical leafturn on one ginkgo tree outside my window.

1985: Canopy thins rapidly. Maples and oaks bright red, orange, and yellow.

1989: To West Virginia: Now it seems to be early peak leaf color just before the real decadence of full Middle Fall. Many catalpas are down, beans dangling. Occasional ash, box elder, tree of heaven, some poplars and sycamores almost bare. Shagbark hickory golden. Black walnuts have dropped their leaves, fruit still hanging. Most all the goldenrod is done blooming, brown but not gray yet. Lush violet smartweed noticed at a rest stop in southeast Ohio, some red clover. All corn and soybeans unharvested. Clumps of mums in the towns. In the foothills: New England asters against a bright green pasture. Crooked stem aster found at rest stop near Athens, *Aster prenanthoides*. Small white asters very common. Patches of Queen Anne's lace still flowering. Sumacs red 30 miles from Athens. Some snakeroot, some jewelweed seen along the road, and banks of low, red, sumac, whole waysides full color, then gaps where the leaves had fallen. 1998: Heavy walnut fall now. Squirrels hard at work.

1999: Yesterday I finally paid attention to the scrub maple that was so gold and orange outside my west window. It had been hidden all summer by a box elder, by some honeysuckle bushes and euonymus vines, shaded by tall locusts and Osage. I had occasionally glanced at it over the past week, noted its turning, but now I saw it push boldly out of hiding and reveal its brilliance. I had dismissed its beauty before. And then yesterday, just before its foliage collapsed in the rain, the maple showed itself completely to me.

2003: Blackbirds clucking in the back trees. Lil's maple and the Danielson's maple are both near full color today. Mrs. Lawson's maple is full and shedding. Janet Hackett's redbud in the north garden is all yellow. Ash, maple, and locust leaves are falling heavily in the breeze this morning, lie in clumps and rows in the streets. It is the early peak of middle autumn.

2005: Katydids and crickets are singing in the warm dry night.

2006: Snow flurries today!

2007: An orange and black woolly bear caterpillar crawled across the back patio at noon. The largest painted lady *(Cynthia)* butterfly I've ever seen came to the zinnias this afternoon.

2008: Crows at 6:30 this morning. Warm 80s today, sun. The sugar maples near Limestone Street are deep orange and maroon now, even starting to shed. The rest of the maples near our house are still mostly green. All of our New England asters have faded today. One monarch butterfly came by early in the afternoon, sailed over my head, the Sun shining through its wings. Eighty daffodils planted along the north wall as the Sun went behind the west trees.

2010: Crows at 6:22 this morning, high near 80 expected today, maybe rain tomorrow. The Danielsons' maple is half turned, but the rest of the maples on the east side of the street are still green. Lil's burning bush is about three-fourths turned. On the north side of our house, the viburnum is a dark rust.

2011: Crows heard at 6:30 this morning, light rain and about 55 degrees. Walking Bella at 8:45, I heard more crows and steady high tree crickets. And Peggy's field cricket was loud, too. Moya's tree of heaven is yellowing and shedding. All the redbuds in the neighborhood are gold and starting to come down. Maples are bright but going quickly. The viburnum on the north side of the house is full red and dropping its leaves. The Korean lilac is a pale orange and mauve, a few of its branches showing purple flowers. Only one rose of Sharon flower seen. One pink and one yellow tea rose in bloom, and the Knockout roses remain lush in full bloom. Many of the mums are wilting now, and the New England asters are closing. Dahlias producing the most full and beautiful flowers of the year. Crickets are much less prominent tonight than last night, fewer windows of grating crickets, a few tree frogs, a few field crickets, one wavering castanet cricket, no katydids at all.

2013: Northern Indiana: Early full color all the way from Yellow Springs to Angola, Indiana. Mild temperatures near 80, clear skies finally clouding up at sundown. On the side of one tree near the lake, red box-elder bugs had hatched and were massed along the bark, the cluster maybe a foot long, three inches wide. Walking along the lake, we saw numerous red-winged blackbirds, probably migrating.

2014: Cardinals singing and robins peeping as I walked Bella just before 8:00. Chilly, sunny morning, becoming milder and cloudy in the afternoon, still bright and warm enough to bring out a few cabbage whites and painted ladies. Carl's maple is the most spectacular now, full gold-orange. The Danielsons' maple leads the east side of the street in gentle gold, followed by Mrs. Timberlake's. The patch of orange on Moya's maple next to my yard grows larger and larger.

2016: Sun and warm in the 70s today, very little butterfly activity for a while, but patience finally paid off with a few: one bright orange polygonia, three silver-spotted skippers, a pair of cabbage whites, a glimpse of an azure. Throughout the village, the maples are yellowing; the park is a gentle ochre, the walk under the canopy golden; white snakeroot is done blooming at John Bryan Park.

2017: Yellow Springs and northwestern New York state, temperatures cool in the 60s, breezy, clouds. Early Middle Fall along Keuka Lake – greener than the mountains to the west. No frost in Ohio or west to the ocean, no frost in the long-range forecast.

2018: Frost last night in Yellow Springs: one plumeria tree damaged, but castor beans and dahlias safe.

2019: First frost on Jill's car this morning. Chris reports ice from north of here a ways, and Mike had frost in Oxford. Sun and high only in the middle 50s this afternoon. One small painted lady seen in the zinnias, no monarchs for several days. Early Fall has finally begun in the countryside with patches of rust and gold blending with the ochre of September. At least six sizeable murmurations of starlings seen as I drove to and from Cincinnati, and at home, the sparrows were loud and nervous, flocking down to feed, up at the slightest alarm, down again chirping the whole time. From Lanesboro, Minnesota, my nephew John sent photos of his lilac bush in full boom, the first time he's ever seen the second bloom.

2020: *The hill…is a voyager standing still. Never moving a step, it travels through years, seasons, weathers, days and nights. These are the measures of its time, and they alter it, marking their passage on it as on a man's face…. Time is told in it mutely and immediately, with perfect accuracy, as it is told by the heart in the body. Its time is the birth and the flourishing and the death of the many lives that are its life.*

From "A Native Hill" by Wendell Berry

A friend of mine got me started, sending me the quotation above. And I sit on the back porch this evening, watching birds, images and feelings moving across me in waves. I am the "voyager standing still."

The day before, a neighbor had told me about a poem in which a meditator sits with Jesus until his ego disappears and only Jesus is left. Wrapped in sensation, I become the hill. I become the Jesus of the poem, losing myself in the autumnal measures of time:

All day long, the peak of maple color spread across the town and countryside. South of the village, great flocks of blackbirds in the cut-over soybean fields. I would actually like to sit with Jesus (Jeanie?), but she's gone, leaving me behind with my stream of consciousness. Sweet and painful memories, suppressed, shelved, superimposed on sensations of autumn passage. At my feeders. sparrows alternate with black-capped chickadees, with aromas of plants and fruits I can't name or recall, layers of other autumns, the flickering of years that have no names.

In the garden in front of me, three small, orange Mexican sunflowers stand bright against the neighbor's dark woods. Two pink canna lilies remain from the summer. Earlier in the day, I had seen that almost all the leaves of TK's maple tree were down, that the Danielsons' maple had turned overnight, that Lil's tree, the latest maple on my High Street block, was suddenly ochre. It seems that keeping track of one tree or another over the years keeps the collapse of summer more manageable. It is enough that these particular trees come down, parts for the whole, short-circuiting the awareness that everything is falling apart; only these trees are dissolving.

I write down what I see over and over again, unable to

catch the anniversaries that seem to land on me and crawl across my body, gathering up the spent seasons, cementing and then letting go of the mottled shrubs to my right that are matted with yellowing hops and false buckwheat and knotweed. In all my notes: the frustrating absence of enough or the right words that would allow meaning to emerge, the absence of sharing that would allow my true emotions to reveal themselves.

My ego pursues meaning, existential explanations about role and persona and value: these, too, are late flowers brought in from the coming cold, seeds saved and set aside in old envelopes, leaves salvaged to press. Now the sunset though the backyard trees matches the dusky, sweet-peach breasts of my October chickadees, measures the time against Berry's hill, and at dusk I prove to myself once again that I exist, and that I look for God, wondering if the geese fly will over again in the early dark like they did yesterday, so many things still unnamed, unworded for winter.

2021: Even with sun and 70s, only one cabbage white butterfly all day. A robin seen at the edge of High Street, the first robin I've seen since summer. The Danielsons' maple is bare, probably diseased. From western New York, Mary Ellen reports full leaf color, while Yellow Springs shows only light to moderate changes. Tonight, a hearty chorus of crickets, high static from tree crickets and intermittent loud whistling crickets. No field crickets or katydids heard.

2022: Peak leaf color intensifies throughout the village, golden canopies over most of the streets. The barometer has been dropping all day. Wind is blowing. Leaves are sailing through the yard, some maples on High Street shedding heavily. Robins peeping off and on.

2023: Very little leaf color so far, radically different from last year. Geese flew over around 8:00 this morning. Time count: still ten canna blossoms as leaves start to mottle the yard and the asters fade. At the Koogler wetlands, six to eight pale gold sulphur butterflies were playing in the red-stemmed purple asters (the only asters besides the small whites in bloom). Drought has shriveled much of the preserve, and leaf color throughout the county is dull and pale.

Different atmospheric conditions – different kinds of weather – are, precisely different moods. Wind, rain, snow, fog, hail, open skies, heavy overcast – each...affects the relation between our body and the living land in a specific way, altering the tenor of our reflections and the tonality of our dreams.

David Abram

October 13th
The 286th Day of the Year

Now retrospect and prospect have their share,
For autumn like the Janus of the year
Holds spring to spring in double-handed keeping.

Vita Sackville-West

Sunrise/set: 6:43/5:59
Day's Length: 11 hours 16 minutes
Average High/Low: 67/45
Average Temperature: 56
Record High: 86 – 1975
Record Low: 27 – 1988

Weather

Frost occurs this morning 40 percent of all the years in my records, the highest percentage so far this fall. Twenty-five percent of those freezing temperatures are in the 20s, so this is the first really dangerous day of the year for tender garden vegetables. Daytime highs rise into the 80s fifteen percent of the years, but that is the last time for such a percentage until April 20th. Chances of 70s are 15 percent, for 60s twenty percent, for 50s forty percent, for 40s ten percent. Rain: one day in three; skies are clear to partly cloudy 80 percent of the time.

The Natural Calendar

In wetter and warmer autumns, glow worms still flicker in the grass and in the shelter of pebbles and crevices. Crickets and katydids still call through the night. Out in the fields, however, almost all the wildflowers have gone to seed. Wild cucumber fruits are dry and empty. The final sedum blossoms are closing for the year. Goldfinches have lost all their bright plumage; they are brown for winter. Only occasional cabbage whites, painted ladies, swallowtails and fritillaries visit the garden

Daybook

1982: First, the black walnut leaves and buckeye leaves fall, then box elders and the cottonwoods, then ashes and then the sycamores and then the maples and then the oaks.

1983: A long flock of geese flew over at 6:30 p.m. Russet buds prominent on the pussy willows. Chicory, red clover, a few Queen Anne's lace, small-flowered asters, a few late goldenrod blooming. Tomatoes still ripening. Celandine still open.

1984: Locust trees at Wilberforce suddenly lose their leaves. New buds are prominent on the pussy willows. The maple in front of the house is three-fourths gone, Mrs. Lawson's almost all gone.

1985: Jacoby: Winter foliage: fresh garlic mustard, dame's rocket, sedum, catchweed, chickweed, mint, ragwort, dock, sweet Cicely, wild ginger, and avens. Purple deadnettle that sprouted a month ago is two inches tall now. River low and quiet, crickets still loud. Bare trees stand out stark against the mist, oaks thinning like the sycamores, reflection of leaf gold mixing with green water cress in the sloughs, white berries prominent in the red dogwood. The sun, dim and low through the last leaves and the blue-gray clouds, sets the woods glowing. Doorweed found blooming in the lawn at home.

1988: South Glen, 10:00 a.m. After two mornings of heavy frost, trees are burned, lamb's quarters rusty red, ash and tree of heaven leaf clusters falling with the melting ice. Osage leaves black and crisp clattering down.

1989: Katydids still loud at night. Milkweed pods have burst all the way from here to Morgantown, West Virginia. Some scattered sundrops blooming. The last white snakeroot has faded at Cooper's Rock, WV, just like here in Yellow Springs.

1990: Some forsythia blooming on Elm Street.

1992: Slow leafturn continues. Buckeyes and black walnuts are bare, but most other trees holding well. Lil's maple is coloring now, earlier than most years; ours has lost a third of its leaves. Peak of mum bloom. At South Glen, shiners steal my bait. As I sit on the riverbank, a small flock of robins comes through the woods behind me with bursts of song, loud explosions of peeps.

1995: At Grinnell Pond, the white snakeroot is seeding. Heart-leafed asters are still strong, but zigzag goldenrod petals are sagging. At the pond, the large-flowered beggarticks have been gone since the first days of the month. In the triangle park, I noticed the tips of the spruce have fresh growth. At Wilberforce, most of the young locusts and ashes have come down, but the golden ash at the park just reached its peak yesterday, is starting to shed today. Lindens there have been earlier than the box elders, leaves darkening to a muddy brown, curling up, then falling.

1998: Downtown: Crows pass through at 7:11 a.m. Sparrows start calling at 7:15 a.m.

1999: Geese fly over in the middle of the afternoon. Katydids heard last night, still strong with the crickets. Peak leaf color throughout the area now, many of the first and second foliage tiers holding as the maples turn.

2000: Now the maples are really coming on. Very late New England asters seen. Three red water lilies are still open in the pond.

2001: A long flock of blackbirds flew over the house this morning at 8:45. They cackled and swarmed in the back trees then moved on east, their passage taking almost fifteen minutes. This afternoon, I found the witch-hazel in bloom.

2002: First Christmas cacti are budding in the greenhouse. A flicker or pileated woodpecker has been calling in the back woodlot for a week now.

2003: Two painted ladies and maybe half a dozen cabbage butterflies in the garden today.

2004: Mrs. Lawson's maple is full yellow-gold, Lil's maple just barely starting.

2005: Jeanie said she heard Albert, the green frog, croak once today. In the Northeast, heavy rains and flooding. Across the countryside, more maples are coming. Some corn and soybean fields are still uncut. New England asters hold here and there. Locusts and ashes are peaking in Wilberforce, full and falling. The cusp of time between early and Middle Fall still holds.

2008: Crows called at 6:30 a.m. again. A huge blackbird flock settled into the back trees around 10:00, stayed for about three and a half hours. I identified some red-wings and some grackles in the flock. Suddenly at 1:25 p.m., a blue jay called, the sparrows at the feeder disappeared, and all the chatter from the birds in the trees ceased; they had all apparently moved on. To Dayton later in the afternoon: Full early middle leaf turn throughout the countryside. The frog finally seen again after weeks in hiding.

2010: Crows at 6:23 this morning. Clouds gathering, the heat wave ending this evening. The leaves of the witch hazel tree are turning pale yellow now, and all the flower buds have opened. Liz sent a note saying she had seen a flock of bluebirds at Ellis Pond last week. Jeanie said she had seen some kind of blue bird in the yard last week – maybe from the same flock.

2011: Crows at about 6:20 this morning, the pair of cardinals at the tall feeders just a few minutes later. Rain due tonight, a cool wave putting an end to a warm spell that has lasted since late September. From Vermont, Cathy says that trees have remained green throughout September and early October, are just now starting to turn. "I wonder what that means for this winter," she wrote. Some rain this afternoon, then the wind picked up a little. Tonight, the crickets were loud in spite of the cool temperatures (about 58 degrees). No katydids, but tree frogs, castanet crickets (again by the green house), a few field cricket chirps, and many grating, high tree crickets.

2012: To St. Clare in Cincinnati: Turkey vultures floating through the sky throughout my trip. Many ashes, cottonwoods, black walnuts and box elders down along the highway, maples full color into Cincinnati – then at the monastery, the ashes have kept most of their leaves, and the woods is rich and golden. Intermittent cricketsong tonight, lasting well into the morning, the morning crickets seeming less tentative, less intermittent.

2013: Northern Indiana to Yellow Springs: More sunny skies. The soybean harvest was underway all the way home. River birch leaves turning quickly over the past two days, hickories completely gold. Grackles and red-wings at the feeders. All along the highways to southern Ohio, trees remain at early full color, many woodlots so bright. Some maple trees reaching their best and holding their leaves. At the Mill, a variety of violet leaved aster with dark centers similar to *aster sagittifolius* and Short's aster common in the undergrowth, honeysuckle berries prominent, deep red, the hardy smartweed breaking down. No robins seen or heard. In the yard, zinnias continue to bloom, but their foliage is spotted with disease, and the number of blooms is about a fourth of what it was this summer in the circle garden, half of what it was along the north wall. While we were gone, the first white Christmas cactus bloomed.

2014: Rapid change on Moya's maple, almost full now. The Danielsons' has peaked, solid golden orange. The chicory stand at Stafford and Limestone has only a few blossoms left. Mateo's black walnut: a dozen fruits remaining. Through the mild afternoon, a couple of cabbage whites and numerous painted ladies in the zinnias. Lil's maple not quite ready but seems on the edge. But her burning bush is bright red. The upper leaves of the backyard cherry tree are down, the lower leaves still green. The crabapple tree at the southeast corner of the yard is bare. The giant beggartick plant I've been nurturing is coming apart, seeds falling when I brush against them, leaves purple like the leaves of the smaller beggarticks and large-flowered bidens at Ellis. At Ellis Pond and arboretum, the ashes have all come down now, and the sugar maple grove is gathering momentum, rich gold-orange, the bald cypress trees are fully turned to a rusty orange, the tulip tree foliage is pale but completely colored, and in the distance, I can see that the oaks are starting to show their age. One yellow sulphur at the pond. Tonight, humid, 60 plus degrees, katydids and tree frogs and chirping crickets and cricket songs like static, a great summer valediction. Maggie reports from eastern North Carolina that the leaves are in perfect early-full color today.

2015: One yellow sulphur seen at the Antioch campus today, no others noticed in the yard. Jeanie's river birch has suddenly produced many yellow leaves, and the cherry nearby is almost bare. Full color spreads through town. Leah reports two quarter-size toads hopping across her driveway. Crickets intense tonight.

2016: Cool in the low 60s and sunny. Only one small fritillary seen in the zinnias and two cabbage whites in randori. On the north side of the house, the viburnum is a rich purple red; half of Lil's burning bush has turned; the Danielsons' maple has turned a pale orange; Moya's maple has started at the top; Don's serviceberries are almost bare; Mateo's black walnut is down to a few leaves, outlined in maroon by the Virginia creeper vines that have taken over its trunk and branches.

2018: To Yellow Springs from Keuka Lake in New York: Milkweed pods open, silver seeds tufted, full early color of ashes in the mountains of western New York, bright green fields, a sunset in which the hazy sun had bookends of sundogs set in splays of violet and cream cirrus and altostratus clouds, pierced at an angle from on high by one low contrail.

2019: The second light frost of the autumn, still no damage to the flowers. Crows and cardinals for a few minutes around 6:25 this morning. Bright sun and chilly through the day. In the chilly morning, yellow jackets stiff, huddling at the sweet openings of the hummingbird feeder. One painted lady, several small bumblebees and cabbage whites in the zinnias. The sweet gum fruits in the tree on the way to Jill's house are turning from green to brown. The sparrows were screaming and feeding and flying back and forth around the feeders all afternoon. Slight turning of the leaves at Ellis, violet-red on some dogwoods, vague purple-brown on the ash grove, some bare black walnut trees (except for their fruit). About three dozen geese were working the field across the road from the pond when I drove by.

2020: After three mild, overcast days and nights, last night brought a thunderstorm, and this morning is clear and bright, 42 degrees. The variegated garden with its zinnias and marigolds is being swallowed up, minute by minute, it seems by the shining leaves, multiplying, falling, piling, becoming flowers themselves. Jogging close to a mile beyond Ellis Pond, crickets and grasshoppers leaping this way and that around me, I saw a black swallowtail, a cabbage white and three or four sulphurs. (Ann told Jill she had been amazed at the number of small grasshoppers on the path, as well.) One medium-size flock of blackbirds above the cornfield. In the garden, a painted lady browsed with a cabbage white and a few honeybees. Moya's maple is at least half shed now, the hackberry beside it thinned, fragile. At the doctor's office west of town, the decorative locust trees are almost bare, reminiscent of my parking lot at Wilberforce, decades ago. Some geese at the pond, more around the college building on East Enon Road. Robins peeping in the yard; they have been around through the autumn. Tonight, we found a black woollybear caterpillar on the kitchen floor.

2021: Sun and cool 70 degrees, one cabbage white. Crows restless throughout the morning. The white bindweed flowers have spread across the front hedge, reminders of July's rose of Sharon blossoms. Robin peeping heard in the yard, the first time since Middle Summer.

2023: Time count: 10 canna blossoms hold, New England asters fading quickly, hops leaves browning, beggartick foliage dusky violet adding to the October garden color, very little leaf fall or bright color in the area. Hostas transplanted before tomorrow's rain.

The ditches have ripened into pale ocherous colors, shades of russet intermixed, and in the fields where soybeans have already been harvested, the stubble lies slicked back like an old man's crew cut. The corn...still stands in rows, dry, skeletal ruings of the plant it was in mid-August – it suggests cool weather, sharp nights....

Verlyn Klinkenborg

October 14th
The 287th Day of the Year

As the crickets' soft autumn hum
Is to us
So are we to the trees
As they
To the rocks and the hills.

Gary Snyder

Sunrise/set: 6:44/5:58
Day's Length: 11 hours 14 minutes
Average High/Low: 66/44
Average Temperature: 55
Record High: 91 – 1899
Record Low: 27 – 1979

Weather

Today is sunny to partly cloudy eight days in ten. Mild conditions usually prevail, with highs above 70 fifteen percent of the afternoons, 60s occurring about half the time, 50s a fourth of the time, and 40s just once in 15 years. Even though nights are ordinarily in the 30s and 40s, frost comes only one morning in ten on this date. Showers occur one day in three.

The Natural Calendar

Blueberry bushes are red. Vineyards are yellow and brown, only a few grapes left. Some ginkgoes are pale golden green, some just a little faded. Large patches of sky shine through the tattered canopy. The domestic plants of local ponds shrivel in the frosty nights: the water lettuce, hyacinth and pickerel plant.

Daybook

1983: South Glen: Sweet, dank, bitter smell of fallen leaves. I came across a small flock of robins on my walk. Buzzards are still flying, crickets loud. Chicory is still blooming, along with the nettles that were cut over in the fields. Burdock still open, red clover, small white asters, white and pink smartweed still in bloom, but some of the pale violet asters are gone. Zigzag goldenrod still open but late; white snakeroot bloom is over, bell-flower leaves yellow and tattered, touch-me-not leaves mostly fallen: today seems the beginning of the last decline. The tall canopy is weakening, the undergrowth losing its leaves too. Ashes are gone, oaks, maples, box elders, Osage, elms are thinning out. Black walnut trees are bare. Dogwoods reddening. Ginger and sedum and sweet Cicely growing back now, and I found two autumn violets flowering.

1984: Covered Bridge: Buzzards flying, crickets loud. Oaks, maples, Osage, elms thinning, walnuts gone. Newborn grasshoppers in the fields. Tattered pokeweed bent with fat purple berries. Touch-me-nots have lost almost all their leaves. Catchweed growing back and blooming. Rose hips are orange. Some sumacs gone. One violet blooming. Wood nettle, pale and yellow, still dominant in the underbrush. Small flock of robins passes through.

1985: Spring's purple deadnettle is lush, four inches tall in the garden. Major leaf drop about a week early this year, locusts half yellow, half gone. Ginkgoes a rusty faded green. Half the maples are falling.

1987:   For some reason this morning, I finally believed what I was seeing and writing down. The world was deliberate and precise. I could measure its movement and slide my hand across its contractions. Flowers bloomed the same day every year. Larvae watched the sun and followed its declination to the minute. Time was visible and concrete. Everything was accessible and at hand. Meaning had shape, scent and color.

1988: Catalpas, burned from two nights in the 20s, fall across the road in the wind, half gone in a day. Grape leaves are black, tree of heaven black, leaf stalks melting from the branches. Osage leaves at South Glen burned and crisp, coming down through the stronger leaves that survived the frost. Crickets still singing. Around six o'clock this evening, sparrows burst into some dispute in the cherry tree.

1989: Locust leaves flutter down in clumps this afternoon. Peach almost gone, and tree of heaven, red mulberry. Sparrows vociferous, cardinals strong off and on, grackles cackling and chattering in the back trees, robins moving through the thinning shrub line. Full leaf color today in Yellow Springs and east on my drive into West Virginia. Loud and clear days and nights.

1990: Red mulberries weakened, maybe half gone, and gnarled even without a frost. Raspberry leaves yellowing. Lil's maple has started on the north side, a patch of color maybe six feet wide. Box elders have come down quickly this past week.

1991: Ginkgo fruits turning rose color, will drop all at once in six weeks.

1992: No ginkgo fruits at all this year.

1995: Yesterday temperatures in the 80s, the leaves dry, falling in showers through the afternoon. I worked tarring the tin roof as the tree of heaven came down into the sticky coating. Clouds covered the sky by evening, then light rain. This morning, Yellow Springs is in the dip of a low-pressure system, the cold front still a hundred miles away. The moon, just past full, is shining through the eye of the front. I have the back door open. Outside in the dark, leaves keep clattering down, and the wind is gusty.

1998: Crows fly over 6:13 a.m. Cardinal sings 7:42 a.m. The greenhouse is lush now with winter tomato and pepper plants, only a few whiteflies, and those easily controlled. Full color has begun now in town all at once.

2000: Crows before dawn, 6:23. Tonight, katydids and crickets still singing.

2001: Yellowing leaves on the ironweed.

2002: First light frost.

2003: The peak of the ashes has just passed, and even many of the maples are coming down. The Osage leaves are bright yellow, compensating a little for the growing bareness of the tree line.

2004: Great flocks of blackbirds passed over me as I drove south. At one point in the city, the birds filled a grove of bare cottonwoods, their black bodies appearing to replace the fallen leaves.

2005: At South Glen this morning: a few tall bellflowers had purple blossoms still, but the zigzag and the tall goldenrods were finished. A few small white asters and Short's and heart-leaved asters remain in bloom. The foliage of the undergrowth, the wood nettle, the wingstem and the ironweed is thinning quickly, and the early trees of the canopy have shed their leaves. The river is very low. One hawk heard in an hour's time, one crow.

2007: Another long flock of blackbirds flew over the yard about 2:00 this afternoon. The stagnation in leafturn continues: neither Lil's maple nor the Danielsons' has started to show any sign of fall. One autumn violet seen in bloom at the side of Peggy's house.

2008: Full maple color and maple fall has begun along Limestone and Dayton Streets, the ground covered with leaves in some yards. In the alley this morning, I approached the apple tree and saw a squirrel with a huge apple in its mouth. He tried to escape with his prize, but the apple tumbled to the ground after he made just two hops. Along Dayton-Yellow Springs Road, the cottonwoods are pretty well down. Ashes, though, are hanging on, bringing full Middle Fall a particular richness.

2010: Crows at 6:30 this morning. Full color of the Danielsons' maple and our northeast corner maple, and Carl's middle maples are brilliant orange. Considerable maple shedding around town, and honeysuckle leaves are coming down quickly. Our ash keeps its gold leaves. The tulip tree sprout that has survived two years in its pot has turned yellow.

2011: Crows at 6:25 this morning. Wind steady, leaves coming down everywhere in town, leaves covering the sidewalks and streets. The Danielsons' maple and Don's are completely bare. Only a handful of fruits on Mateo's black walnut tree. One of our hackberry trees is bare, the other pale gold and shedding. Moya's maple is half gone. At the south end of town, sweet gum trees have full color, some leaves red, some gold, some purple, all shades. Throughout the area, all the cottonwoods are down. The sparrows were boisterous, flocking in the front honeysuckles yesterday and this morning, for the first time in quite a while, maybe an autumn pattern of talking and coming together.

The sun came out later in the morning, and after lunch, Jeanie and I saw three monarchs, a small fritillary, a sulphur and three cabbage whites in the zinnias. We picked more lush dahlias and had a final handful of large, sweet raspberries. The last of the white autumn crocus at the northwest side of the patio dropped its final blossoms today.

This afternoon a Cooper's hawk sat on the bird feeder for a while, and then flew off into the woods. I planted sweet William sprouts along the north edge of the garden. A very large flock of starlings seen on the way to Beavercreek this afternoon, birds lining the high wires and large groups flying across and around the road. The wind picked up this evening, and I could only hear a few crickets braving the cold and the gusts.

2012: The Danielsons' maple is bright orange and half down, Mrs. Timberlake's shaded with gold, holding full, Lil's maple just starting, our crab apple about down, Moya's maple and the secret maple full, one of the hackberries is down, the other with maybe half its leaves thinned, the viburnum at half, the redbud at maybe a third, hops seeds finally turned brown, wings on the Japanese knotweed, tree of heaven down, Ruby's white phlox producing a few more blossoms, two white bindweeds peering out from the tangle of weeds and perennials, many hosta leaves yellowing.

Into South Glen in the wind: Zigzag goldenrod and all the asters fading, maybe half gone, the canopy opening way up, tattered leafcup with late flowers, smartweed blanched by frost only a few red flower nubs left, drifts of white snakeroot to seed, brown and gray, drifts of goldenrod all rusted with the flowers and leaves matching now, wood nettle mottled, spotted, drooping, shredded, eaten, wingstem and ironweed leaves all twisted and brittle, climbing bittersweet all emerged, bright, undressed, pale underside of blackberry leaves up in the warm east wind, one buffeted white cabbage butterfly, one downy woodpecker call, one buzzard circling, crickets steady and high.

From Goshen, Indiana, my sister Judy wrote that a week ago (October 7) robins and red-winged blackbirds were flocking near her condominium, and that now the birds are gone.

2013: As full moon comes closer, the first major snowstorm of the season buries South Dakota. Here in Yellow Springs, clear blue sky, temperature in the 70s.

2014: Full color now in Yellow Springs, even the Zelcovas joining in. Judy writes concerning her trip to France last week: "France was not nearly as far along as we are in progressing toward fall. Everything was in bloom—oleanders, dahlias, impatiens, daisies, geraniums, you name it. The palms in the northwest were absolutely lovely, and ferns looked happy as well. Trees were still green, with some beginning to show color along the roadsides in Normandy."

2015: Cold weather deepens, frost predicted within the next few days. Migrating robins peeping outside my window yesterday and this morning. Several monarchs came through looking for the tithonias this afternoon. Three cabbage whites were already in the flowers. At John Bryan Park, the grove of black walnut trees was bare, and the maples were brilliant orange. When I walked Bella last night, one cold field cricket was rasping steadily, slowly, but the chorus of a few days ago was silent.

2016: Brisk light wind and sunny: The ashes at Ellis Pond still hold their color and most of their leaves, the maples still just starting to turn. In Tom's parking lot, the persimmon, ash and hackberry are rusted but holding on. Throughout town, a few trees are down, a few fully turned, most still green, a mottled autumn display. Three cabbage whites at intervals today, one small skipper, one silver-spotted skipper.

2017: After five days away, I come back to find little change on the High Street maples, only a slight browning of the Danielsons' tree. On this recent trip, I paid attention to the way I missed home and summer, and I thought about what caused the discomfort at leaving both behind.

Since my wife died five years ago, I have tried to understand how to come to terms with home. I have become overly attached to the place where I live and to my story contained in its rooms and gardens. It is hard for me to go away.

On the other hand, once I am on the road and look closely at the different landscape, I like the freedom and take comfort in what I find. I do not become detached so much as I befriend the new space and time.

Spring and summer have always been my favorite seasons, and I miss them now. But when I am too sad to see the leaves come down or too fearful of abandoning the safety of my yard, the grip is too strong.

Homesickness comes from holding on and from being held too much. Befriending is an acceptance of what appears on the other side of home. Each pole is a mentor. Each year, I try to learn from autumn and the road not to hold summer and my home too close and to make friends with the cold and absence.

2019: South thirty miles to Caesar Creek to camp. Full early leafturn throughout. Only a couple of small white aster plants in bloom, one chicory.

2020: Deepening autumn, the air sharp in the morning, such gold everywhere, crows before dawn. I dug canna lily roots, brought in a few in pots, amazing plants, making the greenhouse glow in the afternoon sun. Thirty-two geese on Ellis Pond this afternoon, a large flock of blackbirds in the high trees. The ash grove on the other side of the pond lost its leaves in the night.

2021: A box of tulips and daffodils arrived this afternoon: 300 bulbs to plant before winter. Craig Jaynes from the English Garden Farm in Jamestown, about 20 miles from Yellow Springs, sent a picture, taken today, of 13 monarch butterflies on a clump of his large purple asters (*Aster "Jindai"*). He said, however, that butterflies had not been plentiful this year - even though blooming had been profuse in his elaborate garden acres.

2022: To Lincoln, Nebraska: Yesterday and today, full of hard headwind and sun, the full color at Yellow Springs spreading west across Indiana, Illinois and Iowa, the landscape defined by the end of harvest all along the drive, and the rich foliage reds and golds remaining until Nebraska, when greens and ochres prevailed. Ash trees, however, were deep maroon and holding, having escaped the plague of disease that decimated the Ohio woods. And sumac foliage was still dominant along the highways, deep scarlet-purple. Only a few murmurations of starlings, one sulphur seen in Lincoln.

2023: To Cincinnati: The trees lining the freeway were in full color, and the St. Clare Monastery grounds were golden. The change seemed so quickly over the past two days. At the discussion with my Lay Cistercian group at the monastery, most everyone had been thinking or reading about death; appropriately autumnal, I said. At home, the hackberry has thinned by maybe a third, and Moya's maple has shaded from the top down. The New England asters are almost gone. Time count: Ten cannas in bloom as the yard's plantings grow scruffier and tattered. Two cabbage white butterflies, in spite of the light rain

Lil's maple is pale gold now,
And the Danielsons' bright orange
Across the street.
Every fall, I watch the passage
Of those trees through October,
Even though Lil died,
And the Danielsons moved
To a nursing home years ago.
Each tree is a guide
That shows a different time in place.
Lil's maple is later than all the others on High Street,

Often waiting to turn until the first day
Of November. Lil's maple is the far anchor
Of middle autumn, and when Lil's comes down,
I know the ginkgoes have fallen
Near my old office window in Wilberforce,
And the white mulberry behind our house
Will be bare within a week.
So I could stay here at my window
And attend to nothing else,
Knowing all the world was spinning by design,
And I could never lose my way again.

bf

October 15th
The 288th Day of the Year

One's own landscape comes, in time, to be a sort of outlying part of himself; he has sowed himself broadcast upon it, and it reflects his own moods and feelings.... How has the farmer planted himself in the fields; builded himself into his stone walls, and evoked the sympathy of the hills by his struggle!

John Burroughs,

Sunrise/set: 6:45/5:56
Day's Length: 11 hours 11 minutes
Average High/Low: 66/44
Average Temperature: 55
Record High: 91 – 1899
Record Low: 28 – 1939

Weather

The 15th is usually pleasant, with clear to partly cloudy conditions prevailing 80 percent of the days. Rain passes through just one day in four. Highs in the 80s occur five percent of the time, 70s thirty percent, 60s forty percent, 50s twenty-five percent. Morning lows reach the 30s or 40s half the years, and frost strikes one to two dawns out of ten.

The Weather in the Week Ahead

While most afternoons are in the 50s and 60s, the weather does warm up sometimes: the 15th and 16th each have a 35 percent chance of highs in the 70s or 80s, and the other days at least have a 25 percent chance of such temperatures.

Lows in the 20s or 30s are most likely to occur on the mornings of the 19th, 20th, with the latter date carrying the highest chances of a freeze so far this season: a full 30 percent chance of a light frost, and an additional 20 percent chance of a hard freeze.

Most days this week have a 30 percent chance of precipitation, with the 16th and 17th being the wettest (with a 40 percent chance). The times most likely to produce snow are the 18th through the 20th (but only five to ten percent of all the years).

The Natural Calendar

The chemical changes in the foliage that became noticeable six weeks ago accelerate until the fragile landscape seems to turn all at once. Shagbark hickories, maples, sweet gums, sassafras, and sycamores reach peak color. Black walnuts, locusts, buckeyes, box elders, hackberries, pussy willows, ashes and cottonwoods are almost bare.

Daybook

1983: Arrowhead is brown at Ellis Pond, asters sporadic through the village. Leaf color has peaked in the countryside but not in town. Small flock of red-winged blackbirds at the pond today, the only fall migrating flock of them I've seen. Sunflower field north of town: heads dark, bent toward the ground. A field of winter wheat, just sprouted, fresh spring green.

1984: Peak leaf color ended today, the maples shedding quickly.

1985: All the leaves fell from Mrs. Lawson's maple today. In our yard, more than three-fourths of the maples are down.

1986: The landscape just barely turning.

1989: When I left town on the 12th for West Virginia, leaf color was just gathering momentum throughout southern Ohio. When I returned to Ohio on the 14th, no question - it was the center of leafturn. Today, it's late peak. Locusts, box elders, most ash are gone - the end of the first phase of leafdrop which occurs during the height of the oaks and maples. In a day or two, Middle Fall all will be over.

1990: A mild, gentle peak of leaves in Yellow Springs. My maple and many others are full. The woods down Grinnell Road is thinner now. At dawn, the road is lighter, the sky showing through. All the goldenrod has rusted; all the yard's asters have been gone for a week or more. Patches of Queen Anne's lace still hold in bloom along Wilberforce-Clifton Road. No frost yet. Impatiens continue to flower with the mums. Woolly-bear caterpillars are suddenly everywhere.

1992: Ash leaves coming down in the center of the first major shedding and the beginning of peak maple color.

1997: Finally all the Japanese beetles are gone.

1998: The Japanese beetles have been gone for weeks this dry autumn. Mosquitoes have been few. In the greenhouse, even the whiteflies are less threatening. I find only a couple of dozen a day on more than two dozen tomatoes. Those tomatoes are lush now, especially the ones that haven't set their fruit. Their foliage is soft and deep green, their stalks fat and succulent. The tomatoes that matured early and have large green fruit are wizened, their leaves tough, their new blossoms not setting; they look old and worn out.

2000: Rapid onset of Middle Fall. Full song of the katydids tonight.

2001: Flock of blackbirds passed over at 8:20 this morning. At school: my red maples have turned completely; my grapevine is unchanged; the white oaks still green. Most redbuds are down. Across the countryside, the weekend's rain has taken the ashes and dulled the early tier peak. Now the second phase: full Middle Fall. In Madison, Wisconsin, about 300 miles north of Yellow Springs, Tat said they were still at peak leaf color, the last stage of mapleturn.

2002: A cool evening in the 40s. Only a few crickets. Days and nights so quiet.

2003: The Danielsons' tree is shedding from the top, foliage about a third to a half down. Lil's tree now full gold. No butterflies seen today. Maple leaves all over the lawn and sidewalks.

2004: One monarch seen on the way to Springfield. Peak maple color is occurring now as the ashes pass their best. The "secret maple" is full bright yellow, as is the new maple at the northeast corner of the yard. The Danielsons' maple is patchy gold and green.

2008: The Danielsons' maple is suddenly a fourth dark orange, Lil's just starting. The last purple crocus in the alley has disappeared. A few of our white crocus still stand.

2009: Weeks of cool and cloudy weather, temperatures three to five degrees below normal all month. Lil's maple, the Danielsons' and Mrs. Timberlake's are all reaching early gold at the same time as the maple in the alley and Don's maple. Lil's burning bush is all red. Cold rain and wind yesterday brought down most of the black walnuts from Mateo's tree – maybe two dozen or so left. Asters are fading, and the chicory plants only produce a few blue blossoms these mornings. Honeysuckle berries have been falling for several days, and this morning there were bittersweet berries on the sidewalk for the first time. Faint starling chatter in the distance. No crows in the rain, and the pre-dawn cardinal song has stopped completely. No frost yet. No butterflies for days, and the chilly, damp nights have quieted the field crickets.

2011: A mild sunny day with a steady wind. Crows came at 6:20. Honeysuckle berries noticed on the sidewalk this morning. There are no bittersweet berries in front of Carl's house at High and Limestone - the great vine was cut down this past August. Lil's burning bush has lost most of its leaves, and our viburnum's red leaves are almost all down. Tonight, only four crickets heard, slow intermittent chirps, temperature 52 degrees.

2012: Peak maple color now throughout Yellow Springs, the soft rain and dove-gray sky adding sheen and context. The burning bush shrubs are bright red. Lil's maple has deepened overnight, richer orange-gold spreading through its branches. Mrs. Timberlake's maple is turning and shedding a little, but the color is pale. Along Dayton Street, the serviceberries have lost more than half their leaves, but their rusty brown color complements the maples. On the east bedroom window screen, the orb-weaver still waits.

2013: Don's serviceberries have shed more than half of their foliage. The Danielsons' maple is full orange, Moya's full mottled yellow, leafturn moving steadily throughout town (but Lil's tree and Mrs. Timberlake's haven't started yet). Starlings chirping and cackling in the alley canopy at 8:00 a.m. Under the front porch light, an orb-weaver without much of a web, set up overnight. No frost yet, the long Indian Summer due to end tonight. Throughout the way to Wilmington south, the landscape is at full maple color.

2014: As I was going out the front door this afternoon, I disturbed an orb-weaver that had no web. He was on the edge of the screen door, panicked and dropped down. Leah reports thousands of Asian lady beetles, mixed with some red lady beetles, arriving at her property today in Clark County a few miles north of Yellow Springs. Rain and chilly today and tonight. Only intermittent insect calls, none of the steady tree cricket songs, only what sounds like mournful field crickets, no katydids like last night.

2015: Camel cricket in the bathtub when I woke up. Walk through the village before sunrise, the sky just starting to blush, Orion clear in the south, Venus high in the east, Jupiter following behind a little to the northeast. "Chits" (call notes) from cardinals, and one sparrow at 6:20, crows at 6:24, sparrows in rhythm at 6:44. Full color growing on all the maples. Don's serviceberry trees have shed their leaves, and his river birch has thinned, and the leaves are twisted as though some disease – other than autumn – has taken them. Through the countryside, the tree line is mottled, but still predominantly green; the loss of the ashes has dulled the autumn's show. Several silver-spotted skippers in the zinnias and tithonias today, several mating. One monarch in the morning, one in the afternoon. Crickets louder tonight, steady grating of one species, guttural rhythmic chirping of another.

2017: Storm coming, wind and mild, bamboo restless, back and forth. The first of the old Christmas cacti has two large buds. The white autumn crocus is down to one floppy stalk and bloom.

2018: Canna lilies, zinnias and tithonias still survive in the garden, two purple spiderwort flowers. One cabbage white in this cool and breezy afternoon. The milkweed pods open from the rain and frost. At John Bryan Park, only violet arrow-leaved asters, some small white asters and blue-stemmed goldenrod in bloom, a couple of zigzag goldenrod blossoms. Casey reported that as he and Irene were walking to town this afternoon, they watched a bald eagle soaring over the North Glen area.

2019: After a third day in a row of light frost: sun and mild just over 70 degrees this afternoon, several honeybees, monarchs, painted ladies and cabbage whites nuzzle and suckle the zinnias. Pink smartweed climbs through the spent New England asters. The August-green, forest-green leaves sway in the breeze.

2020: New moon, perigee and the October 12-15 cold front chilling the afternoon with wind into the 50s, birds feeding frantically in the back yard.

2021: A sharp change in the weather: rain today and chilly forecast for the week to come.

2022: Jill sent a photo of a tiny toad, not much bigger than a tadpole, on her house siding.

2023: Leaf color peaking in the countryside, much less change in the village. Time count:10 cnna blossoms hold. Cloudy and chilly, breezy.

If people could only disintegrate like autumn leaves, fret away, dropping their substance like chlorophyll, would not our attitude toward death be different? Suppose we saw ourselves burning like maples in a golden autumn?

Loren Eiseley

October 16th
The 289th Day of the Year

Now do ye dream of Spring when greening shaws
Confer with the shrewd breezes, and of slopes
Flower-kirtled, and of April, sweetling guest....

Siegfried Sassoon

Sunrise/set: 6:46/5:55
Day's Length: 11 hours 9 minutes
Average High/Low: 65/44
Average Temperature: 54
Record High: 89 – 1897
Record Low: 28 – 1991

Weather

Today's weather statistics are very similar to those of the 15th, with highs in the 80s coming five percent of the time, 70s thirty percent, 60s thirty-five percent, and 50s thirty percent. The likelihood for clouds and rain increases slightly: showers fall 30 percent of the days; the Sun shines 70 percent of the time. Frost strikes 15 percent of the nights, but only half those frosts are hard.

The Natural Calendar

To live a pure life, to live for the sake of life in total happiness, is to adapt oneself completely to the universe, as the trees live.
Graça Aranha

The first week of Middle Fall is the center of Burning Bush Turning Red Season. Hosta Seedpod Splitting Season is underway, black seeds ready to fall in a storm. Corn and Soybean Harvest Season and Winter Wheat Planting Season develop in the countryside. New England Aster Season comes to a close in town.

Daybook

1982: Crickets grow silent near eleven tonight as the temperature drops toward freezing.

1983: One village ginkgo is pale yellow green, others mixed, and some just a little faded. Many milkweeds are bursting their pods. Peak leaf color is starting, with shagbark hickory, some maples, sweet gum, scarlet oak, sassafras, sycamore, ash, and cottonwood leading. Quickweed still provides a deep green border to the paths. A few lance-leaf and zigzag goldenrod still hold. Asters still common, with chicory and scattered Queen Anne's lace.

1985: Starlings are in full song outside my window at Wilberforce. At South Glen, thimble plants have broken up like old cattails.

1986: Leaves continue to turn very slowly. My aloe plant in the greenhouse is ready to flower.

1987: Mrs. Lawson's maple is completely golden orange, ours more than half bare. Full color throughout the countryside.

1988: Far Hole, river low, 10:00 a.m., windy: One large carp caught. Last week's frost has curled and paled all the box elders and hackberries. Sycamores, wild cherry, dogwoods have been hurt, too. The whole landscape here has turned rust and tan, with the goldenrod showing a last few flowers. Almost half the asters gone.

1990: More woolly-bear caterpillars appeared along the road to work today. Leaves still not peak color. Blackbirds cackling in the back trees through the sunny afternoon.

1991: After maybe five days of peak color, leaf-drop suddenly accelerates.

1992: Six to ten inches of snow in Duluth and northern Michigan, first major storm of the season.

1995: First frost this morning. At ten o'clock, I heard tapping on the wood siding beside my office. I went out the front door, came around in back to see who it was: a yellow-bellied sapsucker looking for insects. It's been years since I saw the last one here. To and from work today: the road was filled with orange woolly-bear caterpillars. There have been more this fall on Grinnell Road than

I've ever seen. Tonight, Peter reported that Massachusetts had been at full maple color a week ago.

1998: Crows were late this morning, 6:23. A warm and sunny day. I found a small brown grass snake on the outside sill of the south wall windows. In the pond, our koi are getting a little slower, more reluctant to rise for food. Water lilies still have 18 leaves, no flowers.

1999: Crows at 6:30 a.m. sharp this morning. Last night: katydids still strong. Full leaf color throughout, fall slow and rich this year. But the cottonwoods are coming down, and some long rows of ash are bare. Lil's burning bush is bright red. Most all the small white asters in the yard are done. Last year's mums are still in full bloom; zinnias and snapdragons continue to blossom. A few water lilies still bloom, 23 leaves showing.

2000: At school in Springfield, the oaks are starting quickly, the birch accelerating, one poplar suddenly auburn gold. Red maple almost gone. The Danielson's maple is a third down, Lil's maple just starting to turn. The linden in the park is full yellow, the beech on Dayton street red and green.

2003: Mike reports that he heard white-throated sparrows this afternoon. They have returned to the area for winter.

2004: Leaf-fall accelerates in hard wind and about an inch of rain.

2005: Lil's and the Danielson's maples hold at just a few leaves turned. Lil's burning bush: half red. In the south garden, the yellow rose is finally gone, and all the New England asters have faded. Two new purple coneflowers have bloomed, but their petals are not well developed, and their stalks are short. In the east garden, the dahlias have never been stronger. The sedum, though, has gone to seed. The mums have just passed their brightest. In the High-Stafford Street alley, clusters of small violet asters are still blossoming.

2007: Most of the maples are still late-summer green throughout town. In the alley this morning, Mateo's Jerusalem artichoke leaves were turning beside the yellowing honeysuckle and rose of Sharon. The great ragweed leaves have nearly all disintegrated. Goldenrod leaves are turning, flowers tufted. In the north garden, the New England asters are done, have started to go to soft gray seeds. Silence when I started my walk; then, a few starlings started to whistle about 6:55. Jeanie said she and Chris saw maybe a dozen buzzards in a bare tree along the bike path. Along the way to Wilmington, the maples are still holding off, but some woodlots are in early full turn. At Wilberforce, the ashes and locusts stopped shedding the first week of October, are holding at maybe only a third of their leaves down.

2008: A cool front came through last night, after an oppressive day in the 80s. Today, the sky is full of sun and gray clouds, wind, leaves falling. In the alley, the apple tree still holds a dozen apples, and Mateo's violet chicory stand out against the thinning foliage. Along the east fence, the red-gold poison ivy leaves are half down. One red rose bud in the north garden. At the east garden entry, the sedum is still red, still blends with the new bricks. The red viburnum has finally started to drop its leaves. The foliage of Moya's late hostas is browning quickly.

2011: Windy, mild, full of sun: crows at 6:30, a cardinal song heard at 11:35. And four monarchs, one red admiral, two beautiful yellow sulphurs, a handful of cabbage whites visited the garden zinnias this afternoon. Shrill tree crickets sang throughout the day, and in the evening, intermittent crickets were almost drowned out by the vociferous katydids.

2012: Soft wind and sun, robins constantly chirping through the honeysuckles. Peak color holds all the way to Columbus, even many cottonwoods keeping golden leaves. In the Phillips Street alley, the Japanese knotweed foliage has yellowed overnight, and leaf clusters of the tree of heaven are falling to the roadway.

2014: Cool, cloudy: On my walk with Jeff at the quarry, intermittent rattling/buzzing from a few crickets. In the quarry pools, a great flock of geese, maybe a hundred in all, and around them: killdeers calling and calling. At home, clearweed is becoming translucent, all its seeds dropped. The viburnum, deep purple-red, is losing leaves quickly now. Across the street, the Danielsons' maple is in full color and starting to shed, as is Moya's, Mrs. Timberlake's is not too far behind. Lil's maple holds with only tints of gold. At Ellis Pond, the sugar maple grove is almost full orange and gold, the cypress trees deeper rust, the red and scarlet and swamp oaks well on the way to turning, intermittent purr of crickets, continuing through the evening.

2016: Warm and breezy, high in the 70s: A monarch stayed in the north garden throughout the afternoon, flying from one zinnia to another. A yellow sulphur, a few cabbage whites and a silver-spotted skipper appeared from time to time. A robin seen in a crabapple tree along Limestone Street, and occasional migration peeps heard in the morning.

2017: The coldest day so far in the autumn, but one painted lady butterfly stayed tasting zinnias at least half the day. I found bright yellow witch hazel flowering along Pleasant Street. Frost advisory for tonight, the first of the autumn.

2018: Leaving for Italy this afternoon. Deep frost forecast here for tonight. The elephant ears still on the porch will have to be cut off when I get home.

2019: Chilly and rainy, first all-day fire in the stove. Barometer low pulling in the north wind. Cardinal "chit" call in the alley at 6:30, then a sudden male's call at 6:35, then silence. In the backyard honeysuckles, sparrows continue to swarm. One robin whinny heard in the afternoon, but no sighting. At the hummingbird feeder: no ants and very few yellow jackets. Another step in the Sixth Extinction? The Champney's maples near Limestone Street have turned almost all the way now and have started to shed, and the Danielsons' maple has just begun to turn. The other maples on the block hold green.

2020: Last night, the first fire of the autumn in the wood stove. Then this morning, the first light frost, but the castor beans, marigolds, cannas and zinnias survived without damage. Such bright sun in the greenhouse today, plants glowing. The Danielsons' maple and the middle maple of the Champneys are almost down, black walnut trees in the alley bare. Robins peeping in the honeysuckles. The catalpas along Polecat Road are deep yellow-gold. At the pond, more than 50 geese floating on the water, the winter flock gathering now for fellowship before January and February pairing, a movement toward spring.

2021: The first cold day in the 50s since spring. In a drive to Jamestown, very little color change noticed in the trees, but a large flock of starlings seen above an uncut cornfield. Low in the upper 30s forecast for tonight.

2022: Lincoln, Nebraska to Hannibal, Missouri: Overcast and in the 60s most of the morning, windier in the afternoon. Yvonne's garden in Lincoln was still strong with annuals and tomatoes unhurt by the one frost they had had. A robin heard peeping in the bushes, just like at home. East to Hannibal, the leaf color was dulled by the lack of sun, but the progress paralleled that of our trip out on the 13th and 14th.

2023: Gray, chilly, damp. Fallen leaves speckle the garden, increase the tattered sense of the shrubs and remaining zinnias, castor flowers and zinnias. Time count: eight canna blossoms, bedraggled. Only Jeanie's Endless Summer hydrangea's soft pink clusters seem defiant, unfazed by the gloom. Jill reports more road kills than she's ever seen on her drive to Dayton this morning. Peak leaf color is definitely underway. Curiously, on October 3 - 4, 1991, peak leaf color coincided with an unusual number of opossums killed on the highway overnight.

> *Nothing is foreign; Parts relate to whole*
> *One all-extending, all preserving Soul*
> *Connects each being, greatest with the least*
> *Made Beast in aid of Man, and Man of Beast*

Alexander Pope

***October 17th**
The 290th Day of the Year*

*Autumn is a second spring
When every leaf is a flower.*

Albert Camus

Sunrise/set: 6:47/5:53
Day's Length: 11 hours 6 minutes
Average High/Low: 64/43
Average Temperature: 54
Record High: 86 – 1910
Record Low: 25 – 1977

Weather

There is a 25 percent chance of highs in the 70s today, 50 percent for 60s, another 25 percent for 50s. Skies are totally overcast, and rain is recorded 40 percent of the time. A 15 percent chance exists that lows will reach the 30s, ten percent for a freeze in the 20s.

The Natural Calendar

*Yin and yang cut brief autumn days short. Frost and snow
Clear, leaving cold night wide-open at the edge of heaven.*

From "Night at the Tower" by Tu Fu, translated by David Hinton

The temporal countryside takes on its autumnal contours from the increasingly violent movements of the Earth's atmosphere as it tilts away from the Sun.

Tapering floral sequences and the gradual surge of leafturn occur amid the remnants of Early Fall. From the broad lowland of spring and summer warmth with its six months of birdsong and its hundred days of insect calls, the Sun pulls the land up into the foothills of the year where asters and goldenrod bloom and where trees are gold and red.

Middle Fall strips away foliage, puts buds into dormancy, burns away the undergrowth and reveals the dark hillsides. At the end of Late Fall, December's great range of cold and snow fills the horizon. Beyond it lies the high plateau of Deep Winter in which nothing ever seems to grow or change until the ground crumbles and gives way, shattered by thaws, and time tumbles down into March.

Daybook

1982: Jacoby: Cattails are breaking up from repeated frosts. Only two asters left blooming by the swamp. Beggarticks stuck to my shirt this afternoon.

1984: Some ginkgoes completely green, some gold, some bare.

1985: Covered Bridge: Half of the Osage leaves are down. Dozens of robins migrating south along the river.

1988: The first line of leaves did not fall early; now all the trees seem to be coming in together. Maple in the yard is at its best, bright orange.

1989: Dramatic loss of leaves. Suddenly it's Late Fall in the middle of October. Afternoons loud with robins and sparrows. Starlings are boisterous in the trees at Caesar Creek. Kingfishers continue their year-round commuting back and forth along the water.

1992: Kalamazoo, Michigan: The northern leaves are brighter, thicker than those in Yellow Springs, deeper reds, more striking oranges and golds, the undergrowth even more brilliant than the upper canopy. Milkweed by the side of the road: none of the pods have opened yet. At home, the last few rose of Sharon bushes (which had grown from seed this spring) are in bloom.

1997: Silver olive trees hold green along the freeway, but they are starting to have speckles of yellow. Christmas cacti by the back door have been budding for at least a week, and the New England asters suddenly all turned brown a few days ago.

1998: Warm and bright today, woolly-bear caterpillars all over the freeways and back roads. Early full leaf color now. Crows at 6:13

a.m. west of town. A cardinal sings at 6:28 a.m. Descending whinny of a screech owl at 7:45 a.m. About a fourth of the south hedge has shed its leaves, the neighbor's house showing through. In the pond, arrowhead leaves are all shriveled, its seeds floating in the water.

1999: Katydids last night. And this morning at 4:35, they are still rasping slowly in the 65-degree dark.

2001: Cardinal sings at 6:28 a.m. Witch hazel leaves are turning yellow on Dayton Street. Some sugar maples full color, some half down. Along the road to Columbus, the bare ash and cottonwoods give a sense of Late Fall. The fencerows are bare except for yellow-green grape foliage. Goldenrod and false boneset seasons are over. Cattail foliage is yellow-brown. At my school window, the red maple is mostly gold, shedding from the top down.

2003: A lush bouquet of zinnias and two perfect yellow roses picked from the north garden.

2005: Light frost on the back window of the car this morning. Doves and cardinals were calling at 7:00 a.m. The day was warm, and a few katydids called when I walked Bella at 7:30 this evening.

2006: Impatiens and coleus killed by frost between the 10th and the 13th. All butterfly bushes gone. New England asters are ending in the yard. Reddening of the viburnum. Black rose of Sharon seedpods. Moya's maple full gold and shedding. Hackberry trees are two-thirds down. Peach half down. Astilbe and hosta yellowing. Korean lilac and trumpet creeper ocher. Grape vines very yellow. Bittersweet berries dark. Lizard's tail dropping leaves, water willow yellow green. No rose of Sharon flowers. Quince fruits in the pond's filter. Danielsons' maple full, Lil's a fourth. Oaks gold and russet. Some woodlots mostly green. Knotweed seeds all but a few are gone. Many sweet gums full. In the warmth of this wet evening (63 degrees at 8:30), a few katydids were calling, some crickets.

In the countryside, mum sales are coming to a close. My classroom ginkgo is ochre. Dogwoods are deep red, full maples, artichokes waning, some locusts only fringed. Windfall apples down everywhere. Burning bush full red. Teasel stark and brown along the freeway. Pale tan of the corn. Landscape past its best in the morning rain, the loss of the ashes creating a significant change. Goldenrod has rusted but has not tufted. Geraniums, a few hosta, a few marigolds still bloom

2007: Another mild day in this mild October. Starlings whistle along the alley. In the yard, the yellow rose has one bud, pink rose full bloom, Shasta daisies with two flowers, one new purple coneflower, half a dozen pink dahlias. A tinge of gold on Lil's maple and the Danielsons'. Frost does not appear in the forecast.

2010: I walked Bella at the school campus in the afternoon, the leaves down all along the sidewalk before they had been raked into rows or piles, the peak of leafturn ceding to leaf fall.

It was their postures and textures that interested me most. Not yet soaked from rain or flattened and darkened with age, they fell and lay in a way so different from the way they had held to their branches. Instead of the green uniformity of their summer nature, the leaves became individuals. Separated from their source, they showed an independence in their disarray. Like snowflakes, no two were alike. Like snowflakes, their distinct nature would last for only a brief time.

Some stood out because of their brilliant colors. How many different shades of brown and gold and yellow and orange and red, each shade slightly different! Some were blighted, some spotted, some patterned like butterflies. And they were so light and fragile, no longer held in place or given strength by their source, finally loose to sprawl and be taken up by the wind.

Some leaves lay balanced against grass or other leaves, forming joint designs, combining their fallen characteristics. Some were curled, never exactly the same degree of curl as the others. The tips of some leaves pointed up, the tips of others down. On some leaves only half of the leaf was curled. Some were giant and imposing, others tiny. Some were right side up. Some were upside down. But only in this new state did I notice how free they were, and how, to my eye, they could stand out, they could show themselves separately instead of massed together on summer branches.

2011: Cool and bright today, the sun warm against the south garden wall. One red admiral seen, but no Monarchs, no cabbage whites. Dahlias and zinnias and knockout roses continue to fill the garden with color. First beeches rusting, several ginkgoes along Xenia Avenue starting to turn. Tonight, only soft, slurred, intermittent tree cricket calls. Moya served a big bowl of her own raspberries at Jeanie's meeting this evening.

2012: Another soft and sunny day, robins continuing to peep migration songs in the neighborhood. A surround of chatter from squirrels and starlings. At the old Mill Dam site, Bella and I walked along the river, Bella exulting in the clattering leaves. Here the high canopy is about gone, the gold of young maples shining through the woods. The river was low, three great carp seen lazing near the bank. I looked and listened for robins migrating along the Little Miami where they had been so many years ago, but even though they were moving through Yellow Springs, I didn't find them in the woods. At home, the orb-weaver still waits in his web by the southeast bedroom window, and one of Jeanie's purple clematis has flowered on the trellis.

2013: Robins peeping in the alley, starlings working at the gutters of the white house on Limestone Street. The first morning this autumn in the 30s. On the road to Wilmington, full leaf color all around. At Ellis Pond, more changes: the sugar maples have suddenly turned rust and gold and red-green. The sweet gums and the black maples have started to shed. Many dogwoods pink or deep violet. Catalpas pale. The outer fringe of the small, arrowhead-like Korean pear foliage are brilliant scarlet. The hickories are yellowing. Along High Street, Carl Champney's middle maple is bright orange and losing leaves quickly.

2014: More brilliance, more unraveling. Mrs. Timberlake's maple and Moya's are half gone, the Danielsons' and all of Carl's and the Secret Maple holding at peak; and it is peak color all around the village. Lil's maple quickly catching up. The star magnolia next to Mrs. Timberlake's house is pale, sweet yellow, the Japanese maple behind it deep red. Only three black walnuts left on Mateo's tree.

Fresh violet crocuses in bloom along Dayton Street. Honeybees at the zinnia blossoms. Mildew on the zinnia foliage. Day lily leaves streaked with decay, hollow stalks holding stubborn. New quickweed in full bloom, taking over one of the old gladiola beds. Three yellow wild strawberry flowers.

2015: This morning, for the first time since spring, the koi did not rise to feed when I dropped in their food. I checked the water temperature: 45 degrees. I remember now how October and November brought an end to my success when I fished for carp in the river back in the 1980s. Then, in April, the first strike of the year!

2016: The Danielsons' maple is early full, as is Moya's. Now much of the landscape has turned a little, and leafdrop is underway for the yellowing locusts and many precocious maples. Emily reported seeing a flock of cedar waxwings, hundreds of them moving together through the south end of town.

2017: Cold in the upper 30s this morning, but by noon, in the 50s, there were six or seven painted ladies and a couple of cabbage whites in the zinnias, and the hummingbird feeder was feeding dozens of honeybees. At the northeast end of the property, Moya's maple has not turned but has lost most of its foliage, something similar happening to the Danielsons maple. Rick sent a message this morning: "Looks like last night's chill brought an end to the glow worms, which still were making a weak effort in the gravel along our drive the night before, which I guess means fall is finally here."

2019: Several dozen geese in the field across from Ellis.

2020: Drive in the countryside south of town, full maple color, the landscape pale full in so many woodlots, burning bright in others, few trees bare except for black walnut trees, some ashes and box elders. Along the fields by Ellis Pond, newborn grasshoppers still hopped as I jogged to the big tree, accompanied by Ranger and many sulphur butterflies. Working in the yard as the sun disappeared, an old melancholy came over me, like a thick dream residue filling my blood.

2021: Bright sun and cold today in the lower 50s. Blue jays, cardinals, black-capped chickadees, bed-bellied woodpeckers, tufted titmice, house sparrows and nuthatches compete for seed at the feeder. I name them, feeling that they may not be here next year, disappearing like the butterflies.

2022: Return from Nebraska near dusk, Moya's maple half down, Lil's maple full orange, the Danielsons' maple, the secret maple and Mrs. Timberlake's are almost all gone. Flurries in the area. Terri reported that someone saw snowflakes this morning.

2023: High Street maples thinning and ochre. Time count: Nine canna blossoms, and canna transplanting begun as I attempt to keep the plants growing and maybe even blooming through the winter. A greater number will be stored as rhizomes. Joe Pye transplanted to beside the phlox. Each day, I become more engaged with the garden design and future. I wonder about the connection of that intensifying practice to Jeanie's memory presence and my instinctive-like need to keep things the same or at least reminiscent of the past.

Journal
*It is as bad to **study** stars and clouds as flowers and stones....*
Be not preoccupied with looking. Go not to the object. Let it come
to you.
Henry David Thoreau, *Journal*, September 13, 1852

      As the sun moves across the late autumn sky, it shines further and further into my south-facing window. Paying attention to where and when it enters my house allows me to track the seasons toward and away from winter solstice.

      When I watch the sunlight move across my walls, I feel like I am not only following time made visible, but I am also finding myself in relation to the tilt of Earth.

      My relationship with the sun is different when I am outside. Out in the yard or the woods or on the road, the Sun is diffuse, has no limits. It shines everywhere, belongs to everything and to every creature. Even the warmth of the Sun on my face on cold mornings seems accidental and impersonal.

But when I am inside watching it on the wall in my room, the Sun feels more intimate. Shaped by the frame of my south windows, its light is not only tame but mine. It has come to me. I am the only one who sees it here now. It is not so vast and almighty as it appears filling the sky. It is not the indifferent prime mover of the day and night.

Instead, it seems a bright blessing and a personal ally against the winter ahead.

A man dwells in his native valley like a corolla in its calyx, like an acorn in its cup. Here, *of course, is all that you love, all that you expect, all that you are.*

Henry David Thoreau, *Journal,* November 1, 1858

October 18th
The 291st day of the Year

A springful of larks in a rolling
Cloud and the roadside bushes brimming with whistling
Blackbirds and the Sun of October
Summery
On the hill's shoulder,
Here were fond climates and sweet singers suddenly
Come in the morning where I wandered and listened
To the rain wringing
Wind blow cold
In the wood faraway under me.

Dylan Thomas

Sunrise/set: 6:48/5:53
Day's Length: 11 hours 5 minutes
Average High/Low: 64/43
Average Temperature: 54
Record High: 86 - 1910
Record Low: 24 - 1976

Weather

There is a 30 percent chance of highs in the 70s today. Sixties come another 30 percent, 50s twenty-five percent, and cold 40s fifteen percent. Clouds hide the sun 40 percent of the time, and rain falls 30 percent. From the 18th through the 20th, for the first time since the middle of April, there is a steady ten percent chance of snow flurries. Frost strikes one night in five on this date.

The Natural Calendar

St. Luke's Little Summer, a traditional time in Europe for clear, dry weather starts today and ends the 28th. Something of a parallel exists on the western side of the Atlantic: October's average daily precipitation in the Lower Midwest declines noticeably towards the end of the month.

1979: Peak leaf. color today at home.

1982: Wild cucumber fruits are empty. Lone tall bellflower seen: one blossom, no leaves. Not even a hint of yellow on the goldenrod. One pink bouncing bet open.

1984: Yellow jackets swarm near the pussy willow in the sun, green-bottle flies with them. At some parts of Jacoby, especially in the swamp, the canopy is almost gone. Asters have seeded, zigzag goldenrod done, watercress coming back and filling the shallow streams. Sycamore leaves hide the paths. Many oaks still strong, a third of the slippery elms hang on, Virginia creeper finally fallen. Maples in front of our house and at Mrs. Lawson's are completely gone, McDaniel's maple full color and falling, Lil's still full green except on top.

1987: Peak leaf color yesterday and today throughout the county. Leaves are coming down more rapidly now. Catchweed is flowering again, watercress and swamp mint growing back. Orange bittersweet is opening, all its foliage fallen. Robins migrating in small clusters. At Grinnell Swamp, most of the sycamores and poplars are gone, spicebush and shagbark hickory yellow.

1988: Full peak leaf color today in Yellow Springs. Then a heavy thunderstorm filled the back yard with leaves.

1992: Peak leaf color continues throughout Ohio, but most of the leaves on the front maple came down yesterday. Dave Jensen calls, sees ants swarming in his back yard. Were they, perhaps, termites – which often swarm after a hard autumn rain?

1993: The peak has passed now, the maples falling quickly. Crickets are strong at night, but I haven't heard katydids for a couple of weeks. The birds come to the feeders less these days; are there more seeds about, the full harvest of dried fruits coming in? Only cabbage butterflies out on the sunnier days. No Monarchs for maybe ten days. One black swallowtail last week, one fritillary in the garden a few days ago. Spiderwort finally down to just one or two flowers a day. Pink spider plants continue to flower, and all the annuals still hold. Hard frost came 125 miles north of here close to Toledo on the 10th, but no killing freeze yet here.

1995: The tall ash at the triangle park is complete today, hardly a leaf left. The first phase of leafdrop seems about over, but the maples are still moving towards their best color – that will be this week. At South Glen, pink smartweed is the last of the late flowers. Here and there, some remnants of the pale blue tall bellflowers. Driving to school this afternoon, I wove back and forth trying to miss all the woolly-bear caterpillars. They love these warm, sunny days.

1999: Crows at 6:30. Heavy frost on the roof and on the car windshields, freezing temperatures moving across the central part of the state for the first time this fall. On the television, I see that low temperatures in northern Minnesota are in the 20s, and I think about the family homestead, the church at Gentilly, the graveyard at Crookston, my parents' graves, and Uncle Bill's grave in the cold.

2000: This is the peak, the surge in the maple color. Linden full yellow at the park.

2001: Cardinal sings at 6:25 a.m. First Christmas cactus flowers open: one pink, one white. Chicory, Queen Anne's lace, New England aster, dandelions still blooming around the block.

2002: To Archbold in northern Ohio: Here in Yellow Springs, the first tier of leaves is just aging slightly, the landscape dusky across central Ohio like in an average late September. As I drive, I see some ashes are peaking, some hickories, and oaks joining in. Scattered maples are red. Cottonwoods have held on, contributing to the sense of early – instead of middle – fall. Most black walnuts have come down. A hundred miles north of home near St. Marys, some woodlots are fully turned, but some cottonwoods nearby are green. Yellow poplars half turned only. Low, warm sun, cirrus high, wispy, whole tree lines of green. Long blackbird flock over the freeway. Haze, gold, gray, and soft. Fields harvested, many plowed. Great faded fields, dry, plowed, dun. The land flattens above Van

Wert. I drive past a fox killed on the road beside winter grain all green and glowing, some champagne cottonwoods. In Paulding, some bright green catalpas. Many locusts full yellow green, black beans hanging from them. Lots of yellow hickory. Some red oaks turning, definitely twice the color in northern Ohio as in Yellow Springs. Returning home, I see the line between Early Fall and Middle Fall lies exactly between Van Wert and Piqua.

2003: The north hackberry's foliage is withered but still attached; the south hackberry, a younger tree, is bare. Janet's redbud is yellow, mottled, ready to fall. The New England asters are declining quickly. I heard robins chirping in the honeysuckles this morning, starlings cackling, whistling, flocking in the woods near Greg's house.

2005: Walking Bella along the alley at 6:45 this morning: Doves calling, cardinals singing, sparrows chattering. Behind Mateo's property, the small white asters have all gone to seed. The Jerusalem artichoke leaves are mottled, their flower petals gone. On the road to Wilmington, maples are at early peak, many ashes still holding. Four flocks of starlings seen spiraling in sync across the sky. At school, my ash tree is completely bare.

2006: Crickets sing softly just before dawn. At Wilberforce, the small maples are full red, the larger maples bare. One ginkgo tree, the one by my classroom, is full ochre. The ginkgo by my window is still strong green. At home, the Danielsons' maple is full, Lil's is reaching almost half, and Mrs. Timberlake's is just starting.

2007: The road to Wilmington is in early full color. The ashes and locusts at Wilberforce hold at close to half fallen, and it seems the ashes in the country are holding partially as well. Many maples are bright orange and red, but Lil's maple is just a little ochre, and the Danielsons' is still deep green. One of our ash trees along High Street is almost down; the other at the southeast corner of the lot is full, deep, dirty gold. In the alley this morning, about fifteen starlings were sitting in Don's black walnut tree, and two flocks of starlings seen soaring near the community college.

2008: Drove through John Bryan Park this afternoon: many high trees gone, redbuds, sweet gum, sycamore, yellow poplar, sugar maples at full color – mostly yellows and oranges. Some bright Osage leaves, some paling honeysuckle. The alley maple is half shed, and the secret maple is golden. Crows this morning at 6:30 and even one cardinal call.

2010: Crows at 6:27 this morning. All the ashes and locusts are down at Wilberforce, the maples there bright orange, my ginkgoes just slightly pale. Throughout the area, the tree line shows the absence of the ashes, cottonwoods, box elders, black walnuts. Out in the country, the canopy appears dull without the bright ashes. In Yellow Springs, sweet gums and maples are still strong. Carl's maples are bright orange and gold, shedding rapidly, the Danielsons' maple mostly turned and starting to come down. Huge flock of starlings seen heading north at 5:30 p.m.

2011: Crows at 6:45 this morning. Jeanie working in the yard today heard only a few, sporadic cricket calls. No butterflies seen. Rain in the evening, only a couple of crickets heard.

2012: In the field by the Antioch School, a handful of milkweed plants, pods splayed open, silky seeds shining in the late afternoon sun.

2013: As the sun came up over the Glen, I was walking Bella and heard a cardinal singing at the west edge of town. All around me, robins gave their migration signals.

2014: Moya's maple and Mrs. Timberlake's maple are almost down. The Danielsons' is a rich gold, the leaves so fragile, seeming almost ready to collapse. Lil's maple maybe half turned, early, it seems to me.

2015: The autumn's second frost burned most of the upper castor bean leaves, brought down all of the paulownia's. Now Jeanie's river birch is turning more quickly, foliage falling more intensely. Lil's maple and the secret maple have not started to show color, but the Danielsons' is orange-gold, and the top leaves have fallen. Mrs.

Timberlake's maple is just starting, Moya's still full color, Don's coming in. Ed Oxley mentioned to me today how he had not seen the huge flocks of crows he used to see north of town, and he recalled the great flocks of red-winged blackbirds that used to arrive in the spring. And I thought about how no long flocks of grackles have passed over Yellow Springs this fall, and I've only seen one swooping cluster of starlings.

2016: Heat and sun continue, and record highs are expected throughout the East today. In the north garden, only one skipper and a couple of cabbage whites, a few honeybees and small bumblebees seen. Janet's redbud is half yellow, leaves blending with the grape leaves. The bittersweet berries are burnished gold now, almost matching their foliage. Pokeweed berries are drying up, hops vines and false buckwheat done flowering and seeding; the winged knotweed seeds are thinning. Tree of heaven branches have turned an ochre-green and have started to come down. One small fritillary at the Glass Farm this evening.

2017: Sun and cool: Honeybees at the hummingbird feeder, half a dozen or more painted ladies in the zinnias throughout the day, a white-spotted skipper and a cabbage white from time to time. The hackberry at the south side of the yard is almost completely bare, and the north hackberry has sparse, withered foliage. So many more trees without color and twisted foliage. Pokeweed berries shriveling, New England aster seed heads brown, the white autumn crocus finally prostrate, the cherry tree has dropped most of its leaves.

2019: Sun and cool 50s, honeybees in the zinnias, only one butterfly, a pale yellow sulphur. Robin whinny heard again today; they are back. At Ellis Pond, 42 Canadian geese, one white goose on the water, the first time I've seen them there this fall. Neysa in Italy says the land is "green, green, green" all the way from Spoleto in Umbria to Milano in the northwest. Here in Yellow Springs, Middle Fall explodes. The soybean fields have just been cut, and the corn is coming down.

2020: Peak leaf color continues, oaks ruddy, maples advancing quickly, one Cypress tree all brown but the others full green at Ellis. In Wilberforce, the ginkgo by my classroom is half yellow, but the one by my office window is still completely green. Past the southwest side of house, the secret maple is still golden. The Virginia creeper that took over the north side of the house has died back now, and the New England asters are down to maybe a fourth of their blossoms, a few cut-over spiderworts matching their color. The zinnias and the tall marigolds are absorbed into the background of weedy grape, spent goldenrod, false buckwheat, hops and knotweed.

2021: No peak color yet. One cabbage butterfly in the sunny, cool garden.

2022: Most all of the New England asters have gone to seed now, only a few late, cut-over patches still in bloom. Wild lettuce plants and cup plants have shriveled, most seeds gone, stalks blackening. Large-leafed hostas are rich gold. Sleet light this afternoon, a few flurries mixed with rain this evening.

2023: Leah reports painted lady butterflies at here garden; they are not all gone yet! In my yard, I begin the autumn clearing and planting. Still, the time count of canna lilies is nine.

Journal

The very notion of giving meaning to something is premised on a cosmology in which things don't have it yet, in which form is to content as spirit to matter, men to women, God to nature.
Rebecca Solnit

     Last autumn, I was working in the garden and I noticed a small golden maple tree shining in a neighbor's yard several lots away. It stood surrounded behind taller but less dramatic trees, some green, some brown, some bare, but none so glorious.
     I had not noticed that maple before, although obviously it had been growing there for several years. And for a reason I can't remember, I called it a secret maple, using a childhood language, a private naming that seemed right at the moment.

Now, when I come upon golden maples shining through the skeleton of the woods, the canopy above and around them shattered or empty, I think of them as virtual offspring of the private maple, parallel plants reminiscent of that moment when I suddenly found myself startled and comforted by the apparition of such beauty.

When I walked along the river during October this year, I discovered the landscape full of those parallel children, revealed by the course of Middle Fall that had taken down the box elders and the cottonwoods and ashes and the black walnuts, and these secret trees rose out of and above the honeysuckles for their own season, filling my heart and pulling my sight further into the woods than it would have ever gone without them.

I realized then that my fondness for these creatures had other meanings and associations for me. I saw that my feelings about them had to do with the rush of surprise, an excitement of being touched, the gift of uncovered things like unexpected flowers in bloom beneath foliage suddenly exposed by the brush of my hand.

Journal

The season is sending messages. Migrating flocks of birds, sometimes large enough to stretch across the sky, remind the commuter and trucker that ice and snow lie ahead. The urgent call of the geese, common at this time of year, evokes an autumnal restlessness. As the days shorten, sheep and goat owners pay attention to the signs that their does and ewes are cycling. And even human conceptions are said to increase as the weather cools.

The hormonal changes that are related to these phenomena can also produce a seasonal "high" of several weeks or more between the transition time from late summer to early fall and the beginning of late fall (after most of the maple leaves come down).

Optimism can often run wild during this period. Projects that seemed impossible or inadvisable in the oppressive afternoons of July now appear feasible. Career choices, decisions to take on a second job, to apply for a promotion, to propose marriage or to retire are often made more easily at this time of year. Buoyed by the surge of autumn energy, we feel we are invincible.

Every fall I conclude that I will never really be who I might be unless I follow all the reckless intuitions that accompany leafturn. During that time alone, I sometimes think, I know myself the best, am least afraid, least hesitant, most honest, most daring. What if I could always be like I am in late October, I ask myself. I would live with anticipation, ready and willing to become all the things that my body tells me it could become. Unbound by things such as reason and economy, I might break free and find the answer to all the promises biology has programmed deep inside me.

As the recognition of autumn comes suddenly, in a moment, so one day you first hear the geese....Bound for the south, these birds seem to me a strange point of fixity...for in a sense they don't move at all. They take to altitudes to stay in one place, not migrating, but hovering while the equinoctial tilting of the earth rocks the poles back and forth beneath them. The geese remain, an index of what used to be where, and of what will return again. Their seasonal appearance denotes your passing, not their own.

Ted Leeson

October 19th
The 292nd Day of the Year

The days shortened. The air grew frosty. Nights were loud with the honking of geese, and suddenly the leaves were down before gusts of wind. The days were noisy with blowing, and the house filled with the sound of crickets' thighs.

James Still

Sunrise/set: 6:49/5:50
Day's Length: 11 hours 1 minute
Average High/Low: 63/42
Average Temperature: 53
Record High: 84 – 1910
Record Low: 23 – 1992

Weather

Today is another pivotal day on the way to winter: For the first time since April 18th, there is a five percent chance of high temperatures only in the 30s. Another landmark: Chance of low temperatures in the 30s jumps above 50 percent. Highs are in the 70s thirty percent of the afternoons, in the 60s twenty-five percent, in the 50s thirty percent, in the 40s fifteen percent. Showers and overcast skies can be expected one day in three; flurries occur once in a decade.

The Natural Calendar

The sugar beet harvest begins near this date all across the northern states at the same time that grape harvest is done along Lake Erie. The third and final cutting of alfalfa is complete throughout Ohio (although farmers take a fourth cut in the most favorable years). Winter wheat and winter rye have been seeded. Soil temperatures fall into the middle 50s, and earthworms go a little deeper into the ground to avoid the cold. Gardeners divide peonies, lilies, and iris, then plant crocus, daffodils, tulips, snowdrops and aconites.

\\

Daybook

1983: Wild asparagus is yellowing by the roadsides. At the mill, buzzards are sitting on the same sycamore as last October 20th, huge flock of about 50 birds. Last milkweed beetle seen. Fresh mint, six inches tall. It is quiet in the woods at first; then up the hill, suddenly the trees come alive with the sound of robins. They are in the high branches, loud like starlings, hundreds of them. A few minutes later, they're gone. At night, the crickets are still strong.

1984: Sweet gum and redbuds falling, canopy disappearing. Peak color is past.

1985: All-day rain punctuates the end of major leaf color.

1986: Covered Bridge: Robins, bobwhites, and blackbirds calling. Sycamores gold all along the river, geese flying back and forth, a great blue heron gliding up river, skunk cabbage three inches high for March, cottonwood leaves spiraling down like birds, frost melting off the trees like rain. At the edge of the woods, a whole field full of violets covered with frost! Although leaf color is slow to change this year, the late wildflowers have come and gone exactly on schedule. Tonight, only one cricket heard as I walked the dog.

1987: Color starting to turn past its peak, dramatic thinning of the leaves.

1988: Peak color pivot seems to be today.

1989: Record five-inch snowfall in Dayton today.

1990: To Wisconsin: Sunny and 35 degrees, departing Yellow Springs at 8:00 a.m. sharp, full leaf color, cornfields brown and uncut, barometer steady, cardinal singing, flock of crows going over, winter wheat up and fields green in places, so many trees still green. A low bank of clouds lying over the Great Miami river valley like a range of hills or bluffs. All the goldenrod is gone along the highway, milkweed standing stark and disheveled, uncut soybean fields rich orange, scattered Queen Anne's lace. Better leaf color seen near Indianapolis, one patch of asters at Urbana – one in 265 miles, hundreds of yards of red burning bush, harvest of corn and soybeans occasionally complete, spots of helianthus, one woolly bear caterpillar above El Paso, Illinois, crown vetch bright green, more asters near Rockford, leaves holding on the trees north into Madison below the vast mare's tails sweeping up from the northwest.

1992: Most ginkgo leaves fall today after frost.

1997: Crows pass over at 6:30 a.m., a little better than twenty minutes before sunrise. Last night I went into the shrubbery along the east side of the yard looking for Buttercup, our bulldog; I came out covered with beggartick burs.

1998: Huge flock of crows comes over the house at 7:15 a.m.

1999: Yesterday Barbara Preis showed me her praying mantis that lived in her bushes through the summer. Now, she said, he was starting to fail, and when she introduced him to me, he was on his side, wedged between leaves. She says he usually makes a sound "kind of like a cricket," and the same one has been there at least since June. They come back year after year, she says.

2000: Peak color Yellow Springs to Wilmington. The landscape solid gold in the low evening sun.

2001: Portland, Oregon: Trees at least ten days behind Ohio. Honey locusts, white birches, and a few ash are just starting to peak. Maples and aspens are yellowing, but no trees are bare. Burning bush full red. California poppies seen in full bloom by the roadsides. Some periwinkle and yarrow open too.

2003: East to Athens, returning through southern Ohio along the Appalachian Highway: Leaf color was inconsistent throughout. The fall of the first tier of leaves had left the tree line stark in places. In other locations, especially in the east, the hills were a soft yellow, orange, and gold, and many wood lots were at their center of leaf-turn. Several woolly-bear caterpillars seen, a few sulphur butterflies, one painted lady (*Cynthia*). The bodies of many young raccoons seen along the highway; the raccoons seem especially susceptible to being run over these middle-autumn nights.

2005: Hurricane Wilma spins in the Caribbean, has hit Jamaica and is heading toward Florida. This morning it had the lowest barometric pressure ever recorded for that area. The 2005 hurricane season is now tied with the 1937 seasons for number of named storms.

2006: I went out into the woods and fields this morning: Small cups of gossamer were shining with dew, hanging to the tips of the dry wingstem. In the mist, the grass was yellowing, and the woods appeared like it does in April, bright leaves like new flowers. Seeds were sprouting in rotten tree stumps, the sweet smell of autumn ground all around me. The low Sun rested in the treetops. The silver winding river, the fallen logs invisible in summer, lay below me. I saw a small flock of robins at the riverbank, and then further upstream, the trees were full of robins. Fat green Osage fruit lay all over the ground. In one dark patch of ironweed stalks, a few blue tall bellflowers were blooming; off to the side, parsnips were flowering, and some red clover and small white asters.

In the bottomland, poison hemlock was growing back, with chickweed and sedum. A peppercress plant was blossoming as though spring were going to arrive in a few weeks. In one corner of the pasture, wild lettuce, leaves shriveled, displayed dozens of prominent white seed heads, each maybe an inch and a half in diameter. When I touched the heads, they dissolved between my fingers.

Grackles and starlings passed over the woods heading southwest before lunch. One monarch butterfly came by early in the afternoon, sailed over my head, the Sun shining through its wings. A few loud, slow katydids sang tonight, maybe their last songs of the year.

2007: Leaf color is reaching its peak along the freeway, many bright ashes holding everywhere, contributing to one of the best October colorations I can remember. Lil's burning bush is tinged with red. The bittersweet vine at the corner of High and Limestone is holding its leaves, its berries pale orange.

2008: First frost this morning, many coleus burned, but most plants did well. A black and orange woolly bear caterpillar was exploring the front porch when I went out to check the mail. A dozen daffodils planted by the west redbuds this afternoon.

2010: Maples in Yellow Springs still hold at just past their peak, but my sister Tat, calling from the highway to Janesville, Wisconsin, said that all the leaves came down about five days ago in the wind that brought rain here last night. Looking out across the landscape, she said she could see no color at all. Tonight, slow, low cricket calls heard all along my walk with Bella, but there was no high chirping like a few nights ago.

2011: Mateo's red mulberry tree is about a third gone, its remaining leaves mottled gold and ochre. His black walnut tree has lost every one of its walnuts. One tall coneflower still in bloom in the alley. One cardinal song, long and beautiful, heard at 8:55. Across the countryside, the peak color is long gone, but occasional maples still offer bright golden foci. Some oaks are red along Xenia Avenue, but the Mills park oaks are still completely green. Out our south bedroom window, the witch hazel is in full bloom underneath the overarching honeysuckle, leaves yellowing. Steady rain throughout the day. Camel cricket seen in the kitchen and another in the laundry room today. Wind storm in Chicago.

2012: Rain off and on and cool today. A few Jerusalem artichokes hold in the Phillips Street alley. Lil's maple full gold, the Danielsons' maple almost completely down, Mrs. Timberlake's not far behind. Peak color still holds throughout the area, but leaves are shedding quickly. Some coloring has begun on the Dayton Street beech tree. Zelcovas along Xenia Avenue are deep maroon, and the Zelcova by the post office is half down. A cardinal was singing when I walked Bella this morning before 9:00.

2014: Very light freeze on the car windshield this morning, the first freeze of the autumn – but no damage to the flowers. As I walked Bella after sunrise, robins were whinnying all around, their migration through town obvious. Crows were boisterous, some starlings were whistling and scrawing, sparrows were chirping, and there was a sharp birdcall I didn't recognize. Carl's maples half down, Moya's and Mrs. Timberlake's decimated. I noticed that Don's pie cherry tree was completely bare – I missed its progression this year.

2015: I cut down the castor beans today after three nights below freezing. Now the whole garden, except for a few red petunia blossoms, has darkened. Throughout the village, leaf change spreads, quickened by the frost.

2016: To Dayton this morning in sun and soft wind: Full early maple leaf color throughout. The locust plantings in the city are all gold, still fully dressed. No frost so far. The last white autumn crocus flower wilted overnight. The zinnias sag but continue to blossom. The castor beans still provide red accents to the north garden. The town's Zelcova trees have still not started to turn, but the Kentucky coffee tree by the shop is golden and ready to fall. At Ellis Pond, the maples are darkening, the ashes still keeping all their purple leaves. This afternoon, a small checkerspot, a painted lady and a silver-spotted skipper in the garden. Light rain this evening, thunderstorms coming from the southwest, tree frogs high buzzing crickets, trilling crickets, all pushing hard against the coming cold.

2017: Kentucky coffee trees: withered foliage dropping. More sun and mild, some painted ladies remaining in the zinnias. Katydids and crickets loud as we walked home from the movie around 8:00 p.m.

2019: Sun and cool in the 50s today, only one yellow jacket seen, no honeybees or butterflies. The viburnum is a dusky violet-red beneath the maroon and dirty gold Virginia creeper on the north side of the house, Lil's burning bush still has just a few reddish leaves. A soft but chilly evening, katydids sluggish, tree frogs still buzzing, some field cricket chirping. At the mill habitat, a flock of crows in the distance, but no vultures or robins seen or heard. From Spoleto, Italy, Neysa sends photos of cyclamen and several other flowers I haven't identified yet. And a *Porcini* mushroom (she hopes).

2020: A drive to the dentist south of town: today is definitely the peak of the best maples. A ginkgo is even turning on Xenia Avenue. The maple grove at Ellis has also reached its best. In my column for the *News*, I answered (melodramatically) a question from Reilly: "As to why one should pay attention to or look forward to peak leaf color, I suppose that also is a matter of feeling. In my experience, when the last best leaf color finally disintegrates with the collapse of the ginkgoes, the white mulberries, the decorative pears, the sweet gums and the Osage, then summer, with all it means, is really and truly gone. I think that realization is the gateway to winter and all its psychological baggage. I believe we are what we perceive; only memory keeps our bodies from despair over the cold and gives us the strength to transform the growing darkness."

2022: More thinning: Moya's hackberry tree is catching up with her maple. leaves coming down in the steady wind, filling the yard and sidewalks. Hosta foliage turns from gold to caramel in decay. Climbing false buckwheat is dark and wrinkled in the cup plants and wild lettuce. Hops flowers and leaves are dusky brown. Grape leaves are pale lemon. My viburnum foliage is losing its brightness, sagging and limp on the edge of the end of peak leaf color. Beggartick seeds are dry and ready to fall.

> *Now constantly there is a*
> *Sound, quieter than rain,*
> *Of leaves falling.*
> *Under their loosening bright*
> *Gold, the sycamore limbs*
> *bleach whiter.*

> Wendell Berry

October 20th
The 293rd Day of the Year

The flowers do fade, and wanton fields
To wayward winter reckoning yield.

Walter Raleigh

Sunrise/set: 6:50/5:49
Day's Length: 10 hours 59 minutes
Average High/Low: 63/42
Average Temperature: 52
Record High: 84 – 1953
Record Low: 24 – 1952

Weather

Today is often one of the cooler days of October, with a 40 percent chance of overcast skies, and a 30 percent chance of rain or light snow. Highs climb above 70 only five percent of the time (the first time odds for heat have been so low since April 11th. Most afternoons reach the 60s (a 40 percent chance) or the 50s (a 50 percent chance or that). Also: a five percent chance of just 30s. A light frost strikes most gardens five years in ten, the highest likelihood so far this fall.

The Natural Calendar

The day's length falls below eleven hours for the first time since February 21st during this week of the year. Peak leaf coloring is just beginning throughout the middle and southern Appalachians, but in the lower Midwest, the best of Middle Fall is often over. Some years, however, the land still looks and feels like September.

Daybook

1982: To this point, fall came gently, with a cool spell the second week of August, then the ragweed and goldenrod, a few trees with patches of yellow, the black walnuts thinning, then buckeyes. Buzzards gathering for migration at the bend of the river past the mill. Now, everything is poised for violent change. Another week, one more heavy frost, a storm, and Middle Fall could be over.

1983: From scattered notes: Peak of fall leaf coloring occurred today in 1979, 1980, 1981, 1982, 1983.

1986: Crickets continue singing in the warmer afternoons. Whip-poor-will calls are common.

1987: Major leaf fall in the last two days. Peak is gone. My maples hold just a fourth of their leaves. Pussy willow foliage coming down, some Osage. Cherry mostly gone. Magnolias yellow quickly. Rapid early turning of ginkgoes. Sweet gum thins quickly. Catalpas mostly gone. Half the trees are bare along the road to Wilberforce. Winter wheat sprouting.

1991: Uncle Bill calls from Gentilly, Minnesota: Ground white with the first snowfall of the season.

1992: Most all the ginkgoes at Wilberforce fell yesterday and the day before. Frost brought them down in 1988, too. Ashes are bare, but they held on late. Now the locusts follow. Lil's maple has turned completely - that's early for her tree. Snow bursts this morning. By late afternoon, peak leaf fullness is gone, the village on the other side of Middle Fall. On the way to Springfield, 6:45 p.m., I saw a long line of blackbirds flying southeast, both ends of the flock lost in the distance.

1995: The witch hazel on Dayton Street, leaves yellow and two-thirds gone, bloomed overnight. Peak leaf color in the maples now. I drive north to Chicago in the wind and rain: The tree line is dull, but not empty. With ashes and cottonwoods finished, the color depends on the quantity of maples or oaks in a grove. In northern Indiana, the number of oaks seems to increase, bringing more dark reds and browns to the landscape. Every 30 or 40 miles a flock of starlings rises far in front of the car, swoops and dives with the wind.

1998: To Wisconsin: starting from the height of leaf color in Yellow Springs, I drive west and north. At 7:45 a.m., not a cloud in sight. The landscape shines. Oaks and sweet gum turning gold, ashes maroon, hickories golden green, ash trees red. Tarnished grape leaves, scarlet poison ivy, yellow locusts and redbuds, blushing spicebush. Tattered box elders, orange maples. Honeysuckles untouched by fall, and some white oaks, silver maples also summer green. Some very late goldenrod flowering. Cattail leaves browning, last year's cattail remnants ghostly and puffy, heads swollen and broken. Black teasel. Purple barberry bushes. Scattered crows, a few last red-winged blackbirds. At Richmond, 60 miles west of Yellow Springs: one buzzard.

At 92 miles from home, cirrus wisps appear in the south. Tightly cut soy fields, gray beige, low stubble. Corn all brown, much harvested, color of old wheat. Primrose seen past Indianapolis. Queen Anne's lace then occasionally, peak leaf color staying through western Indiana. Deep blue farm ponds reflect the sky. At a rest stop near Danville, Illinois, one burning bush is completely red. At 1:00 p.m., the sky remains clear, except now there is a long band of altostratus and cirrostratus in the far southern horizon. Barometer continues high.

A patch of wild sunflowers near Urbana, sow thistles too, and a few cutover goldenrod. Blue chicory past Mahomet, and scattered New England asters near Bloomington. At 2:30 p.m., the cirrus clouds have moved overhead. The west is hazy with cirrostratus. Full harvest in progress across northern Illinois. Now flocks of starlings every 40 miles or so. Scattered asters seen about parallel with Chicago. Three deer killed on the road near Rockford, rutting season here. Above the Illinois border, more leaves are down, the tree line much more brown, duller. Late color here, maybe a week from Yellow Springs.

Now cirrus are dominant in the sky. Geese on Wisconsin ponds. White clover seen at Beloit. Milkweeds more open and tattered here than in Ohio. The land so drab approaching Madison. Thickening clouds by sundown, altocumulus, altostratus. Barometer dropping.

1999: Drive through Xenia and Wilberforce. My ash is completely bare, my ginkgoes no longer rich deep green. In the parking lot, most of ash and locust trees are down. Maple foliage maybe a fourth down, and throughout the drive in the countryside, the peak of leaf color has passed. The mornings keep bringing light frost on the roof and on the car windows, but no plants have been hurt so far in the garden.

2000: Burning bush shedding. Ginkgo and the pink-flowered quince are half yellow, linden a third to a half down.

2002: A cardinal sang at 6:30 a.m. A flock of robins passed through the yard a little after 7:00. Blackbirds filled the back locust trees at 9:30.

2004: Cardinal heard at 6:35 this foggy morning. In the countryside, maples hold their color. Tonight at home, a few sluggish katydids, a few green tree frogs, the air soft and damp, temperature mild.

2005: Wilberforce: Ashes and locusts shedding heavily here. One ginkgo is very pale. Deep red orange maples here and there throughout the campus.

2006: A good-sized camel cricket was in the bathtub when I got up this morning. Starlings seen in Don's tree when I walked Bella. Killdeer seen at school in Wilmington. So many maples peaking, my maple in the alley full gold. A few tall coneflowers bloom by the fence. At Wilberforce, my classroom ginkgo is full gold.

2007: The alley sugar maple is full yellow, two maples on the corner of High and Limestone full color – one bright orange, the other bright gold. Our ashes still holding gold. Lil's maple and the Danielson's have started to develop a few autumn patches. Starlings whistling. One cabbage butterfly.

2008: A second frost this morning, more coleus hurt. Driving to Beavercreek, I saw the ash trees shedding, maples still full dusky color. Tonight, a few katydids were calling, in spite of two cold nights.

2010: To Kettering: Full maple and oak color continues, as does the shedding. Lil's maple is turning suddenly now.

2011: Steady rain continues, wind picking up. Crows late this morning, 6:50. Moya's maple is about gone now, as are Carl's up the street. Lil's maple is maybe a fourth turned. Rachel's ginkgo is fringed with gold. The Korean lilac has lost three-fourths of its soft violet leaves. The oaks in the woodlots on the south side of town are rust and red and brown - full color. One ginkgo on Xenia Avenue is beginning to shed! Songbirds feeding heavily in the rain, but I haven't seen a single flock of blackbirds or starlings flying over so far this fall.

2012: Hard rain this morning, then scattered clouds and sun. When I walked outside before sunrise, after the storm, I saw and heard a great flock of robins and starlings and blackbirds moving southeast across the village, and the passage lasted and lasted, was going even when I walked Bella two hours later. Now Moya's maple is down, and the Danielsons' and most of Mrs. Timberlake's, Lil's still holding at peak, but the Lawsons' and Carl's maples are shedding quickly, their lawns all covered with golden leaves. The secret maple holds, but is losing leaves quickly, too.

2013: Jeff reported that a cutover field on Grinnell was white with frost this morning. But there was no freeze here in Yellow Springs.

2014: Robins still in the neighborhood, whinnying and chirping, but much quieter than yesterday. Leaf fall intensifies. Lil's maple three-fourths gold-orange. Violets blooming in the college lawn.

2015: One yellow sulphur butterfly at John Bryan Park this afternoon. The village remains at the very top of its color (including Mrs. Timberlake's maple; although Lil's maple has just a slight tarnish, and the Danielsons' maple is three-fourths down). In the pond, the fish rose to feed this mild, sunny afternoon. I checked the water temperature: 52 degrees instead of the inhibiting 45 of a few days ago. Tonight, after a day in the 70s, one high-trilling cricket, long calls, then silence, then more long calls.

2017: Another mild and sunny day, a white-spotted skipper and painted lady noticed in the sun early, temperature at 50 degrees. As I walked the back yard for a few minutes, I heard grackles clucking in the high locusts and robins peeping and whinnying their flocking songs.

2019: Crows at 6:30 this morning, cardinals far off about ten minutes later, robins peeping and whinnying around 8:00. Moya's maple started to turn in the night. One monarch seen this afternoon, one sulphur, three cabbage whites in sunny but breezy 70s.

2020: Third day in a row of overcast skies, highs and lows in the 50s, and this afternoon it seems yesterday's peak leaf color is spreading, rather than declining, turning the whole village gold. Across from Ellis, a sizeable flock of honking geese landed in the cut-over soybean field when I walked Ranger there after lunch. Steady buzzing and whistling of tree crickets in the misty night, but no katydids heard.

2021: Driving to Keuka Lake in New York: Color is very light and spotty, still in September, from Yellow Springs north to Cleveland and into western New York. The hills toward the lake are still mainly green in some places, become dull gold and bare in others. It is a subdued autumn, except for scattered scarlet sumacs and bright yellow white birches. Here at the cottage, most of the leaves are still on the oaks that surround the property. The weeping willow is still summer green. The white birch near the dock is almost bare. From northern Minnesota, my nephew John reports close to peak leaf color and late shedding.

2022: The first serious freeze this morning, castor bean plants drooping. More leaf fall: High street is tattered now, the Champney's maples almost all down, the Danielsons' tree about empty, and T.K.'s too. Lil's holds on, a beacon of Middle Fall, Mrs. Timberlake's close behind. Honeysuckle leaves are blanching and shedding steadily. The speed of the coming undone! The southeastern midmorning sun gilding the hedge in front of my window. One buzzard circling over Stafford Street, and I noticed the tight tufted mesh of the autumn webworms that still hung to a bare black walnut tree there. The zelcovas downtown were at their best, and Xenia Avenue is still at peak color with even a few ginkgoes turning early. Burning bush at Lil's: deep scarlet. Overall, however, the height is beginning to subside, empty branches competing with oranges and reds and golds.

Unlike simple geographical locations, which exist objectively, places do not exist until they are verbalized, first in thought and memory and then through the spoken or written word.

Kent Ryden

October 21st
The 294th Day of the Year

Up the slope, the wind:
asters bend, the brown grass trembles,
air is chill.

August Derleth

Sunrise/set: 6:52/5:47
Day's Length: 10 hours 55 minutes
Average High/Low: 62/42
Average Temperature: 52
Record High: 85 - 1953
Record Low: 23 - 1974

Weather

Today and the 12th are the two October days in my history most likely to bring clouds: 45 percent of the days are completely overcast, 30 percent carry rain. One in ten afternoons has a high above 80, twenty-five percent of the days are in the 70s, twenty-five percent in the 60s, twenty percent in the 50s, twenty percent in the 40s. Frost comes one morning in five, lows in the 20s one morning in 20.

The Natural Calendar

One of the invasive species that grows throughout our village is the wintercreeper vine, or *Euonymus fortunei*. An Asian native brought to the United States one hundred years ago, it has probably thrived in the Lower Midwest for at least half a century. Wintercreeper has dark green, oval leaves and often climbs local trees and outbuildings. It keeps its foliage and its color even through the most bitter Januarys.

Like all perennials, this *euonymus* has a growth cycle that fills twelve months. Most of its phases are easily observed, and it is a steady companion with which to follow the path of the Yellow Springs year. At the end of October, the vine shows off white or pale pink fruit that formed in early August. By the first weeks of November, the fruit capsules begin to break open, revealing their orange seeds just as ginkgo and white mulberry trees lose their leaves.

When honeysuckle and forsythia foliage finally gives way by the middle of December, the wintercreeper berries start to break away from their hulls, continuing to fall to the ground, joining the decaying Osage fruits to measure out the first three months of the year. Then, when snowdrops and aconites flower in our dooryards, when pussy willows are full of pollen and maple seeds sprout in the garden, the *euonymus* vines put on new growth, and the seed capsules themselves come down.

By the middle of April, when large-flowered trilliums cover the Glen floor, the fresh wintercreeper leaves have almost reached full size, and throughout the spring and early summer, their tiny buds gradually take shape, clearly visible when lilies blossom in village gardens. In the third or fourth week of July, the buds break out in clusters of five-petaled yellow-green flowers that last until the middle of August. Then they form their white capsules that open when all the maple leaves are gone, displaying once again their orange seeds that slowly fall like hourglass sand to fill the cup of spring.

Winter's Orion is fully emerged from the east by midnight, streaked with the Orionid meteors on or near this date. The Big Dipper is low along the north horizon then. To the west, Hercules is sets behind the Corona Borealis. Pegasus is overhead in the Milky Way. Cygnus, the Northern Cross, follows summer's Vega south.

Daybook

1982: Mill Habitat: I had gone for a walk expecting to find the end of everything. Instead the Glen was full of robins chirping and fluttering: I had never seen the woods so alive. Buzzards, maybe fifty or sixty of them, uneasy when they saw me, rose and settled on one sycamore then another, their reflections in the water like huge berries on the branches.

1983: Mill Habitat: Parsnips blooming here, and some red clover and small white asters. A small flock of robins at the riverbank, and then further upstream, the woods full of robins. And I counted 60 buzzards perched in a sycamore tree at the bend of the river. In the bottomland, poison hemlock was growing back, with chickweed and sedum. One peppercress was blooming as though spring were going to arrive in a few weeks.

1984: Redbud leaves falling, some gone, catalpas faded but most are holding, Osage half yellow, some coming down.

1985: A spring peppercress found blooming at the mill.

1986: 4:39 p.m., 70 degrees, barometer dropping, moon in Taurus, the sky clear. Buzzards circling. A big carp caught on homemade dough balls, fish biting as fast as I could cast.

1988: Rain hurrying the leaf fall. High Street maples coming down more heavily now, and the box elders, and the Osage orange in the back yard.

1990: Madison, Wisconsin to Yellow Springs: As I drove, I saw flocks of blackbirds every hour or so, one flock of seagulls. Under overcast skies and with a north tail wind, the grass seems wintry to me, the trees duller and thinner than just two days ago when I drove in the sun, pushed north by a south wind. Late autumn came overnight, the cornfields gray, the underside of the remaining leaves up in the wind, hiding the brighter colors. But the wheat glows in the rain.

1992: Red mulberry, knotweed, and tree of heaven leaves blackened from a hard freeze. Dave Jensen calls, still finding fireflies (he calls them glow-worms) by the side of the road, in the grass along the edge of the Vale.

1993: Rain yesterday, then wind started about nine o'clock at night, blew hard through this morning. Clearing now, with maybe half of the maples gone, all the ash, locust, box elders. Autumn came so slowly through the first part of the month. The trees browned so subtly in the sun. Suddenly the peak came, and then the wind last night, and everything collapsed.

1994: The last of the stonecrop is gone now in the east garden, passed its peak more than a week ago.

1995: With the pieces of autumn come moods, motifs that are tied to the shapes and the smells around me. I feel a need to close and to let go, to accept old failures. I'm ready for new adventures, feel a tensing of my body for new encounters, for things about to happen now that the leaves are almost down. Whitman says that landscape is language. Seasons are language, too, each day with its own syntax, its own vocabulary.

1999: Robins heard in town for the first time in quite a while this afternoon. In the yard, the south hedge is holding; even though the black walnut is gone, the red mulberries, the poplar, lilacs and rose of Sharon are still mostly green. The honeysuckle hedge: maybe a third thinned, revealing the street along the north line. Geese seen flying near the bright orange sunset.

2002: Blackbirds cackling in the back yard trees at 10:00 a.m. Cardinals sing off and on through the morning. To Wilmington, 30 miles south of Yellow Springs, in the afternoon: Some New England asters still open, peak ash color in places. At Wilberforce, my ginkgo is pale, my ash three-fourths shed. In the parking lot, all the ashes are down, the locusts almost bare, maples full color, the landscape maybe at the end of the first week of October.

2003: Turkey vultures seen through the day on my drives to Washington Court House and Dayton. More than a dozen buzzards were perched on a sycamore roost near the covered bridge at 9:30 a.m.

2004: Blackbirds flying over at the north edge of town, starlings clucking in the back trees. The maples hold in the rain, the Danielsons' tree is full gold and starting to shed. Lil's maple is a pale gold, patches of summer green still showing through. The secret maple is about half gone. The town settles into the end of middle autumn, quiet in the fog and mist, leaves bright on the soft, wet earth.

2005: To Cincinnati to look for another wood stove. Peak leaf color throughout the area, many ashes holding on and blending with the bright maples, bright in spite of the steady rain. The Danielsons' maple has turned a dusky gold over the last day or two. Lil's maple has one corner half yellow. The secret maple is just barely starting.

2007: Peak leaf color throughout the area, ashes and hickories holding on and complementing the maples. The secret maple is mostly gold. Lil's and the Danielsons' are only just starting in patches. Two monarch butterflies seen today in the garden, one in the morning, one late in the afternoon. A yellow tea rose opened a day or so ago, is huge and brilliant.

2008: On the way to Wilmington this morning, I saw a great flock of vultures circling the river near Old Town. On the way home: A sizeable murmuration of starlings swooped and played in the wind, wide, graceful group acrobatics. In the yard, I brought in the jade tree and the two angel-wing begonias: lows in the 20s tonight. Two autumn violets were blooming in the north garden

2011: After the passage of a cold front last night, finally sun and milder temperatures in the middle 50s. Stacking wood in the afternoon, we saw one red admiral butterfly, one painted lady (*Cynthia*), no cabbage whites. Only one cricket heard during the day, high in the honeysuckles. A few autumn violets in bloom among the white mulberry leaves. Jeanie and I cut dahlias and zinnias in advance of threatened frost tonight. No crickets heard on my night walk with Bella.

2012: Around the yard: Blueberry foliage holding red. Violets blooming in the circle garden. Robins peeping through the trees. Late red mums just starting. Cherry leaves half down. Secret maple two-thirds down. Blush on the oakleaf hydrangea. Still a few lace vine flowers. One bright yellow sulphur. Four deep purple spiderworts. Lamium coming back. Lil's maple two thirds gone, Moya's down. Red leaves on crepe myrtle. Almost all the New England asters gone, Janet's redbud gone, small white asters half gone. Some new yellow flowers on wild strawberries, one ripening raspberry.

At Ellis Pond, most of the sycamores down, silver maples palomino gold, tulip trees dirty gold, veins outlined in brown. The large scarlet oak is scarlet-sienna full, black oak full brown with red veins, saw-tooth oak rich light brown, white oak burnished red brown, sawtooth oak green with yellow streaks, red oak yellow green brown, shingle oak, green brown, chinquapin almost all down and brown, bur oak bare. Six dandelions to seed, willow dulled, sugar maple grove yellow brown and two-thirds down, hickory yellow brown, three fourths holding, bald cypress rust and full, birch three-fourths down.

2013: I brought in the last elephant ear plants and cut the last of the best zinnias in anticipation of a freeze tonight. Steady mild wind throughout the morning and afternoon.

2014: Wind and rain for the past couple of days. Most of the leaves are down on Mrs. Timberlake's maple and many of Carl's. The Danielsons' has maybe a fourth of its foliage. Fallen leaves all over the place. Lil's maple has reached full color.

2015: A walk before dawn, Venus, Jupiter and Mars triangulating in the eastern sky, Orion due south. At 6:08, I heard a bard owl's "Who cooks for you?" as I turned off the bike path into downtown. Near High Street, a lone out-of-season cardinal call at 6:58. When I got home, I found that one of the bird feeders in the back yard had been tipped over by a raccoon or opossum or bear during the night. In the house, mice had ransacked the two pantry shelves, knocking down dog biscuits and boxes of tea! I mix these together: what apophenic conclusion can I draw? The evening was mild, the high trilling cricket steady and strong.

2017: Early this morning, looking for the Leonid Meteors, not a one seen in a clear, moonless sky. The day: sunny and in the 70s: cutting back zinnias in the north garden, I saw three painted lady butterflies. The hummingbird feeder, almost drained in the past two days by honeybees, was still attracting them. The pokeweed plant by the old peach tree has started to turn, its leaves deep red. Late this mild afternoon when I was transplanting hellebores, I saw a monarch butterfly in the zinnias – even though the sun had gone behind the trees and the garden was shaded. On Walnut Street: a patch of Jerusalem artichokes in full boom. On the way to Fairborn, we saw a very large blackbird flock heading south.

2018: Fontanelli, Italy: A quiet stay at Neysa and Ivano's little villa in the hills above Spoleto. I left a green world still green in Ohio, arriving at about the same season here. The drive from Rome: all summer-like, but only a few blossoms on the oleanders. Around Neysa and Ivano's house, ancient oaks watch over the landscape, deep green. A few trees have turned a little on the property of the condominium, as Neysa calls the area: a red maple and a dogwood on the western side of the house are blushing, and some of the grasses have yellowed. There is a mottled blend of ochre and summer in the woods outside my bedroom window.

The ginestra clusters are bare, but their thin green stalks blend perfectly with whatever is around them, show no promise of spring. There are pines, though, and several varieties of live oaks and holly that will keep the landscape from the worst of autumn and winter. Along the driveway to the house, I found two small cyclamen blossoms, one violet, one creamy white, and one larger blue bell flower. The property is full of volunteer oaks and a variety of weeds and shrubs I haven't identified yet. I did see basal great mullein leaves and wild strawberry foliage here and there around the yard. According to Ivano, the grapes, olives and chestnut harvests are complete now. We have new olive oil for the bruschetta and new red wine, and last night Ivano roasted chestnuts over the fire.

2019: In the night, the Danielsons' maple and Moya's maple turned full ochre-gold, Lil's just with a tinge of color, the north hackberry a pale ochre. (There were no hackberry butterflies this year, as I recall, but many in 2018.) This afternoon, a large hawk dropped on some kind of prey near the bird feeders, but I couldn't tell what it caught.

2020: A feeling of autumn acceleration, even in the warm and wet morning: the tattered hedge between my house and Moya's revealing her porch after months of it being hidden, the garden zinnias and marigolds sparse and thinning, in disarray, accenting the aging that is mottling the grape leaves, the pokeweed dropping withered leaves and berries, the tree-of-heaven saplings losing their foliage, the ruddy foliage of the primroses disappearing into the tangle of spent grasses, the overnight shedding of early pale white-yellow honeysuckle leaves, the beige redbud leaves coming down more obviously, the viburnum reduced to maybe a tenth of its maroon leaves, the back yard becoming less protected from neighbors and the street, one lone cardinal call, robins peeping. Crickets buzzing and trilling at the Glass Farm wetland, one red-winged blackbird yodel heard. Small white asters were in full flower at the edges of the path; out in the fields, they were withered and brown. Canadian thistles and hemlock growing back strong beside them.

2022: After several days of wind and then frost, zinnias killed (but the castor beans still strong), the weather is warming. One cabbage white in the patches of New England asters that are still in bloom.

2023: Crows at about 6:30 this morning. Time count ended today as I cut away all the remaining zinnias and canna lilies. I began bulb planting in hopesof filling the lawn with flowers next year. Now leaf fall is intensifying throughout town. Lil's maple and the Danielsons' maple are half thinned, Moya's maple is full red and gold, the secret maple yellow and orange. In the countryside, many leaves bare, soybean fields cut to the ground, corn still waiting.

In winds, and trees, and streams, and all things common,
In music and the sweet unconscious tone
Of animals, and voices which are human,
Meant to express some feelings of their own;
In the soft motions and rare smiles of woman,
In flowers and leaves, and in the grass fresh-shown,
Or dying in the autumn, I the most
Adore thee present or lament thee lost.

Percy Bysshe Shelley

October 22nd
The 295th Day of the Year

Out of the matted roots of the turf and from the gray soil beneath, innumerable forms of life resembling those that have vanished will spring to light – creatures of a thousand beautiful shapes, lit by brilliant color, intense in their little lives, forever moving in a passionate, swift, fantastic dance. And we shall see it all again, and in seeing renew the old familiar pleasure.

William Henry Hudson

Sunrise/set: 6:53/5:46
Day's Length: 10 hours 53 minutes
Average High/Low: 62/41
Average Temperature: 52
Record High: 82 – 1920
Record Low: 25 – 1887

Weather

Today is the last day of the year on which there is a ten percent chance of a high in the 80s. From now on, temperatures remain below that mark at least until the first week of April. Highs come into the 70s fifteen percent of the days, into the 60s twenty-five percent, into the 50s forty-five percent, and into the 40s five percent. Chances of rain are 40 percent; overcast conditions occur four to five days in a decade. Frost strikes one morning in five.

The Weather in the Week Ahead

Highs are usually in the 50s or 60s, with the odds for 70s near one in five. The danger of frost remains similar to that of the third week in October; about one night in three receives temperatures in the upper 20s or lower 30s. But by this late in the season, the chances of a hard freeze have risen past 50 percent, and the odds get better each night for killing lows.

This week is generally a brighter one than last week. Chances of sun are about 70 percent throughout the period, and some of the driest October days are the 26th, 28th, and 29th (each having just a fifteen percent chance of precipitation).

The sixth high-pressure system of the month usually arrives near Halloween. If it is approaching on the 31st, that evening will be warm, with maybe a little rain. If the front arrives on the 29th or 30th, the eve of All Saints Day is usually brisk..

The Natural Calendar

The last weeks of October usually bring an end to the best of Sugar Mapleturn Season. Oakturn, Osageturn, Mulberryturn, Silvermapleturn, Magnoliaturn and Ginkgoturn Seasons intensify. As foliage thins, Eastern Phoebe, Catbird, Turkey Vulture and House Wren Migration Seasons deepen. Cattail Breakdown Season opens as Aster Season closes and Fall Raspberry Season gives up its final berries.

Daybook

1980: Peak leaf color in town.

1983: Mill habitat: Robins past the mill, this time on the ground and quiet until I walked through. Twenty buzzards counted on the roost at the bend of the river. Parsnips in bloom, yarrow and winter cress growing back. Thin and broad-leaved zigzag goldenrod still blooming. At home, a violet in the grass. Along the north hedge, peach leaves green but falling.

1984: Mill habitat: Robins found about 200 yards beyond the river bend, buzzards also in a different sycamore, large flocks swarming before heading south. In the rain, the grass was yellow green, the woods like it seemed in April, red leaves like new flowers, and the faded elms glowing like the fresh leaves of spring. In town, the maples are in full decline, yellow poplars and redbuds all gone.

1986: Leaves holding late this year, front maple full yellow, just a third dropped, Mrs. Lawson's maple only half turned.

1989: Dahlia bulbs dug, tulips and daffodils and lilies planted.

1990: Through the countryside, colors are intensifying, coming to a head about a week later than last year. Lil's maple about a fourth turned. Mrs. Lawson's is deep and fragile, as are mine. A Canadian thistle seen blooming at Wilberforce. A sundrop primrose flowering along Grinnell Road.

1993: Dozens of black woolly-bear caterpillars crossing Grinnell and Route 68 today, the only day in the year they've been so restless.

1994: A monarch butterfly came to the zinnias today, the last of the year?

1995: Coming back to Yellow Springs from Chicago, I can see little change in the leafturn. Along the freeways in northern Illinois, goldenrod is still in bloom, sunflowers still open. But here at home, all the flowers are gone.

1999: The south hedge suddenly rusts and sheds quickly, my privacy dropping away all at once.

2000: Crows at 6:34 a.m., clear, quite dark. In the garden, the last veronica and phlox die back, gaura still in bloom. On the road to Hillsboro, I found the peak of leaf color to be well past. At home, the Danielsons' maple was three-fourths down, but Lil's was still at its best. The south hedge around the house is slowly collapsing, revealing the neighbors.

2001: The red Christmas cactus is about a third open.

2002: A large flock of grackles in the back trees for several hours in the late morning.

2003: The landscape is dull on the way to Wilmington, even though so many of the maples and oaks still hold most of their foliage.

2004: A cardinal was singing when I walked out the front door this morning at 6:35. The Danielsons' maple is deep orange gold, aging but still holding. Lil's tree is a rich new gold. At South Glen, 8:00 a.m., small cups of gossamer, shining with dew, hang to the tips of the black wingstem, are common throughout the cut field grass. Robins are passing south along the east ridge. Osage leaves are bright yellow (fat green fruit all over the ground); sycamore leaves are rust-brown-gold. In one dark patch of wingstem stalks, a few pale blue tall bellflowers are blooming. In one corner of the pasture, wild lettuce plants, leaves shriveled, display dozens of prominent white seed heads, each maybe an inch and a half in diameter. When I touch the heads, they dissolved between my fingers. This afternoon, I planted late-spring tulips in the northeast garden around the hydrangea.

2006: A few late violet flowers on the fall hostas seen today.

2007: Venus shining huge in the deep blue, predawn east. A cardinal sang at 6:35 as I walked Bella in the alley. As Jeanie and I drove to Dayton about 6:50 this morning, we saw a long flock of blackbirds high above the freeway. The flock began at the northern horizon and continued across the clear sky into the southern horizon.

2008: Crows at 6:50 this morning. Low of 28, three degrees from the record. The alley maple, the High-Limestone Street maples, and Don's black walnut are almost bare. Don's maple full color. Lil's maple hardly started, Danielsons' holding at a third. Caladium bulbs taken inside this afternoon, Shasta daisies transplanted to prepare for lily tree bulbs.

2010: First light frost of the year this morning, frost on the windshield of the cars and all across the lawn. The elephant ears and the impatiens, though, were not hurt. When I was swimming in Xenia at about 8:00, I looked out to see a long flock of blackbirds maybe half a mile away, and they continued to pass over the buildings in my line of sight as I swam along, a huge flock! The secret maple and the northeast maple are just about all down; the Danielsons' maple deep orange, half shed; Lil's maple maybe a third turned; serviceberry trees are holding; the north viburnum is down to about a tenth of its leaves. One ginkgo on the south end of time is full gold-green, while most of the others have barely started to change.

2011: Light frost this morning, identical to last year's frost on this date. When I walked with Bella in the alley and along Stafford Street, robins were whinnying and peeping all along the way. On the High Street sidewalk, many more green Osage fruits had fallen in yesterday's rain. Stacking wood this afternoon, Jeanie and I saw at least three monarchs, a buckeye and a painted lady (Cynthia). Jeanie heard one or two crickets before supper, but on my walk tonight, the neighborhood was silent.

2012: To the hills of the Red River Gorge in Kentucky, 200 miles southeast of Yellow Springs, the land in late full color throughout the drive, many hillsides really strong, others quite thin. The oaks are red and brown now, and many maples still bright orange and gold. In the woods, zigzags have gone to seed, only a few white asters in bloom. Giant pawpaw leaves had just fallen recently, probably burned from the frosts of last week. Ghostly trilling of a cricket behind the motel tonight, like the one I heard at home walking Bella last night.

2013: The first light frost in town this morning, cold front moving in briskly, gibbous moon in the clear west. On Limestone Street, starlings cackle high up in the black walnut trees, almost indistinguishable from the walnuts themselves. Down Stafford Street, robins talking migration. Coming home from Wilmington today, I could see that the peak had just passed, the ashes and cottonwoods empty, leaving the more common maples and sycamores and tulip trees to stand almost alone. At Ellis Pond this afternoon, the sugar maples had deepened a little more, and the bald cypress close to the west end of the pond had turned rusty brown, other tinges of color on several others. The bur oak and the red oak were starting to show yellow along the edges of their leaves, and the tulip trees had more gold, tattered. When I got home, I noticed that the remaining zinnias had all lost their brilliance from the frost. The remaining butterfly bush flowers were brown. The roses were the only plants in bloom.

2014: More and more maples coming down in the neighborhood. And orange berries on euonymus shrub on the corner of Phillips and Limestone Streets have started to emerge from their white hulls. At the Ellis Pond arboretum: Sweet Hart chestnuts yellow green, half down; ginkgo turning (and they are fully turned in town, glowing); sycamores gold and weathered-green; sweet gums streaked with red and gold and purple and green; Zelcovas turning at various stages, some rich, chocolate rust; hickory deep deep gold; pawpaw and lindens both shedding now, foliage yellow-gold tinged with violet; some dogwoods with sagging red-purple leaves, some dogwoods with just a few leaves left; weeping cherry yellow-green, three-fourths down; beech dark black-green, holding near full; wild plum, Katsura tree, Maackia trees bare; the maple grove orange-brown and half fallen.

2015: Sun and high clouds, temperature in the upper 70s. Crows at 6:33 this morning, the sharp call notes of a cardinal at 6:38. The hackberry tree at the south edge of the yard has lost most of its leaves; the north hackberry is still thick and palomino gold. In Clifton Gorge and Bryon Park, the hillsides were still at late peak color, but leaf drop had gouged huge holes in the canopy. The only flowers were a few violet asters, *Aster spectabilis*. One painted lady butterfly, several Asian lady beetles seen. Only crows, one pileated and one cricket heard my whole five-mile walk. This afternoon, the koi relished their food in the warm sun. Leah reported a small toad hopping along her living room rug! Tonight, soft and mild, a few crickets: several raspy field crickets and one higher-frequency trilling cricket.

2016: A blustery day after the passage of a cold front. The north yard is full of hackberry leaves pulled down by the wind and rain, the tallest castor bean plants fallen over, the zinnias leaning closer to the ground, the garden so tattered, ready to be cut away. Into south central Ohio: the land was at early-full leafturn, subdued by the scarcity of sunlight, but the sky was fast with chopped white and gray cumulus clouds opening off and on throughout the morning into pools of blue-green. At Conkle's Hollow, the trees still held. Once in a while, a violet arrowhead aster still bloomed. In the afternoon, the clouds overcame the blue, turned to banks of stratus, increasing and chilling the wind.

2017: Jill's vincas brought to the greenhouse this morning. We prepare for the frost forecast for a week from how. Behind my new red vincas, the first red-orange Christmas cactus flower has come open. In the zinnia garden: two monarchs, a bright yellow sulphur and at least one painted lady at 9:00 a.m. Honeybees still work the hummingbird feeder.

2019: Mild and calm in the morning, then brisk wind and chilling through the day, two monarchs in the zinnias, despite the fair-weather cumulus clouds that kept cutting off the sun. Robin heard in the front yard. Two relatively large flocks of geese near Ellis.

2020: A day of sun and warmth in the 70s: I dug all the remaining canna lily beds, made up two more pots of plants to bring inside and two large bags of rhizomes to start in February or March. Windy all day, birds scurrying from one hedge of honeysuckles to the bird feeders, back and forth. Buzzing crickets, trilling crickets, barometer dropping, three buzzards circling, broken cumulus and stratus clouds fast over Janet's spent redbud, withered false buckwheat, wisps of milkweed clinging to the graying goldenrod, euonymus berries white, bittersweet berries light orange, crab apple branches naked. One or two cabbage whites and one large bright yellow sulphur butterfly in the remaining zinnias. Lil's maple and Moya's tulip tree are both deep full gold, rich honey-gold-brown like the older hosta leaves. Some ginkgoes are full yellow now along Xenia Avenue, and there are some unbelievably purple-brown-red sweet gums. At Ellis, a gathering of starlings in the English elms. I raked leaves at Jill's, the sugar maples almost all the way down, the silver maples thinning there. Lil's maple across High Street gilding quickly now.

2022: The warmup continues, allowing me to keep working in the yard and garden. One sluggish cabbage white in the last New England asters this morning, and a monarch butterfly at Pearl's Fen this afternoon. The swamp was gray with goldenrod all tufted. The only flower blooming in the fen: the broad purple blossoms of a *Rhexia mariana* or *Rhexia virginica,* Meadow Beauty. In town and in the countryside, late full leaf color continues with almost all the ginkgoes pale gold now and the remaining maples, oaks, sweet gums, zelcovas rich and dark red, orange (Lil's iconic maple the flagship). One Christmas cactus brought indoors from the front porch is fully budded (red).

2023: Full planting of tulips, daffodils and alliums along the north side of the house, 150 bulbs, that portion of the garden looking neat and clean. Tomorrow I take the last of the cannas from thr north side of the path. Then the next day, bulb planting again. Frost forecast for tonight, plants brought in from the porch. Tree crickets chattering throughout the day. My hoodie was covered with beggartick ticks after I walked through the brambles. All the beggartick foliage, pale violet just a few days ago, was dried and crisp and curled.

Journal

Often in this warm last week of October, I sat in the backyard and looked up at Lil's maple, full orange-gold, and at the round, clear sky through the opening in my plantings.

Jill and I had just returned from a trip to my nephew's wedding in Lincoln, Nebraska. We had driven 1,600 miles across great beige plains shorn of their corn and soybeans, and under chilly sun and big sky, and in steady, hard wind.

It was good to be home. I was tired, and I rested next to the last purple asters in the garden, the one cabbage white butterfly, the bees still active, the one monarch butterfly that suddenly appeared.

Here the sky was contained, a porthole through the suburban landscape. We had seen few birds on our four-day trip, but sitting in the yard, I could watch a vulture watching me, sailing in and out of my window perspetive. Small birds passed above me, so high that I had trouble seeing their silhouettes.

They appeared alone or in widely separated pairs or in clusters of maybe half a dozen. They might have been swallows hunting insects, but I couldn't be sure. They might have been migrating, but they seemed, like the buzzard, to be moving too erratically or circling like sandhill cranes sometimes do when they wait for the next crane cohort to catch up with them over Yellow Springs.

Framed by my location and limited perspective, the birds seemed mine. No longer lost in the infinite horizon of Iowa and Nebraska, they and I belonged here. This glimpse of natural history

through a tiny looking glass was more revealing than the vast
options of outer space beyond my yard. Here I could see enough.

*The landscape contains a thousand dials which indicate the
natural divisions of time....*

Henry David Thoreau

\

October 23rd
The 296th Day of the Year

Along roadsides, in abandoned pastures, on open hillsides, hues had turned somber. The flowers of fall lacked the brilliance and freshness of their spring predecessors.... One saw lavender and old lace: the violet-purple of New England Asters alongside the faded white of Umbellate Asters. Queen Anne's Lace had lost its virginal whiteness and gone to seed. In seeming paradox, the once brilliant goldenrod appeared tarnished. Even the textures of plants were those of the aged. Vegetation which before had been soft, smooth, and supple had become rough, coarse and brittle.

Vincent G. Dethier

Sunrise/set: 6:54/5:45
Day's Length: 10 hours 51 minutes
Average High/Low: 61/41
Average Temperature: 51
Record High: 84 – 1947
Record Low: 25 – 1982

Weather

Another step towards winter: From now on, the chances of a high below 50 degrees jump to 30 percent for the first time since April 9th. But afternoons still warm to the 70s twenty-five percent of the time, to the 60s thirty percent, to the 50s fifteen percent. Skies are overcast, and rain comes four times in a decade on this day. Frost occurs 20 percent of the mornings.

The Natural Calendar

Today is Cross-Quarter Day, the midpoint between fall equinox and winter solstice. At the same time, the Sun enters Scorpio as the Sun's declination reaches approximately -11 degrees 30 minutes. Today is the hinge of deep autumn and initiates the most dramatic period of leaf fall. Throughout this final stage of the natural year, the landscape becomes fully primed for the new signs and seasons to come.

Goldenrod flowers darken and turn to downy tufts. Pokeweed berries shrivel and fall. Wingstem turns brittle from the cold. Knotweed withers. Jerusalem artichokes yellow, stalks collapsing. Dahlias blacken.

Hosta leaves turn honey gold. Knotweed withers. Jerusalem artichokes bend in the wind. Dahlia pale in the cold. The blossoms of the latest asters go to seed. The blush of ginkgo foliage anticipates its sudden collapse, which opens the door to the last phase of autumn.

It is the time of threat of early frost. Time for next year's skunk cabbage to peer from the wetlands,. for yellow witch hazel blossoms to appear. More geese, some years up to 100, gather at Ellis Pond for fellowship through February. Robins, having returned from their August and September retreat, cluck in the bushes. The last monarchs sail over the last roses. Winter's craneflies (looking like clusters of mosquitoes) spin in the sun. Asian lady beetles take shelter in bark and siding. Deer mate at night in the protection of village yards.

The middle of second spring also marks this time of year. When the temperature reaches 60, and cardinals sing, and the starlings cluck in the high trees, November seems like April. Waterleaf is strong on the slopes. Celandine blooms in the garden, along with a few dandelions, some roses, some chickweed, some violets, deadnettle and wild strawberries. Seeds sprout in rotting logs.

Mock orange and forsythia are thinning; their leaf fall measures the progress of the last phase of autumn. Even as more bare branches are revealed, the remaining leaves stand out more clearly. Tarnished grape leaves hold to fences. Some scarlet poison ivy and Virginia creeper still hold in the woodlots. Spicebushes blush. Barberry bushes turn purple. Scarlet rose hips shine in the undergrowth.

Sandhill cranes depart their northern nesting grounds in Michigan, the first formations reaching the Ohio Valley sky just days before Sagittarius. The last monarchs sail over the last roses. The last black walnuts and Osage fall. The last raspberry bushes and apple trees give up their fruit. The last autumn violets and dandelions often go into dormancy.

Milkweed and white snakeroot seeds scatter. Christmas cacti flower and fade. Bittersweet and euonymus open. Asian lady beetles take shelter in bark and siding. Deer mate in the night. Wings of the hosta and lilies droop and melt. Black privet berries and rose hips appear as their foliage thins. Winter wheat sprouts and greens the fields.

As distant and unimaginable as the movements of the high firmament seem, so close and tangible and countable are the events of the immediate landscape. Starlike, those events gleam in their earthy setting, pointing to the hour, the constellations of lanky, empty branches following and reflecting in mirror the deep astrology of the cosmos.

Daybook

1982: King Street still looks like September, mostly green. Mulberry trees are keeping their summer color.

1985: A few buzzards, but no robins migrating by the river. Mulberry leaves turning yellow.

1986: Mrs. Lawson's maple turned to full color in only one day.

1987: Mrs. Lawson's maple is completely down. The ginkgo by my window is yellow green, has most of its leaves. Pussy willow thinned by half, tree of heaven gone. Now the tree line is dull all the way to Wilberforce. Flocks of starlings still cackle in the trees outside the ginkgo window.

1988: Walk at Covered Bridge, rain, 50 degrees, most of the leaves fallen here, no bird songs at all, not a robin. The tree line black and brown, bark and branches wet and sharp against the sky. Just one or two crickets. In Yellow Springs, maples hold, but leaves come down heavily in the rain. The peak has turned, but Middle Fall isn't over yet. Mrs. Lawson's maple holds with half its leaves, as does my front maple. Behind the house, the pussy willow, cherry, and apple still have most all their leaves. They turn tan, yellow, orange slowly, speckled with decay.

Late morning, with the fire behind me in the stove, rain on the windows, purple, white, gold mums shining through the greenhouse wall, against old Virginia creeper, mulberry, maple, raspberry leaves, I sit with myself in private society, as hunter-gatherer, leisurely, self-confidently watching from this cave. I could live completely in this present, give freely or not at all, focus tightly, perfectly, on the leaves and rain.

1990: Only an occasional cricket tonight, clear, 40 degrees. Leaves continue at peak, hold strong.

1991: Pear trees are nearly half red, early like the maples were.

1992: Cardinal at 6:30 this morning, promise of spring. South Glen: Osage fruits on the ground and hanging from the branches, leaves blackened by the frost. A few scattered white asters, all the others seem to be through. Robins migrating along the river, like in all the years before. A monarch butterfly leisurely flies up over the gray tufted goldenrod. Pokeweed berries dark and soft, some withering, lanky broken stalks gold and rust like love vine.

1993: Walking Buttercup at South Glen, clear skies, 55 degrees: Just off the road, on the way to Sycamore Hole, the sound of robins migrating, steady whinnies from up the hill and across the river. Most of the high canopy is gone now: chinquapins, ash, hickory, locust, maples, sycamores. Most of the asters are well past their prime, and the zigzag is almost through. Occasional dandelions brighten the field (one of Jeanie's students picked a bouquet of them last week from the golf course). Blackberry leaves are deep red, goldenrod heads have become gray and puffy, ironweed seeds have turned a palomino tan. The half moon is rising through the black wingstem.

1997: Vultures circling over the North Glen this afternoon as I came home from work. Definitive killing frosts yesterday morning and this morning.

2000: At school in Springfield, the ginkgoes, English oak, chestnut, black oak, sweet gum all full color and shedding. The tall, narrow maple is bare now.

2002: A cardinal sang before dawn this morning. Lil's maple is just starting, her burning bush half red. On the green at Antioch, fall dandelions are common. To Wilmington: Close to full leaf color in many places, the first and second tier of trees coming to their peak together. Woolly-bear caterpillars are out in the sun crossing the highways.

2003: My ginkgo at school is still a solid green. One ginkgo beside it, however, turned yellow more than a week ago; now, it's almost bare.

2004: The secret maple, the northeast maple and Mrs. Lawson's maple all came down yesterday. The Korean lilac leaves are yellow green, the goosefoot leaves a deep red. Mexican sunflowers, Russian sage, the purple hollyhocks, and the small, late-seeded zinnias still bloom. Blackbirds suddenly filled the trees at 11:20 this morning.

2006: Cold and gray with flurries this morning, and one camel cricket in the bathtub. Lil's tree and the secret maple are full now. Danielsons' maple half shed, Moya's maple mostly gone. The mother tree of heaven is losing foliage, but the tree of heaven hedge along the south border is holding green. Throughout town, major maple leafdrop underway. Mateo's Jerusalem artichokes have finished blooming.

2007: A mild all-day rain dulled the leaf color, but peak foliage stayed on quite well. At Wilberforce, the maroon ashes continue at about a third, and the maples are becoming brilliant orange and red-orange. The ginkgoes are all summer green. When I drove into the river valley below Wilberforce this morning, I came on a flock of wild turkeys feeding in the grass by the side of the road, close to a dozen birds.

2008: A very quiet morning. Only eight apples left on the alley apple tree. Sun throughout the day. The landscape holds at full color, but pale. Lil's tree is still not turning, but her burning bush is red all across the top half. The Danielsons' maple is approaching its best. The viburnum at the north side of the house has lost about half of its leaves. Jeanie put in the tree lilies on either side of the trellis this afternoon. Tonight, Venus in the far west, Jupiter approaching from the south, two very slow katydids calling near the park after dark.

2009: The last two nights have been warm and damp, the crickets trilling softly and steadily.

2010: Crows heard at 7:37 this morning. Sporadic chirps from sparrows and nuthatches as I walked along Dayton Street. The witch hazel foliage by the south window is a rich yellow and has started to shed. This evening, the air was warm and the crickets steady and soft.

2011: Coyotes heard howling about 3:00 this morning northwest of town. Robins calling in the alley again and flying through the trees after sunrise. Driving to town, Jeanie and I passed a boulevard yellow with dandelions in full bloom. One painted lady (Cynthia) seen at the zinnias this morning. One katydid this evening at the triangle park, gruff, hoarse and slow: kaaaty......diiiid.

2012: A second day at the Red River Gorge in Kentucky, driving the perimeter of the park, walking a few areas deep into the hills, along cliffs and caves, leaf color still very strong, maples falling more now, witch hazel found in bloom off the edge of an overlook. On the drive home, several bright red pear trees seen. Two large starling-blackbird flocks crossing the highway. At home tonight, a high intermittent tree frog trill in the warm darkness, gibbous moon high in the south.

2013: Hard rain for a while after I went to bed last night, and this morning, the first snow of the winter, light and wet, one of the earliest I've seen here. Across the street: Lil's maple and Mrs. Timberlake's maple are finally starting to turn; the Danielsons' has lost half its leaves. Lil's burning bush and many others throughout the countryside are full deep red. The viburnum foliage on the north side of my house sheds gradually, deep red. Late this afternoon, a sleet/hail/snowburst soaked Annie and her dog as they walked the bike path. At Ellis Pond, I counted seventy Canadian geese on the water, holding to a "V" formation as they swam.

2014: Clear and crisp this morning, but still no frost. Robins whinnying through the neighborhood. In the garden, one yellow daylily open, one of Jeanie's yellow roses, several red shrub roses, one Shasta daisy, one deep purple spiderwort. All but a few New England asters are done blooming. The dahlias continue to do fine, but the number of zinnias is greatly reduced; their bloom really affected by cool weather, the plants not blooming again soon enough after having their flowers cut. Gladiolas dug and the bed prepared for spring. In the afternoon, a painted lady (*Cynthia*), a cabbage white and two checkerspot butterflies came out to the zinnias.

Across the street, Lil's maple is full color and shedding quickly. One yellow sulphur seen as I drove to the Mill habitat in the middle afternoon. Robins were there all around near the road in the honeysuckle thickets, short peeping calls. Further toward the river, no sign of robins in the high trees. I made so much noise walking in the fallen leaves that I had to stop to listen even to the water. The only blooming plants in this area were the violet heart-leaved aster (*Aster cordifolium)* and the white-flowered Heath's aster (*Aster pilosus)*.

Throughout town, peak leaf color continues. This evening, Casey called to say he had seen several monarch butterflies in his butterfly bushes today, and they had been coming pretty steadily throughout the summer and fall. Driving to Dayton with Kathy at dusk, we passed under a great, long blackbird flock, the first I've seen this fall. (Of course, there must have been more that I didn't see.)

2015: Crows at 6:44 this morning. Lil's maple suddenly filled with orange and gold, the burning bush beside it as deep red as it can be. Jeanie's river birch dusky mustard, shedding more now. Janet's redbud and one of its offshoots are almost bare. A house finch came to the feeder in mid afternoon. Later, a goldfinch in winter colors fed on the sock feeder. These are the first finches I have seen in a while. They were away molting for maybe a month. Along the west coast of Mexico, Hurricane Patricia turned almost overnight from a Category 1 storm to a Category 5, with winds near 200 miles an hour – perhaps, meteorologists said, the strongest hurricane ever seen in the hemisphere.

2016: Calm and clear in the low 40s this morning, robins peeping in the twilight through the neighborhood. The Danielsons' maple is almost half shed. Charlene's maple has covered the sidewalk with its rusty-red leaves. The hackberry at the southern edge of my property is completely down, the one on the north side still has most of its leaves. The ash grove at Ellis Pond lost all its foliage in yesterday's rain and wind.

2017: The nearly uniform golden-orange of the Yellow Springs maples is starting to be shredded by the rain and wind. The Danielsons' maple and Moya's maple and both my hackberries are bare except for leaves withered by the dry autumn. Lil's maple and Mrs. Timberlake's maple are still green. From Madison, Wisconsin, Maggie reports peak leaf color.

2019: Sun, brisk and wind. Early morning with Orion bright in the south, clarity bookended by pale city lights. Windy and chilly in the garden, but two monarchs and cabbage whites, one painted lady still worked the late zinnias. Bumble bees and honeybees, as well. Downtown, the Zelcova trees are full of color, like the surviving ashes, maroon and gold. The Kentucky coffee trees are three-fourths down and very yellow. Moya's maple is almost done, and the young trees of heaven collapse around it. Several dozen geese at Ellis Pond.

2020: Warm and mostly sunny in the upper 70s today, windy, birds feeding heavily, barometer dropping, only two cabbage whites in the remaining flowers, two flies, one bumblebee.

2021: The weather turns raw here in the Finger Lakes Region, and the tree coloring seems to shift, as well, the greens of the hills turning gold and brown, the differences between sunlight and shade more pronounced, the shadows dulling, the sun revealing the new brilliance. No pleasure boats, fishing boats or jet skis disrupt Keuka Lake when clouds move down from the northwest. The water is gray and cold, the wind chilling. Only an occasional gull flies by, sometimes going south, sometimes north.

2022: Cirrus clouds, swirling mare's tails yesterday, thicken today, and the weather warms. One cabbage white motionless in the New England asters, and, for the first time in weeks, a monarch visiting, too.

2023: First light frost on the car windows. No damage to plants. Moya's maple shines the brightest gold in the midmorning sun;

My window shows the traveling clouds,
Leaves spent, new seasons, alter'd sky.

Gerard Manley Hopkins

As the afternoons grow shorter, and the early evening drives us home to complete our chores, we are reminded of the shortness of life, and become more pensive, at least in this twilight of the year. We are prompted to make haste and finish our work before the night comes.

Henry David Thoreau

Sunrise/set: 6:55/5:43
Day's Length: 10 hours 48 minutes
Average High/Low: 61/41
Average Temperature: 51
Record High: 82 – 1899
Record Low: 23 – 1981

Weather

Today's chances of precipitation: 25 percent. Highs are in the 70s twenty-five percent of the years, in the 60s forty percent, in the 50s fifteen percent, in the 40s fifteen percent, in the 30s five percent. Sixty percent of the days are clear to partly cloudy. Light frost occurs one morning in three or four.

The Natural Calendar
Counting absences
Days without red-winged blackbirds:
Autumn Samadhi

The inventory of autumn is rich in foliage and color, but the approach of late autumn draws down the density and texture of the canopy and strips away almost all the floral barriers to winter. In the same way that spring overcomes February and March with an accumulation of new growth, fall spreads across the summer with an accumulation of loss.

One enumeration of the season is the counting of what no longer holds, a counting of emptiness, cued only by memory and the more durable, woody scaffolding that binds the seasons:

Foliage of apple trees and crab apple trees, ginkgoes, sugar maples, trees of heaven, redbuds, black walnuts, catalpas, box elders, locusts, elms, birches, poplars, cottonwoods, peach trees, cherry trees, Osage, red oaks, white oaks, chinquapin oaks sycamores, red mulberries, sweet gums, silver maples, Japanese maples, white mulberry trees, beeches, magnolias, mock orange and silver olive shrubs, honeysuckles, Korean lilacs, quinces, privets, viburnums, burning bush, dogwoods, spireas, standard lilacs, gone or collapsing –

Silent mornings: no more robins chattering, no cardinal song, no dove song, no red-winged blackbird song, no grackle song, no cicada song, no katydid song, no cricket song –

Hollow milkweed pods, bare raspberry canes, bare blackberry canes, the leaves of hostas and stonecrop melted, innumerable flowers absent, and harvest complete – no wheat, soybeans, corn, tomatoes, peas, beans, cucumbers, zucchini, lettuce.

Shapes of absent plums and peaches, pears and cherries, broccoli and lettuce, strawberries and mulberries, and the cotton of cottonwoods. Bare landscapes of corn and soybeans and wheat. Empty shells of milkweed and hosta, empty canes and branches, seeds eaten and stored, innumerable creatures gone, the harvest complete.

Faded colors of zinnias and snapdragons, sunflowers and coneflowers, goldenrod and purple ironweed, dahlias and tulips. Vanished fragrances of blossoms from roses and Japanese honeysuckles and azaleas and apple trees and mock orange and lilacs, from alyssum and moonflowers and jasmine. Missing calls of doves and red-winged blackbirds and robins, of toads and frogs, katydids and crickets and cicadas.

From a litany of creatures and events no longer present, one might unthink the world, take it down and let it rest. Emptiness is to space what silence is to sound. In the monastic embrace of the quiet, autumnal cell, I watch and listen, counting absences, replacing nothing.

Daybook

1984: Grinnell habitat, clear, 58 degrees: Dogwoods pink, red, and pale green. Small flock of robins in the upper undergrowth, but not swarming through the high canopy. No flowers blooming. Some crickets strong. Buzzards circling, several dozen perching at their roost at the river bend.

1986: Full leaf color now: ashes and maples turn together, red and gold. Full leaf spectrum, with the major leaf drop starting.

1987: South Glen: Robins passing through the honeysuckles, starlings whistling in the Osage, crickets chanting. Some smartweed still blooming.

1989: Covered Bridge: Leaves almost gone now, red rosehips standing out, only a few asters along the path. Waterleaf, grown back luxuriant, dominant across the woods floor. Crickets in constant song. All the zigzag goldenrod gone, scattered foliage of lizard's tail along the river bank, an autumn violet in the shade, several more in the open field, a flock of robins at Far Hole, sycamore leaves tumbling downstream in the clear water, yellow Osage fruits spread over the ground, crows boisterous, Canadian thistles coming back, fresh nettle growing – a good time for greens. At my second fishing hole, a flock of migrating robins fluttered back and forth, seemed lost, separated, disoriented, a pair of male cardinals were sparring near them. Water striders in a pool, bright red barberries seen through the brush.

1993: Cardinal song strong all day, a piece of second spring. One sulphur butterfly at the roses, the only butterfly seen in what seems like weeks.

1994: This afternoon about five o'clock, I stopped with Buttercup at Grinnell Pond below the railroad tracks. A few yards into the woods, I startled robins, and they flew off to the east into the gorge. Further down the hill, more robins, and then I could see it was a vast flock passing through, fluttering, chattering, whinnying, moving south through the high trees along the river valley.

1997: Standing in the back yard at dawn, I could only hear one cricket over in the north hedge. Downtown at eight o'clock, sparrows were loud in the pear trees. Jeanie says she hasn't heard them for a long time. Then later, Neysa said she hadn't heard them from her apartment since maybe the middle of summer.

1999: Leaves come down quickly now, and the wood lots are dull. It must have been the ashes and hickories that made them bright. Mrs. Lawson's maple is completely gone; I missed tracking it this year. By the back workshop, my "secret" maple is bare. The front maple has maybe a fourth of its leaves, still bright gold. In the greenhouse: one bud on a Christmas cactus.

2000: Several Christmas cacti budding, some well along. Between Springfield and Wilmington, the landscape is on the way to Late Fall, ashes and the early trees gone. At Xenia Avenue and Herman Street, the ginkgo is half down. My birch is gold and shedding at school, beech at its rusty best, the dozen maples in my maple grove three-fourths fallen. Out on the freeway, the sky is gray, and the horizon is dull and brown.

2001: The Korean lilac is pale yellow green now. At school, the red maple is three-fourths bare, the remaining leaves yellow. Along Main Street in Columbus, the sycamores are keeping most of their foliage. Outside my window, the grape leaves are suddenly changing to a red gold. The Danielson's sugar maple is down, the ginkgo at Herman and Xenia Avenue is at full color and half down, Lil's maple is fully turned and shedding. The red mulberries are half stripped, and the neighbor's house shows through. In Xenia, silver maples peaking in their dusky gray gold. The sky above the yard is open now, and at night the streetlights shine into the living room.

2002: Still a few of the miniature hollyhocks in the south garden, still a few blue spiderworts survive. Lamb's ear foliage is about a foot high, providing a silver touch to the browning ground. At the entrance to the village, three raccoon kits were run over together last night, so young, born most likely in late September.

2003: At South Glen this morning, the undergrowth was covered with frost, the trees tattered, sycamores bare, some oaks half down, bright yellow Osage leaves falling. Two buzzards circling. Starlings and robins heard in the distance. At home, Lil's tree is in full color, starting to shed. The Danielsons' tree is three-fourths fallen. Butterfly bushes and Russian sage continue in bloom.

2004: Lil's maple is deep, deep gold and starting to shed, the Danielsons' is half down. I pulled up the drooping coleus bed, uncovering the parsley, chives and lavender underneath. Daffodils planted on either side of the new arbor.

2008: Several cardinals in the alley this morning, one cardinal song around noon.

2009: After a day of hard rain, the alley maple is almost all down, Lil's, Don's, the Danielsons' and Mrs. Timberlake's maples are half shed. The maple from our bedroom window is full rich gold. Mateo's black walnut tree has lost all but one of its walnuts. The tall coneflowers are down to two flowers. The summer of the entire neighborhood is collapsing around me. Robins peeping and whinnying, the wind blowing from the west. In the garden, a big handful of raspberries, some of the last of the year. Greg mentioned that hundreds of monarchs had visited his butterfly garden in Centerville late in the month, stayed two to three days before moving on.

2010: I went outside at 5:30 this morning and listened to the green tree frogs, their long lisping trills. Lil's maple almost full yellow; the Don's, Carl's and the Danielsons' three-fourths down; Mrs. Timberlake's suddenly yellowing. Again this evening at about 8:00, soft cricket songs throughout my walk with Bella.

2011: Crows not heard until about 6:50 this morning just at the end of a thunderstorm. Robins peeping all around. Then the sun came out, and the temperature rose to the 60s. In the countryside, the oaks are reaching early full, accented by the late maples, bringing the tree line alive again. One tree along the highway had dropped all its Osage fruit. The secret maple is fully turned, Lil's is almost all gold, and the silver maples are starting to come in, as well. In the greenhouse, the very first Christmas cactus flower opened. No crickets or katydids this evening.

2012: Rain before dawn, now sun and warm. Robins peeping and whinnying, cardinals singing along my walk (and I heard a cardinal at 7:04 this morning). Lil's maple and Jimmy's maple hold at three fourths of their foliage, but the Danielsons' and Mrs. Timberlake's maples and Janet's redbud are completely down, as are the maples at the Lawson edge of the Champney's property. Don's serviceberry trees have finally shed, and the Dayton Street beech has color now on maybe a third of its leaves. In the alley, orange euonymus berries are emerging from their white hulls. Throughout the neighborhood, the sugar maples have fallen over the past two days, including the secret maple behind the house. In the yard, the hops vines are all brittle and brown, a sudden change from last week, victims of the frost. The pink quince is shedding rapidly now, the pond screen full of golden leaves this morning. The witch hazel is full of flowers, just like the one two hundred miles south at the Red River Gorge yesterday.

2013: More stormy flurries and sleet today. Jeff and I walked at Ellis through snowbursts. Today, there were ninety-seven geese on the water, following each other, like they were yesterday, in the "V" formation they use in flight. At home, all the zinnia and dahlia plants are curled and dark from the frost.

2014: Peonies cut back in the south garden. The berries of the bittersweet vine in the alley are emerging, deep orange.

2015: Peak leaf color continues in the village and throughout the countryside. Lil's maple is straw gold and completely intact, the Danielsons' and Moya's more than three-fourths gone, Mrs. Timberlake's at about half. Asian lady beetles all about on the south side of a farmhouse I visited near Beavercreek.

2016: Chilly and windy and sunny: one skipper in the zinnias, several small bumblebees and honeybees. Lil's and Mrs. Timberlake's tree still are not turning. Robins peeping at sunrise. An autumn violet found in flower in the back yard lawn: the first of the fall.

2017: Wind and chilly, fast clouds and openings of sunlight:

Sparrows on the front porch, pecking in the cemented spaces between the bricks, their winter pattern beginning. And they seem early to me this year. In the yard, the redbud trees are yellowing, their dark, long seedpods appearing on the branches now, a stark replacement for the soft leaves. The upper leaves of Lil's maple and Mrs. Timberlake's maple have suddenly started to turn gold, and Lil's burning bush is about all red. Jeanie's river birch is yellowing, too, the foliage of the trumpet vine leading the way. Throughout the village: full leaf color and shedding in the deepening cold. Voles invading the greenhouse to gather spilled birdseed. This afternoon as I read by the wood stove, I saw one scoot across the floor. I told it to go back outside, but it disappeared into the closet.

2018: Return from Italy to Yellow Springs: The maples of High Street are still predominantly green. The Danielsons' tree has lost leaves and is starting to look shaggy; the Limestone-High Street maples have started to show pale orange; I saw a few deep purple redbuds along Elm Street, and a couple of bright sugar maples along Dayton Street (one visible through the back honeysuckles), but the landscape both here and in Italy has not begun to enter Middle Fall. In the yard, frost has taken the zinnias, the tithonias and the dahlias, and most of the castor beans. Jeanie's river birch has lost half its leaves, the remainder gold. Milkweed seeds have drifted into the spent New England asters. The morning glory and the knotweed foliage is twisted and brown. Along King Street: a few robins peeping, moving south, Osage fruits alongside the road. Sparrows on the front porch, working the spaces between the bricks. They had started before I left last week.

2019: Departing Yellow Springs for Amsterdam in Holland: Full early color is dominant in southwestern Ohio, with some shedding underway. The flight to Detroit showed similar color throughout.

2020: A tornado warning, and then a thunderstorm passed through in the night. Today is breezy and cold, broken stratus clouds rushing over from the north, vultures riding the wind, white mulberry leaves yellowing more and coming down. The locust and box elder branches that I see through my high studio windows are completely bare for the first time. Across the street, Lil's maple and Mrs.

Timberlake's maple are tied for deep gold full color. Frank's silver maple and the Danielson's sugar maple are down. The downtown Zelcova trees are deep maroon and half gone. At Ellis, the round maple tree at the water's edge that was so golden all week has collapsed.

2022: A few whistling crickets heard tonight, but no katydids in the neighborhood.

2023: One cabbage white today as I planted bulbs in the north garden. T.K.'s maple is half down, Lil's and the Danielsons' hold a little better. Mrs. Timberlake's maple and Frank's hold without much color. Jill reports the arrival of Asian lady beetles in her house today, perphaps a couple of dozen.

The interior landscape responds to the character and subtlety of an exterior landscape; the shape of the individual mind is affected by land as it is by genes.

Barry Lopez

October 25th
The 298th Day of the Year

The subtle frost hath plied its mystic art,
and in the day the golden Sun hath wrought
True wonders; and the wings of morn and even
Have touched with magic breath the changing leaves.

William D. Gallagher

Sunrise/set: 6:56/5:42
Day's Length: 10 hours 46 minutes
Average High/Low: 60/40
Average Temperature: 50
Record High: 83 – 1963
Record Low: 25 – 1962

Weather

Today brings one more statistical movement towards winter: the chances of a morning freeze in the 20s rises to 40 percent for the first time since late March; and today and the 26th are the two October days most likely to bring a hard freeze. Highs in the 70s occur 15 percent of the years; there's a 30 percent chance of 60s, 25 percent chance of 50s, twenty percent chance of 40s, ten percent for 30s. Rain or snow comes 45 percent of the days. Skies are completely overcast four days in ten.

The Natural Calendar

Last year's cattail remnants rise above the dying grasses, are ghostly and puffy, heads swollen and broken. Teasel is black and stark. The soybean fields are shorn to a gray stubble. The last of the standing corn is ragged and pale.

In the last week of an average Middle Fall, the oaks and the Osage, white mulberries, magnolias, ginkgoes and the late black and sugar maples move towards full color. The second tier of leaves, consisting mostly of the early maples, is coming down. (In the first tier were the ashes and box elders, locusts and buckeyes.)

Harvest continues, with about half of the corn and three-fourths of the soybeans cut in a typical year. Apple orchards have been picked clean of fruit. Throughout the cranberry region of the northern states, most of the berries have been brought in from the bogs.

Even as more bare maple branches appear, the remaining leaves stand out more clearly. Tarnished grape leaves hold to fences, some scarlet poison ivy and Virginia creeper still shine in the woodlots. Spicebushes blush, barberry bushes turn purple.

Daybook

1982: No flowers blooming except some Queen Anne's lace along the roadsides, a few asters and pink smartweed in the woods. Canopy almost gone in some parts of the Glen.

1983: Maples full color, full yellow in front of our house and in Mrs. Lawson's yard. Raspberries are finally past their peak. Only a third of a pint today, leaves becoming purple. Garden still strong, zucchini still producing.

1984: Jimsonweed is still open in the dry soybean fields.

1985: South Glen: Except for the Osage, a few oaks, and occasional sycamores, all the leaves are down. Fields are brown. Robins are gone. It's Late Fall now in spite of the warm, windless days, the lack of killing frost.

1986: Rapid leaf-fall occurring at peak color, sudden climax of Middle Fall. But Lil's maple is late, as usual, just starting to turn.

1988: Magnolias near my doors are turning light yellow green, still have all their leaves. The tall poplar at the south wall is deepening, but still holding near summer color. Pussy willows and cherry are browning lightly. Geese flying south in a "V" at 6:05 p.m. No crickets heard tonight.

1992: Crows boisterous at 6:40 a.m., stayed in the back trees five or ten minutes. One daddy longlegs still hunting on the buttercup foliage in the south garden.

1995: Today I stopped again at Grinnell Pond looking for robins.

This time, the woods quiet, not even a chickadee.

1998: Starting from the height of Middle Fall on the 20th of October, I drove north toward Fargo to see the trees and visit Uncle Bill. The days of Yellow Springs Time fell away the farther I traveled. In two days and 1,100 miles, I went well into Glen Helen November in which color no longer lay on the trees but on the radiant winter rye, the black earth, and green roadsides glowing in the low angle of the Sun.

There were no clouds in the six days of my trip, the whole country held under a vast high-pressure system that warmed the Dakotas into the 70s. And as I drove, the land opened up, the Sun became more powerful, was no longer the filtered Yellow Springs sun.

When I arrived, I made my visits, met a new cousin, was given a tour of Grand Forks, and saw the devastation that the flood had caused there over a year ago. Then, restless, I started home. Leaving town about 6:00 a.m., I turned into the empty darkness south toward Fargo an hour away, not a car for miles, only one or two lights from human habitation.

After a while, there was a hint of pink in the east, and then the glow spread deep into the north and south. Without a bush or weed to stop it, twilight engulfed the whole land and air. Then the Sun rose sharper and bigger than I'd ever seen it, so big it made me uneasy, stirred some primitive fear inside me about solar divinity. Alone on the bare cusp of earth, I felt fragile and vulnerable before the wide, revealing emptiness of the prairie.

By the time full daylight came, I was a hundred miles southeast of Fargo, and I could see how the slightest addition to the landscape - a tree or a house or even a gentle swell in the pastures - diminished the grandeur of the horizon. It was not so much that objects or hills reduced visibility, although they certainly did that, but that each one detracted just a little from the perfection of the prairie vision.

I reached Yellow Springs the next night, and in the morning, I went out to watch dawn over my small yard and pond. Even though the sky was mostly clear, I could only see a soft and filtered urban sunrise over this benign, cluttered habitat. It was good to be home to a safer, less naked place, in which day always came gently from behind the trees, and set, glorious and imperfect, flawed by power lines and people, into the city.

1999: The Danielsons' maple is at late peak, bright yellow orange. Mrs. Lawson's maple is long gone. My secret maple is empty now. The front maple has maybe fifteen percent of its rich ochre leaves. In the pond, the water lily still has one bud, but the leaves are down to fifteen. No killing frost yet.

2000: Redbuds naked now. Major sweet gum fall begins. The ginkgo at Xenia Avenue and Herman is 95 percent down. Most of the burning bush leaves are gone. One woolly bear caterpillar seen; but they're rare this year.

2001: Seasons tied to the fields and woods: space and passage unified. Landmarks containing past and future. Time as explicator of space, space as anchor of time, the visible matter and form of time.

2003: A warm morning before the rain arrives. The bamboo sways against the greenhouse wall (the first Christmas cactus opening inside, jade trees budding). All around the neighborhood starlings and blackbirds cluck and cackle. A few robins calling in the honeysuckles. A flock of crows flies over at 7:30. Two small redbud trees transplanted, the lawn mowed, the zinnias pulled up in the 70- degree afternoon.

2004: The first red Christmas cactus flowers opened today in the greenhouse.

2006: Two camel crickets found this morning, one in the bathtub, another under the bed. In the greenhouse, one white Christmas cactus and one red have been in full bloom for two days.

2007: Christmas cacti, which were left outside until last week, just have small buds. Cardinal sang once at 6:50. Almost all of Mateo's and Don's black walnut fruits have fallen; one tree near the alley still retains most of its walnuts. Redbud leaves are falling. Our small crab apple is almost bare. Lil's tree is still holding back, mostly green; the golden patches on the Danielsons' tree are spreading. Flocks of blackbirds and starlings as I walked this morning, veering and swooping in the windswept day. No robins heard for quite a while.

2008: The Danielsons' maple is full orange and shedding. Lil's is a third or more turned. Two of Don's serviceberry trees are still keeping their foliage; a third is bare. The secret maple is still golden. Roses and late rudbeckia plants continue to offer highlights of color in the north garden. No crickets last night, no katydids. No birdcalls heard.

2010: Deep yellow gold of many hosta leaves.

2011: Crows very late this morning - near 7:00 a.m. A grackle came to the bird feeder this morning, the first I've seen here since summer. A few grackle calls as I left the house, then only distant sparrow chirps throughout my walk. Silver maples are shedding on Stafford Street. Mrs. Timberlake's maple is full gold and shedding quickly, Lil's almost all gold. The late mum plant, a holdover from last year, red with gold centers, finally bloomed. This mild and sunny afternoon, Jeanie and I stacked wood, accompanied by two monarchs, one buckeye, one painted lady (Cynthia), two sulphurs, three cabbage whites, one small checkerspot. Tonight, temperature in the 50s, soft, intermittent cricket song throughout the neighborhood, and several loud katydids at the park.

 2012: A cardinal sang at 6:30 this morning, then again at 6:37. Crows were calling at 6:50. Robins and cardinals heard when I walked Bella before 8:00. I walked at the Siebenthaler Fen this morning with Jeff: We stood at the edge of the swamp and watched robins migrating in the high trees, swooping and chasing one anther, chirping and whinnying. In town, the ginkgoes have begun to shed, most redbuds down, sweet gum still red gold and holding. At Ellis Pond, one cypress shedding, scarlet and bur oaks down, red oak brown and full, sawtooth oak full green, scarlet oak full red, in general, all oaks full to late. At home, the quince is three fourths down, leaves filling the pond net, most of rose of Sharon wilted pale yellow green. The cherry is all down, and the river birch is finally turning, a few yellow leaves, the white mulberry full gold, the red mulberry a little paler and thin, Osage yellowing, Dayton Street birch with more and more rust and gold.

2014: Don's serviceberry trees, foliage rusty brown, hold at about three-fourths down. The star magnolia across the street, leaves all pale, most fallen. The quince in our back yard has kept its leaves to this point, the cherry half its leaves. The redbuds about bare.

2015: Some wind and then a brief, hard rain last night, and now the peak has passed, the canopy dramatically changed. But among the ground cover at the Pine Forest, Jill found a toad – identical in color with the leaves and pine needles. Now October 25 is the latest date for sighting a toad in the area!

2016: The first frost arrived this morning, coating Jill's car and a field near Ed Oxley's house. No plants were hurt, though; even the castor beans seem fine. The pink quince in the back yard keeps its leaves. All of my Christmas cacti have developed buds; some appeared over a week ago. In the north garden, the New England asters have started to develop round, soft seed heads, and the goldenrod paces their transformation with smaller heads lining the end of their stems. Joe Pye seeds are fluffy and falling, motherwort seeds sharp and hard. A couple of small bumblebees and one ragged silver-spotted skipper in the zinnias struggle with the cold breeze.

2017: Frost due tonight, all the plants brought inside. The high locust by my studio has thinned, leaving the second major opening above my windows. The first was the box elder,

2018: Debbie Walker wrote to say that, for the first time in several weeks, she had heard red-winged blackbirds on her property north of town. The latest date for the red-wings to migrate in the area is the middle of November.

2021: The drive from Keuka Lake in New York to Yellow Springs took us through the middle of peak leaf color throughout the region, In just the five days we were at the lake, the whole landscape collapsed into rich gold, orange and red. At home, mixed changes.

The High Street trees hold off for the most part, Lil's maple just starting to turn.

2022: Robins peeping. Euonymus and the northeast corner viburnum blanching like the pale green rose of Sharon bushes. Redbuds and the pink quince tree, like the peach tree leaves, ripe peach color, honeysuckles falling steadily, river birch nearly bare. I keep the tall wild lettuce plants with their white seed tufts, the browning cup plants with their buckwheat tangles, the fading castor beans, for their subtle gathering of autumn decay. One cabbage white butterfly glimpsed late in the afternoon. New moon today foretells tomorrow's end of a week-long mild spell. No katydids or crickets heard in the yard tonight.

Dandelions still blossomed on the hills east of town today, but there was little sound – the voices of juncos, chickadees, jays, and the sound of the cowbell rising from the cattle coming down the slope to the valley above where I sat.

August Derleth

October 26th
The 299th Day of the Year

This tiny corner of the earth that is ours gives a feeling of deep content and security; this is the base to which we can always come back, and be ourselves, alone, completely free from the outside world.

Charles Burchfield

Sunrise/set: 6:57/5:41
Day's Length: 10 hours 44 minutes
Average High/Low: 60/40
Average Temperature: 50
Record High: 83 – 1963
Record Low: 21 – 1962

Weather

Today's chances of morning frost are 55 percent, and the likelihood of rain is only 20 percent. The temperature distribution: 25 percent chance of highs in the 70s, thirty percent for 60s, fifteen percent for 50s, twenty-five percent for 40s, five percent for 30s. Completely overcast conditions occur four days in ten.

The Natural Calendar

In many years, the canopy of county woodlots is almost completely open by this time of the month. White snakeroot seeds come apart in downy clusters like thistle seeds or goldenrod. The final aster blossoms disappear. Craneflies spin in the sun.

Daybook

1984: A second-spring field of dandelions has gone to seed near Wilberforce, probably bloomed a week ago.

1986: Long flock of grackles passes over the house. Rains are stripping the late turning trees. First new green wheat field seen today.

1987: Aloe blooms in the greenhouse. Starlings and blackbirds cackling, whistling and clucking in the back woodlot this morning. Sweet gums falling, half the ginkgo leaves gone. Some Bradford pears are turning. Magnolias at school are half gone. Lawson's maple and my maple empty, Lil's maple burned, half fallen. Pussy willow leaves the color of golden pears, and thinned.

1988: 7:56 a.m.: Geese fly over the house. On the way to Wilberforce: Winter wheat is green, a few stands of goldenrod still late full bloom. Along the tree line, autumn colors are becoming less prominent, more subtle. At school, ashes are gone, locusts gone. About a third of the maples left in the yard. 8:30 p.m. The full Buzzard Moon is rising from the other side of the Catholic church, and all the stars are out. Mars is high in the south, Jupiter leading the Pleiades. Branches more than half bare now, streetlights shining through into the yard.

1989: Almost the same as 1987 in Yellow Springs. On the way north to Lansing, in the last quarter of leaf color, the frequency of bare trees increases as I move toward Toledo, then foliage thicker again in the city (more silver maples). Willows only half turned there.

1990: South Glen, sunny, 48 degrees: Red smartweed still in bloom. Zigzag seeds puffed and fragile, crows and crickets loud. Woolly-bear caterpillars all over the road to the Glen. Hundreds of grasshoppers along the path through the butterfly preserve, milkweed scattered like thistle down. One violet holding. No spider webs. Box elder seeds still hanging, glistening. Half moon up along the eastern tree line. Outside my window, starlings cackle and whistle all day in the sun.

1992: Aloe blooming in the greenhouse, open maybe a day or two. In the warm evening, a few moths seen, then a bat circling the yard at 5:55.

1993: Winter-colored gold finches seem to be replacing the house finches at the feeders now. More woolly bears, completely black, on Grinnell today, but not so many as on the 22nd.

1997: The first Christmas cactus flower opened yesterday. At least half of the cacti are budding now, and more will bloom this week. Along the south hedge, the red mulberries are losing their leaves, hurt by the frost. On Herman Street, the ginkgo has dropped hundreds of green leaves, also, I presume, because of the frost. But out along the roadways, the tree line still seems young. The maples are holding well, and greens still dominate across the area. The corn and soybean harvest is in full swing in the county. It's a good year for pumpkins: a sale at the orchard - two dollars for any size.

1999: As I go back over some of my weather notes, I realize how the practicality of my weather history is different from the practicality of a modern weather forecast. I keep track of the weather not so much to know the future as to know the present and the past and myself better. Or maybe it's a different kind of future I encounter when I chart the seasonal patterns, something of the mystery of fractals that I want to explore.

2000: Full streetlight intrusion into the living room now that the leaves have come down.

2002: Cosmos and Mexican sunflowers remain bright, as do the impatiens. Zinnias all fell to powdery mildew three weeks ago. More sweet William sprouts planted, eight patches so far.

2003: The Korean lilac is yellowing. Redbud leaves have fallen, and Danielsons', maples is almost bare. Red maples in the triangle park are at their peak, full red. Other maples and sweet gum trees in Yellow Springs and Dayton are reaching yellow and red full color.

2004: The Korean lilac has lost more than half its leaves.

2006 The ginkgo at my classroom in Wilberforce is completely bare. My office ginkgo is ochre.

2007: The classroom ginkgo is just turning pale today. The Korean lilac is thinning on the north side of house, but holding at maybe three-fourths. Ruby Nicholson reported seeing the first junco today.

2008: Diane reports a fresh tall bellflower along the river, south near where the swinging bridge used to be.

2010: Crows briefly at 6:50 this morning, barometer has dropped to 29.47 so far, wind in the drying leaves, crickets strong until daylight, third-quarter moon high in the west trees. Lil's tree is full gold now, Mrs. Timberlake's well underway, the star magnolia across the street is as yellow as witch hazel leaves and flowers. Across the West, the first cold temperatures of the season have moved down from Canada and are coming across the Plains. Yesterday and the day before, snow in the mountains, now freezing all the way to Flagstaff and Santa Fe.

2011: Crows at 6:45 this morning, some crickets, too. Mild near 70 today. In town, the sweet gum trees are full red and purple, more ginkgoes are gold and shedding, the Zelcova trees on Xenia Avenue are turning red. Jeanie and I finished stacking the woodpile, watched a pair of monarchs hang out all afternoon in the zinnias, floating back and forth. One buckeye, one sulphur, one cabbage white, as well. Sprawling bouquets of zinnias and roses and dahlias picked before the rain. In the greenhouse, more Christmas cacti are coming in. Tonight, the crickets were strong throughout the neighborhood. I even heard the "castanet" cricket again, intermittent tree crickets and field crickets. Katydids were calling back and forth at several locations.

2012: The days continue clear and bright. Two weeks ago, much of the landscape was still deep, late-summer green. Now, ashes are gold and burgundy, a few maples and dogwoods are orange, or red. Cottonwoods and catalpas and sweet gums and shagbark hickories are yellow. Grape vines and nettles are bleached with age. Locust leaves drizzle steadily to the undergrowth. The serviceberries are almost bare. The black walnut trees keep only their last fruit. Purple poison ivy and Virginia creeper outline the changes.

       In local gardens, the virgin's bower is done flowering. White boneset and New England asters are in decline, but the cabbage moths still swarm around them. A few rose of Sharon and Japanese honeysuckle blossoms hold on. The last jumpseeds still jump when my fingers stroke them. Craneflies swarm, a fraction of their winter size. Dragonflies still hunt in the Metropark ponds. Monarchs and painted ladies and swallowtails come by each day.

In the woods this afternoon, kingfishers were screaming up and down the river throughout my walk. Late goldenrod was still in bloom, along with white snakeroot and the small white asters and the violet heart-leafed asters. The zigzag goldenrod, orange jewelweed and the blue-stemmed goldenrod still blossomed at the far side of their season.

I looked for buzzards circling above the woods. They used to come here by the hundreds, waiting on the high currents for October. I saw only one today. Driving south near dusk, I noticed the milkweed pods were open, their silk shining in the last light.

2013: More frost this morning, faint robins calling. The quince leaves have not started yet, much later than in earlier years. In the greenhouse, Christmas cacti are in early full bloom. A great flock of starlings half way to Fairborn in front of the auto-body shop, swooping and diving, many sitting on the high-tension wires. A few deep purple autumn violets at Ellis Pond. The black maple was almost all down there, and the persimmon trees were completely bare.

2014: Quince leaf fall gathering just a little momentum. Both hackberries are down. Lil's maple continues deep gold, light shedding. T.K.'s young maple is pacing Lil's. The secret maple (so big now) has lost half its leaves. The dahlias in the northwest garden keep that corner anchored with color even as the zinnias slowly decline. The leaves are still late full in the village. In the alley, bittersweet foliage is pale yellow, more bittersweet berries emerging, darkening. In the middle of the morning, the high trees of the neighborhood harbored the chirping of robins and the whistling of starlings. The canopy is more than half gone at the Cascades. Yesterday Maggie said that the southern Wisconsin leaves had pretty much all come down.

2015: Robin migration calls in the honeysuckles. One cabbage white seen. The wind was so quiet at the approach of tomorrow's remnant of Hurricane Patricia. Downtown, the Kentucky coffee trees are almost bare, and the Zelcovas are deep red- orange, ginkgoes yellowing along Xenia Avenue. Throughout the village, the tall remaining sugar maples are so bright against the azure sky. At Ellis Pond, the red oaks are chocolate brown and caramel gold, the sycamores are three-fourths empty, the cypresses are rusting, the silver maples have a few palomino patches, the dogwoods are purple-red and tattered, the tulip trees and sugar maples are half down, still golden. I was about to leave when I looked over to the west end of the pond, and I saw geese slowly coming out of the cornfield, and they came in twos and threes, walking-waddling so slowly, kind of at the speed of walking meditation, and they came toward the west edge of the pond and then deliberately followed each other one by one down the bank, five dozen of them I counted, and they swam out single file onto the still water.

2017: First frost tonight: 29 degrees. Most of the flowers killed, but many castor bean plants survived pretty well. In the warming sun, I saw two painted ladies and a honeybee in the withered zinnias, trying to make something of what was left for them. On the way to the airport, the tree line was mostly green, and as the plane took off over Dayton, the whole land seemed in Late Summer. And that season continued as we flew along the Ohio River and then down into Texas. From Corning, New York, Lois reports forsythia in bloom.

2018: Early full color is spreading across the county now, a major change just since I returned from Italy, brilliant maples dominating, rusty purple-red oaks along the bike path toward Xenia. The Champneys' maples lead High Street color, T.K.'s maple close behind. Burning bush filling in throughout. The Danielsons' maple shedding but with little color, Lil's maple losing its deep green. A few dozen daffodils planted before the rain. Two autumn violets discovered in the circle garden.

2020: A small flock of robins in Moya's bare maple tree this morning. Lil's maple deepening, burnt gold, more dramatic than I remember it ever being. Rachel's ginkgo yellowing suddenly.

2021: Cold and breezy today, but a yellow sulphur butterfly flew past me as I walked the garden.

2022: Cool and rainy today: Jill reports ginkgoes starting to shed. Lil's maple is thinning to about half. John called and left a message about another bald eagle sighting in the area.

2023: Continued mild. Robins peeping in the honeysuckles

Pack the dark fibre in the potters bowl;
Set bulbs of hyacinth and daffodil,
Jonquil and crocus (bulbs both sound and whole,)
Narcissus and the blue Siberian squill.
Set close, but not so tight
That flowe'ring heads collide as months fulfill
Their purpose , and in generous sheaf expand
Obedient to th'arrangement of your hand.
Yours is the forethought, yours the sage command.

V. Sackville-West

October 27th
The 300th Day of the Year

Old October's purt' nigh gone,
And the frosts is comin' on
Little heavier every day.

James Whitcomb Riley

Sunrise/set: 6:58/5:39
Day's Length: 10 hours 41 minutes
Average High/Low: 59/40
Average Temperature: 50
Record High: 81 – 1897
Record Low: 21 – 1903

Weather

Chances of frost are 45 percent, for rain 30 percent, for totally overcast skies 55 percent, for highs in the 70s twenty-five percent, for 60s fifteen percent, for 50s fifty percent, for 40s ten percent.

The Natural Calendar

The week just past and the week to come are among the most dramatic of the year along the 40th Parallel. Thirty days ago, the woods were green. Fifteen days ago, the maples, ashes and locusts were at their peak; today, most of them are gone or ready to come down. The white mulberries, ginkgoes, zelcovas, pears, beeches and the sweet gums dominate the village now. The deciduous year is almost over; the storms that bring Late Fall will finish it.

Daybook

1983: Geese fly over the house at 4:45 p.m.

1985: Geese fly over the house at 4:37 p.m.

1986: Ginkgoes suddenly full yellow, sycamores deep gold along Corey Street.

1988: Sycamores all gold along Corey Street, but most sycamore leaves are gone at South Glen.

1989: Lansing, Michigan: Only the last oaks and silver maples hold. Autumn haze, black tree line against a white, bright horizon, sun highlighting gray goldenrod tufts and flashes of gold from the maples and poplars. Burning bush still holds red, winter wheat is up, shining green.

1990: Leaves past their peak now, but still strong. Primroses, planted in the early spring, are blooming, one red, one yellow, one blue. A cardinal sang off and on while I cleaned up the garden this morning, and geese flew over. After three frosts, the last tomatoes and zucchini gathered. Robins migrating through the yard today.

1992: The first tier of maples has fallen, the second level is full color now, maybe half the trees are bare, half full color. No birds heard today.

1995: At the Mill, robins flocking yesterday afternoon and now this morning, too, steady chirping and fluttering. Near sundown yesterday as I was coming back from the dam, about three dozen buzzards suddenly appeared over the river bend, reminiscent of the way I saw them a decade ago.

1998: Asian ladybugs reported at the schools now, increasing in numbers as the week progresses. And a call from Clifton a few days ago about an invasion there. In the garden, I dug up two chard plants and brought them to the greenhouse for a winter experiment.

1999: The pond is cluttered with leaves. A new frog seems to have come to live there. I haven't seen him, but he dives whenever I approach, unlike the summer frog that sat and watched me from under a rock. Late afternoon: Lil's maple has been turning all day, now is deep golden brown; two days ago it was almost fully green. Mrs. Lawson's far maple matches the color of Lil's.

2000: Cabbage butterfly and small gold skipper seen. In the village, the late locusts are down, ginkgoes starting to shed, pink quince three-fourths bare, some sweet gum trees are three-fourths, catalpas seven-eighths shed. Out in the countryside, the tree line is brown and empty except for scattered bright Osage and maples. In the south garden, late mums, a handful of gaura, spiderworts, two daisies left. Along the stone wall, the yellow roses are the most beautiful they've been all year. In the greenhouse, several Christmas cacti are blooming.

2001: Casey called this afternoon: A giant flock of herring gulls was feeding in a soybean field north of town. The soybeans, he said, had just been harvested, and he'd never seen so many gulls. My books say they are migrating now towards the Ohio and Mississippi valleys; Casey found them.

2002: Full color of the first and second tier of leaves blossoming together. Cottonwoods mostly down. Hostas are yellowing.

2003: The Danielsons' tree is down.

2005: The Danielson's tree is all pale gold and losing leaves. Lil's maple is still mostly green; her burning bush is deep red. The red-orange maple toward Limestone Street is shedding but still vibrant. Mrs. Timberlake's maple is blanching a little, but remains in Early Fall. In the alley behind Mateo's house, chicory was opening at 7:45 this morning. Christmas cacti brought in from the back yard, many of the plants budding. On the road to Wilmington, the woodlots are still in full color, but shedding continues to increase.

2007: Robins chirping and whinnying, starlings chattering in the alley this morning, some starlings in the alley pine tree. The alley maple is shedding hard now. Mexican sunflowers cut back today; they are still blooming, but the stalks have collapsed. To Columbus and back this afternoon, the cottonwoods and many ashes down, but many ashes holding, and peak maple and sweet gum color throughout. Across the street, Lil's maple and Mrs. Timberlake's maple are still green, the Danielson's more than half turned. The ash tree between the Lawson's and the corner is pale yellow and holds all its leaves. Some burning bush in the area is full red; Lil's favors the southern exposure.

2008: After a blustery night, the back yard shows hundreds of white mulberry leaves down, leaves that belonged to branches damaged in the passage of Hurricane Ike in September. In the alley, all but three of the apples have fallen from the ancient apple tree – the last remnant of an orchard that filled this part of town three-quarters of a century ago. The orange of the Danielsons' maple deepens, becomes more transparent, stronger. The McDaniels' maple is still yellow green, half back into summer.

2010: Lil's maple full gold, her burning bush full red. The Danielsons' maple is about down, Mrs. Timberlake's full yellow and shedding, the star magnolia next door to her has dropped all its leaves. Many silver maples around town are still green, many turning palomino gold, some red maples full red. Quickweed, roses, deadnettle, smartweed blooming strong. The pale gold of the grape leaves outline the honeysuckle bushes. One dark maroon and black woolly bear caterpillar climbing up the front steps this afternoon when I was raking leaves.

2012: A reader sent me the following: "Is it just me (I reside in Clark County, OH) or are there fewer, if any, wooly worms this year? I haven't personally seen a single one and have asked many friends and relatives who have said, 'Come to think of it, I haven't either.' Is it a result of the dry summer, will there be no moths/butterflies next year? They have been used to predict the coming winter's intensity in years past, if so what could this indicate?"

I wrote her that right after receiving her note, I found a dark rust orange woolly bear in the woodpile, but it was the only one I've seen this fall. Later, I found several more woolly bears in the woodpile, more than usual, really. Maybe they all just got to the woodpile without being seen!

2013: The Danielsons' maple is almost bare, as is Carl's middle maple, and Mrs. Timberlake's has started to turn near the bottom. (But a handful of her feverfew blossoms have survived in the alley.) Lil's is holding out, still quite green. Quince shedding is accelerating just a little, the pond netting catching more leaves. At the Cascades, no goldenrod or asters seen, only one robin heard, the staccato rattle of a cricket, the canopy half down.

2014: Leafdrop accelerating leaves thick now on the sidewalks and yards. The star magnolia's foliage is almost all gone. Carl's maples are bare. Lil's continues to hold but thinning. At 7:50 this morning, a medium-sized flock of grackles passed over the alley heading southeast.

In the neighborhood, robins still here, chirping in the lower trees. This afternoon, the very first Christmas cactus flower opened, a white and pink one. On Xenia Avenue, the bright golden ginkgo is starting to shed. Near John Bryant Park, Bob Huston reported seeing two fireflies blinking above the soybean field by his house. And Brad Roof found a snapping turtle emerging from its egg.

2015: Before daylight, I stood in the back yard and listened to the steady trill of a tree cricket. Later, Ed Oxley called to tell me he had found (and photographed) two toads yesterday as he was clearing brush from around his yard. That makes October 26th the latest toad sighting so far! Lil's Norway maple is now full and deep yellow-orange, its darkest and richest coloring in years. Maples are shedding quickly now, more with each rain, and the secret maple is completely down.

2016: Jeff from Springfield sent a note saying he had always called the fat, round fruits of the Osage orange "hedge apples." "My grandfather was half Native American, and he used the hedge apples as an insect repellent, mainly for the concentrations of 'lady bugs' that accumulate in the fall when the weather turns. I did not see any real change in the numbers."

This morning, Moya's maple and Mrs. Timberlake's are three-fourths down, Lil's burning bush about full red.

2017: Portland, Oregon: I arrived at the height of leafturn and the second or third day of leaf fall (according to my grandkids, Max and Jack). Throughout the area, Zelcovas and ashes and maples – especially red maples – are full gold and orange and red and falling quickly, and poplars elegant yellow gold, thinning. The color is more dramatic here in suburban Portland two thousand miles from Yellow Springs, but it seems that the stage of breakdown is quite similar.

2018: Deep golden peak leaf color in the rain.

2019: Notes from Amsterdam, Holland: Sightings of ginkgoes at the same stage as in Yellow Springs, the whole golden sphere, and walking in the park with Gracie, Michaels black poodle, finding old friends (plants), encountering home in the familiar burdock, rudbeckia, mouse-eared chickweed, horseweed (everywhere horseweed, surprisingly familiar here on the vast Netherlands delta overlooking one canal after another in the cool wind), and so I am simply home or home is not being alone or less being alone than not being totally alien or out of place, ex-patriotic and then running into Ana and having a conversation in Spanish, and I was surprised at my facility.

And so things fell into place as I stood by the canal, and the dog ate grass, and it came time for me to go back,

And then another encounter:

An Incident in Amsterdam-Yellow Springs
at Bilderdijk Park by the Hugo de Grootgract Canal
Amsterdam, Holland

I was walking the dog of a friend in Amsterdam. It was my first time there, and it was Sunday afternoon, and cloudy and cool and breezy, and we had just come back from the North Sea where the wind had been wild and hard that morning, and the dogs had played fiercely in the waves.

So with everyone else doing something else later in the afternoon, I was asked to walk Gracie, a labra-doodle that looked like a smaller standard poodle, black and curly-haired. Gracie seemed disoriented to be going out with me but gradually seemed to come to accept me in a kind of absent-minded or lost or confused way, perhaps like I was feeling in a strange country.

Gracie eventually ended up eating grass, like an indoor dog will do, and I stood by the black canal and noticed the Yellow Springs plants that still were blooming now at the end of October among fallen sycamore leaves: burdock, horseweed, quickweed, chickweed, the tiny English daisies with their fat small broad leaves, the dried nettle and the sharp burrs of the burdock, and creeping Charley, and on a puff of wind, a honeybee, the only insect I had seen since my arrival, approached my right hand and then came up and hovered for a moment close to my face then flew away.

Later as Gracie and I were leaving the park, a woman so beautiful and tall and old, with blonde-gray hair past her shoulders, blue eyes lonely, with her two small brown terriers approached me, said something I did not understand, and then she so casually deliberately let the leash of one of the dogs fall to the ground in front of me.

2020: A chilly, gray, autumn day, but this afternoon, in the cut-over soybean field across from Ellis Pond, a flock of at least a hundred geese was feeding, fattening for winter fellowship and spring pairing.

2021: First frost of the year in the region, but no damage in my yard. Jeff said he had a "bigly" freeze. Yellow Springs foliage is still early full, still spotty.

2022: Robins peeping in the honeysuckles this morning. Lil's burning bush and others in town are still bold red. The backyard white mulberry has turned pale green almost overnight. The post office zelcova is almost bare, but others hold pretty well. The beech tree on Dayton Street has rusted in the past few days. Moya's tulip tree is deep red and gold. Only a few New England aster blossoms remain in the north garden. My peach tree shed most of its leaves last night. From Madison, Wisconsin, Tat reports that peak leaf color is holding.

2023: Over night: Moya's maple and the secret maple shed the rest of their leaves. Lil"s maple and my viburnum are down to maybe a fourth, the Danielsons' maple and T.K.'s maple about gone. My peach tree has been dropping deep golden leaves into the path all week. Suzie cut down her (Lil's, really) burning bush shrub last month, that landmark gone.

Spatial units are stagnant and there is no "stuff" between the units or frames. The weaving together of these frames occurs in the mind.... In quantum mechanics, "position" is like a strobe snapshot. Momentum is the life-created summation of many frames.

Robert Lanza

October 28th
The 301st Day of the Year

Once you have uncovered a portion of the year's cycle, you can see the past and tell the future. Every day becomes one day. Stasis and passage become inseparable.

bf

Sunrise/set: 6:59/5:38
Day's Length: 10 hours 39 minutes
Average High/Low: 59/39
Average Temperature: 49
Record High: 81 – 1900
Record Low: 23 – 1976

Weather

The period between October 28th and November 1st is typically the best time remaining in the year for late harvest and outdoor activities. The Sun shines more often during this period than on any time for the rest of the year. October 28th is usually the driest of all those days, with the chance of rain dropping to only 15 percent. Skies are clear to partly cloudy 75 percent of the time. Temperature distribution is almost identical to that of yesterday: 25 percent chance of 70s, fifteen percent for 60s, fifty percent for 50s, ten percent for 30s. Chances of frost fall slightly to 30 percent.

The Natural Calendar

Cabbage worms still eat the cabbages and kale, but the seasons of tomatoes, beans, eggplant, and squash are usually over as October ends. Some years, houseflies still get in the back door. The last crickets sing in the milder afternoons and nights. A few cabbage butterflies still hunt for flowers. Grasshoppers and woolly-bear caterpillars are still common. Small moths play in the woods. Asian lady beetles seek winter refuge in crevices of house siding.

Daybook

1982: Covered Bridge: Cucumber beetle sunning on the tip of an old wingstem. Two blue bellflowers cling to a dead stem. Rose foliage yellowing. Canopy about two-thirds gone, woods dry and brown.

1984: To Maryland: Most leaves gone along the Pennsylvania Turnpike, but Washington D.C. and much of southern Maryland seem near late peak of color. Sundrops, Queen Anne's lace, occasional crown vetch, daisies, a few asters, a few rape plants, two or three white moth mulleins, some helianthus still in bloom there. All goldenrod gone, but the South clearly has more leaves and later wildflowers. Buzzards seen in the mountains and near the coast.

1985: Robin migration seems to be done. Only occasional peeps heard.

1986: Geese fly over about 9:00 a.m.

1987: Geese fly over at 9:05 a.m.

1988: On the other side of leafturn and leaf fall: fragments of foliage, the patterns of the bare branches isolated without the confusion and the monotony of summer green or the dramatic power of Middle Fall's color.

1989: Geese fly over at 9:00 a.m. Christmas cactus: small buds noticed.

1990: First white mulberry leaves fell today after three frosts. Ginkgoes paling more and falling a little. Magnolias hold most leaves, yellow green. Lil's maple full.

1991: Magnolias gone, ginkgoes full gold, half to three-fourths gone.

1993: To North Carolina: East at dawn, the Sun, huge and orange through the violet cirrus on the horizon, gives a russet glow to the trees. The autumn reds shine. Through the Ohio piedmont outside of Chillicothe, fields of gray goldenrod, the hills' rust and browns of Late Fall, remaining sycamores pale green, leaves edged with decay. Smell of wood smoke here and there. Past Portsmouth along the Ohio River, some hills of oaks are gold and orange, autumn completely intact a hundred and fifty miles southeast of Yellow Springs. Sumac leaves appear on about a third of their branches, bare trees become less common.

At Charleston, West Virginia, the yellow catalpas, yellow poplars, cottonwoods, and maple oranges become more prominent, setting off and showing off the other colors. I can see that the first step to Late Fall is the disintegration of the brighter leaves.

South toward Beckley, more pines appear, tempering the losses, the blush of maroon and rich yellow ashes comes in at about 180 miles from Yellow Springs. The yellow poplars have all their leaves by now, hickories here too, the sugar gums are full again, their star-shaped leaves red orange.

At 200 miles, the red sumacs have about three fourths of their leaves. Then within just a few minutes, Late Fall returns, hills with different plantings appearing dark and past their prime, then back again to Middle Fall for an hour or two. Then approaching North Carolina, I come into early Middle Fall, with far more green trees, and many of the cottonwoods and poplars still strong, no hint of the fragile status of the season two hundred miles north.

A few clumps of violet asters grew from the cliffs in central West Virginia. Thirty miles north of Beckley, one primrose stood by itself in a narrow segment of soil between the two sides of the freeway. Milkweed pods were open and disheveled all the way from Yellow Springs to Winston-Salem. Once in a while, a goldenrod plant had its September Ohio color.

I called home and talked with Jeanie tonight. She said Uncle Bill had just phoned from northern Minnesota in the middle of the first heavy snowstorm of the season.

1994: At South Glen, nothing in bloom except new, blue tall bellflowers growing in the axils of their long, tattered stems.

1998: Now deterioration speeds up, the fullness of a week ago suddenly collapses in the morning rain. The unity and the cohesiveness of the summer and Middle Fall disappear.

1999: To Xenia: Sweet gum trees red, the silver maples turning palomino-champagne gold, ginkgoes olive green, oaks brown and red and rust. This is the last phase of the peak.

2001: Cardinal sang at 6:45 this morning. Small flock of goldfinches with gray winter breasts seen in the redbud tree this afternoon.

2002: Flock of blackbirds flew over at 8:23 a.m. One jade tree budded in the greenhouse. To Wilmington: the cottonwoods are down, but many maples and oaks keep their full middle autumn color. One golden birch almost bare. Woolly-bear caterpillars are common on the road again.

2003: Lil's maple half gone, the Danielson's all down except for a few hundred leaves.

2004: Lil's maple is half gone. Mrs. Timberlake's is maybe three-fourths fallen. In the yard and out at Duckwall's at the edge of the Glen, robins are chirping and calling, moving south. The Danielsons' tree is down. No woolly-bear caterpillars seen through the entire autumn.

2005: One purple clematis flower opened yesterday or today in the sun. One yellow rose cut for the kitchen table. Pink roses continue to bloom in the northwest garden. The secret maple is suddenly full gold. Danielsons' maple full, Lil's only about a third turned. The leaves remain mostly green on the Korean lilac. A freeze last night killed most of the elephant ears, impatiens and zinnias. Much of the basil survived.

At South Glen, a few scattered aster flowers remain, but little else. The foliage of the wood nettle is shriveled. On our walk this morning, robin clucking in the distance. The spent goldenrod, wingstem, ironweed, and one blooming parsnip were white with the frost. The puffy white seed heads of the sow thistles had disappeared in the rain of a few days ago. Most of the leaves were down along the river.

The sycamores seemed to be the hardiest. Tonight at 7:45, Mars, as large and bright as it will ever be this century, was rising over the village; Venus was huge in the southwest. As I type this, a small mosquito hovers around the computer screen, maybe came in with some of the Christmas cacti I brought into the greenhouse yesterday.

And Cathy sent the following from Vermont: "I can't imagine how we are going to get through the winter here. That doesn't stop the cold weather from advancing on us. The leaves here never turned, not in the normal sense. There are still green leaves and not a lot of bare trees. Some turned a bland yellow beige and dropped off. No reds, oranges. This week we had a snowstorm and were without power, and heat, and many trees and bushes down on our property, and all around. The snow too heavy for the trees with leaves still on. We lost big pieces of a giant willow, and old lilacs, and a mountain ash. All those ancient trees and shrubs. Sad."

2007: First light frost of the fall this morning, but it caused very little damage. In the alley, one robin, starlings chirping.

2008: First heavy northeaster blankets New York and surrounding states with snow. Ruby Nicholson sent me a note: "A kettle of buzzards (28 of them in all) were in a tree at Bryan Park today. Two other trees nearby were equally as well populated with them. They were still flying in at 4:10 p.m."

2010: The witch hazel leaves have turned brown and are withering, but the flowers stay yellow and soft. Sweet gums half down along Dayton Street.

2011: The heaviest frost so far in the fall this morning, but the elephant ears and the zinnias still survived. The cold has silenced the crickets, and an unusual winter storm is poised to cover the East Coast with snow. Robins calling the yard, birds feeding heavily at the feeders, including the first tufted titmouse in weeks. The Zelcova trees are full red-rust-maroon, the sweet gums and the secret maple are shedding, Lil's maple, Mrs. Timberlake's maple and all the town ginkgoes are golden, silver maples are palomino gold (as is so much of the tree line - except the deeper and brighter shades of the oaks and sugar maples fully turned. A flock of starlings seen yesterday, a large flock of blackbirds or grackles today.

2012: Three voles caught in the space of a few hours this evening. They had been squeaking in one of the greenhouse cabinets for several days, were making Neysa a little nervous.

2013: Mrs. Timberlake's maple has turned full gold overnight. The north hackberry holds its leaves; the south hackberry has lost more than half.

2014: A cardinal sang twice at 6:51 this morning. The first and maybe the only one before sunrise. A large flock of blackbirds and starlings flying southeast over the highway when I was driving back from the doctor's. Mateo's red mulberry trees, ochre, are down to maybe a third of their leaves. A vole seen scurrying across the greenhouse floor yesterday. Looking back over my notes, I see that this year's leafturn has been considerably earlier.

2016: At the mill with Emily, 10:15 a.m., sun, mild: We parked at the old mill and walked up river for a ways looking for the robin flocks I used to see years ago. This morning, only an occasional robin peep, a chickadee, nuthatch, downy woodpecker. A few violet arrowhead aster bushes in bloom. The high canopy was almost gone, but the lower trees and the undergrowth were still mostly green. Downtown, the Zelcovas have started to turn at the top, and the Kentucky coffee tree is more than half down. In this afternoon's sun, a few small bumblebees and one bright yellow sulphur visited the zinnias. Before supper, I transplanted the large hydrangea from the south border to near the dooryard garden.

2017: Portland, Oregon: Jill sent photos from the first snow of the year on High Street. She says the day is so raw and gray and cold. On the national news yesterday, coverage of a blizzard in northern Minnesota. Here at Jeni's, two roses are in bloom, just like the rose bush I left in Yellow Springs on the 26th.

2018: In a day, the trees of High Street left summer. Even Lil's tree was transformed, with Mrs. Timberlake's keeping pace. The secret maple and all of the Champney's maples are lush with dense gold. Moya's maple, so green two days ago is changing. A drive through the village and the township showed full peak leafturn everywhere.

Honeysuckle leaves clutter the front sidewalk, make it slippery in the rain.

2020: Hurricane Zeta moves across the Gulf toward New Orleans. Here, the day is gray and soft, peak color departing as more sugar maples come down. Jill's small red mulberry is luminescent gold by her driveway, Frank's mulberry glows gold below his thinning silver maple. All the Champneys' maples are down. Lil's maple and Mrs. Timberlake's maple are both peaking, Lil's burning bush finally fully turned scarlet. Robins peeping in the honeysuckles. At a small park along the bike way, decorative pear trees are deep red-purple.

2022: Pause in rapid leaf drop, brief plateau. Casey called to tell me he'd seen a number of bluebirds at his feeders, but the starlings seemed to be scaring them away.

2023: High Street has turned completely now, the best trees gone, the rest all gold and mottled. The honeysuckle leaves, pale and soft, cover the sidewalk in front of the house. The tulip tree at Moya's yard is full of different shades of orange and yellow and brown, and the mood all up and down the block is one of the final days of Middle Autumn.

The weather of a district is undoubtedly part of its natural history.

Gilbert White

October 29th
The 302nd Day of the Year

Go where he will, the wise man is at home,
His hearth the earth, -- his hall the azure dome;
Where his clear spirit leads him, there's his road,
By God's own light illumined and foreshowed.

Ralph Waldo Emerson

Sunrise/set: 7:00/5:37
Day's Length: 10 hours 37 minutes
Average High/Low: 58/39
Average Temperature: 49
Record High: 82 – 1900
Record Low: 21 – 1925

Weather

The likelihood for sun rises to 85 percent today, and rain comes only two or three times in a decade. Frost occurs 60 percent of the mornings. Highs in the 70s occur 15 percent of the afternoons; 60s forty percent of the time, 50s thirty percent, 40s fifteen percent.

The Natural Calendar

The hay harvest and potato digging are complete today in typical years, and the cutting of corn and soybeans is winding down. Over half of the sugar beet crop has ordinarily been taken up. Farmers are shelling corn, stripping tobacco, chiseling ground. People with septic systems check their septic tanks before the ground freezes.

Daybook

1983: Mill Habitat: A few white and violet asters, some red clover, Queen Anne's lace, chicory. A little new wild lettuce foliage. Chestnut oak gone in some places, holding half in others. Buzzards still circling. Dogwoods mostly gone. The hickories and the tall canopy mostly bare. Honeysuckle still bright green, berries red in groups of four. In the woods across the hills everything is brown.

Chipmunks seen and heard. In the village, where maples dominate, it is still the last phase of peak leaf color.

1985: Cherry tree and the pecan still hold all their leaves. Peach leaves gone. Some ginkgoes a third to three-fourths gone, others holding.

1986: Front maples mostly gone. Some magnolias almost bare. Buzzards circling Grinnell. Across the fields, the tree line is empty, except for the oaks.

1989: A week in the 70s is ending, rivers low, grasses dry, harvest well underway. Most of the leaves are gone (but Lil's holds at half). Goldenrod all tufted and gray. An occasional bright maple in the fields stands out against the dull seeds and stalks. Some Osage have lost their leaves, and their green fruits still hang on the lanky branches. Then on other Osage trees, the fruits have fallen and the leaves have stayed.

1991: Brown finch at the feeder.

1995: Robins passing through the yard today, eating honeysuckle berries in the north hedge. At noon, a late monarch butterfly visited the south garden, heading south. A yellow-bellied woodpecker, chattering like a squirrel, worked at the back locust. Woolly-bear caterpillars were still crossing the highways in the cold sun through the middle of the afternoon. On the way to the triangle park, I saw the witch hazels were in full bloom, leaves down, and the redbud tree was bare.

More growth at the tips of the spruce at the park. The red maple there turned pale gold this past week, is losing leaves rapidly now. All the silver maples are shifting from pale green to a rich palomino tan. Most crab apples have lost their leaves, berries bright and fat. On High Street, the Danielson's maple is through; ours is deep orange, brittle, will be gone in a day or two. Lil's is half yellow and losing leaves. The red mulberries along the south hedge still hold on.

1997: A long flock of blackbirds flew over Beavercreek when I was there this morning. Starlings filled the telephone lines in Xenia. Hundreds of yellow cabbage butterflies swarmed along Wilberforce-Clifton road as I drove by this afternoon.

1998: Fish lie quietly in the pond now, respond only sluggishly to food. Lil's tree suddenly starts to turn. The hostas are yellow green along the edges of their leaves. At Jacoby, a flock of robins. The canopy gone. Twenty-three white puffball mushrooms found on a green hillside in the middle of this sunny afternoon.

1999: To Caesar Creek, high of 75 degrees, sun and wispy cirrus. Fishing up river, explored several new places, but caught no fish. Then back to the hole where John and I caught bluegills this summer. The fish were still there and biting on wax worms. I must have caught thirty or so, kept twenty for eating. The landscape all around was bright and full of color. Even though more than half the leaves were down, the late maples and oaks were coming in together, more dramatic than the early color this year, more intense. Now the ginkgoes are turning all shades from deep gold to pale yellow-green. At the lake, only a few small-flowered asters seen, one goldenrod.

2001: At the Mill: Red smartweed, one periwinkle, a few white and violet asters. In the yard, asters gone, redbud and all the maples bare (including Lil's across the street). Only the Osage remain. Beech half turned on Dayton Street. Burning bush foliage more than half fallen.

On the way to Columbus: one late monarch seen crossing the freeway heading south. Across the countryside, entire sections of the tree line are gray. Five deer killed in 50 miles of highway: rutting season. At school, my red maple is finally gone, and most of my grape vine leaves. The white oak is still stable. In Columbus and at Antioch, the sycamores are thinned but not empty; in the woods along the river, all their leaves have come down. Yellow poplars have shed at Duckwall's.

2002: This morning at four o'clock, a wonderful wind, the bamboo singing against the windows, the red mulberry trees rustling and waving. A crack and thud as a branch somewhere broke in a gust.

The woodpile's tarp was blown toward the south, exposing the logs. The Halloween cold front was on schedule, exciting after so long an autumn without change, so late and mild and dry. The sky was pale from the clouds, then an opening, the third-quarter moon overhead and Orion standing in the southwest, betraying the coming of November. I felt an urgency to get on with winter.

2003: A long flock of blackbirds flew over the neighborhood at 7:05 a.m., continued until 7:10. Jeanie mentioned that she saw two trees full of turkey vultures near the riding center about 7:45 this morning.

2004: In the soft early morning, green tree frogs were calling like muted screech owls as I went jogging. Mrs. Timberlake's maple is shedding hard, still holds maybe a fourth of its leaves. Lil's maple is still deep gold but continues to shed, too. The magnolia next to the Timberlake's is also gold and coming down. The quince at the southwest side of the house is deep gold like the magnolia. In the east garden, the early stonecrop foliage has yellowed. The late stonecrop is still deep green. At the end of the day, Lil's tree is down to just about a tenth of its leaves. Mrs. Timberlake's is gone. Jerry and Lee's sweet gum is half yellow. All the trees of heaven have lost their leaves.

2005: As I sat outside in the sun on the back porch talking to Tat, I watched Asian lady beetles flying by looking for winter quarters.

2007: The second frost of the year came last night, burning all the dahlias. Grackles visited the bird feeder this morning for the first time since summer. The plum tree at Antioch School is maroon-purple, has most of its leaves.

2008: In the clear sky before dawn, Orion is overhead. Morning frosts continue and cool afternoons. Only one apple left on the alley apple tree. Starlings fluttering through the downtown pear trees this morning.

2011: Another freeze last night, the hardest so far of the season, finally took the zinnias, dahlias and elephant ears. Crows at 6:55

a.m. . Major snowfall along the East Coast today with accumulations the heaviest since records began.

2012: Hurricane Sandy is coming ashore just below New York City this morning, its winds and rain reaching all across the Middle Atlantic states to Yellow Springs. Lil's maple is all but maybe ten percent down, scraggly lower foliage. Along Xenia Avenue, most of the ginkgoes are more than half down, one of them completely bare. In the greenhouse, two Christmas cacti are reaching full bloom, and most of the others are getting large buds. And I noticed sparrows again on the front porch, pecking at the spaces between the bricks. They have just started doing that over the past week or so. Will they stop in the spring? I've never noticed!

2013: Successive mornings of frost have withered the Endless Summer hydrangeas, the knotweed, the paulownia and the tree of heaven. Rose blossoms resist the cold, but the bushes produce few buds now. One cabbage butterfly near the pond; one yellow sulphur flying across the cutover soybean field at Ellis.

2014: Many ginkgoes full and shedding, several bare. Sparrows have been picking between the bricks of the front porch. Zinnias and dahlias gathered: frost coming tomorrow night. Primroses transplanted in the north garden. Maybe half of the hosta leaves have turned gold like the maples that are left.

2015: When I was planting daffodils in the circle garden this afternoon, a green frog hopped away. I captured him and set him down in the pond. So far this is the latest amphibian sighting I've made. In the east garden, I cut away hostas that had been weakened by frost. This evening, on the way back from shopping, I saw a vast murmuration of starlings swooping and diving across a cornfield.

2017: Riding through suburban Portland, I saw that all of the ginkgoes were full deep gold, well ahead of the ginkgoes of Yellow Springs.

2020: Middle Fall under attack in a chilly all-day rain. Precipitous drop and then rise in the barometer as the moon waxes, two days from full. Hurricane Zeta came ashore in the night, moving rapidly into the Southeast. Today's high temperatures was only in the high 40s. Earthquakes of 7.0 in the Aegean Sea shake Turkey and Greece, about the same time of year as in Italy in 2016. New moon time that year, full moon time this year.

2021: Like last year on this date, a chilly, all-day rain, and the barometer is at its lowest so far this autumn, 29.40. The foliage is approaching full color throughout the countryide, even though certain blocks in town are still pretty green.

2023: Chilly and rainy. In the netting I had placed over the pond, I saw a small frog caught and being attacked by the koi. In the afternoon, I dug in four dozen daffodil bulbs, robins peeping all around the neighborhood. When I went out to the shed after dark, tree crickets were calling softly.

Whenever we look in the world of matter and events outside ourselves we find that oscillations and wave motions have a significant, often dominant role. It is not, therefore, astonishing to find that waves play an important part in ourselves also.

Archibald Hill

October 30th
The 303rd Day of the Year

The strong, somber colors of the fading leaves, much greenness still, the straight trunks the trees emerging, the skeleton of the woods now revealed.

Harlan Hubbard

Sunrise/set: 7:01/5:36
Day's Length: 10 hours 35 minutes
Average High/Low: 58/39
Average Temperature: 49
Record High: 81 – 1927
Record Low: 18 – 1895

Weather

Chances of a day above 70 degrees double over those of yesterday to a full 30 percent. Sixties can be expected on another 30 percent of the afternoons, 50s on another 30 percent; ten percent chance of 40s. Half the mornings bring frost, and skies are clear to partly cloudy 80 percent of the time; rain occurs on just 20 percent of the days. Between today and April 14th, there is a possibility of a low temperature below 20 degrees.

The Natural Calendar

Along the 40th Parallel, the best of the leaf color has often disappeared from the canopy. As the land drops down toward the coastal plain, however, the high trees begin to fill again with green and gold. Sweet gums and hickories and sycamores return the landscape to early Middle Fall near Colombia, South Carolina. In the Low Country below Charleston and all the way to Florida, Early Fall and Late Summer still hold for a few more weeks.

Daybook

1982: Robins still here. Most peach leaves gone. One dandelion found blooming today. Forsythia is burned red from frost. Celandine and chicory foliage is strong. Mountain maple at Antioch holds its leaves, turning orange. Mums still full bloom.

1983: Starlings in the back yard. Out along Clifton Road, some of the lower leaves still show color, but the background consists of brown branches instead of foliage. Watercress is reviving for Late Fall at Jacoby.

1984: One monarch butterfly seen today, and a couple woolly bears.

1985: My mother sent me a George Cooper poem from my childhood, mourning for the falling leaves:

"Come little leaves," said the wind one day,
"Come o'er the meadows with me and play;
Put on your dresses of red and gold,
For summer is gone and the days grow cold."

Soon as the leaves heard the wind's loud call,
down they came fluttering, one and all;
Over the brown fields they danced and flew,
Singing the glad little songs they knew.

"Cricket, good-bye, we've been friends so long,
Little brook, sing us your farewell song;
Say you are sorry to see us go;
Ah, you will miss us, right well we know.

"Dear little lambs in your fleecy fold,
Mother will keep you from harm and cold;
Fondly we watched you in vale and glade,
Say will you dream of your loving shade?"

Dancing and whirling the little leaves went,
Winter had called them, and they were content;
Soon fast asleep in their earthy beds,
The snow laid a coverlet over their heads.

1987: Sweet gum leaves finally down at Wilberforce, but some still full and red twenty miles away in Byron. Star magnolias about gone by my door.

1988: Two nights near 20 degrees brought down the Osage and white mulberry leaves all at once.

1993: Returning from North Carolina in the rain, the season having changed in a day. When I got to Greensboro on the 28th, the sky was clear and the temperature in the 60s. The next morning, the first Carolina frost (according to the motel clerk) covered my car windows. Now I drive north through the mountains, through fog and low clouds. The hills have lost all their color in the gloom. In Ohio, the first snow of the year is falling, accumulating up to four inches deep by the roadside, sticking on the newly plowed fields. This was Uncle Bill's storm in northern Minnesota just yesterday.

Arriving back home, I've gone from the middle of October into the middle of November. Home in the greenhouse, two Christmas cacti have their first buds. At South Glen, late afternoon, wet snow falling into the dark river, honeysuckles still green, bending under the weight of the snow, the paths slippery, no bird song, the road past the Covered Bridge quiet. By the riverbank, the sound of the snow dropping from branches, plopping into the water.

1997: Brown Asian ladybugs swarm on every building at Wilberforce, all over the southeast wall of Wesley, and at the dorms and at the library. At home in the pond, the fish do not come up to eat the food I throw out to them.

1999: No Asian ladybugs at all this year. Was it the drought? Were they delayed or destroyed by the Late Summer's lack of rain?

2000: On the lawn at school in Springfield, a bright yellow sulphur butterfly flew around and about, finding dandelions blooming here and there, sharing them with bees.

2001: Starlings in the back trees cackling, crows in the distance at 7:30 this morning. Tonight, occasional trill of a cricket, temperature at 40 degrees.

2002: In spite of yesterday's storm, the full late Middle Fall color holds. There are more bare trees, but not a significant deterioration of the tree line. Some New England asters are still blooming along the highway. This afternoon, Mrs. Lawson's maple began to come apart, but the Danielsons' maple is still full gold, and Lil's is just beginning.

2003: Robins clucking in the honeysuckles at 7:30 this morning, grackles chattering throughout the neighborhood. Lil's tree half shed, bright gold in the sunlight. Three woolly-bear caterpillars on the road to Wilmington.

2004: A warm, hard wind all day, temperature reaching into the upper 70s. Lil's tree is down, and the Korean lilac. The magnolia is shedding quickly. Maple leaves pile up against the forsythia, pushed there by the wind. Lilies planted along the northeast garden.

2005: Cathy continues our conversation from Vermont: "I want you to understand that this leaf thing here is no just a mild complaint about off-ish color. It's a sci-fi-weird phenomenon. Even old native Vermonters say they've never seen anything like it. It's a green fall. There were so many green leaves on the trees in this snowstorm this week that the power company said they had over 100 trees-on-lines just in our little area. But if you saw it, you see why it happened -- branches of green leaves loaded with wet snow, bent to the ground or broken. We never have green leaves the beginning of November. The oaks are usually getting brown now and I saw one this week still all green. We haven't had a bad frost yet. A friend told me tonight that her eggplant was blooming again. The nurseries we sell ads to are complaining that people aren't buying mums because there is so much still blooming in the garden. The field and yard grass are bright emerald green and growing like crazy. The recent fall has been everyday wet. Rain and fog. Just beautiful to see. But lots of floods and septic problems (including ours). Earlier in the fall we had 90- degree weather in September."

2006: The russets and browns of the oaks now dominate the landscape up through northern Indiana, the maples having disappeared from the woodlots. In villages and urban areas, almost all of the silver maples and many sugar maples hold, as they still do a little in Yellow Springs. But Lil's maple has started shedding, the

Danielsons' maple is bare, and Mrs. Timberlake's maple is bright yellow and coming down. Certainly leafdrop is way on the other side of peak throughout the lower Midwest. Bittersweet has opened at the corner of High and Limestone Streets, and in the alley robin calls are loud as migration intensifies. Small flocks of sparrows move through the honeysuckles. Trumpet vine leaves are suddenly down, Korean lilac and the red viburnum three-fourths bare. Two Shasta daisies in bloom. Blue privet berries are showing more and more now. One forsythia branch winding through one of the fences has yellow flowers, and three blossoms remain on the tall coneflowers. The blue bindweeds, however, have disappeared, and the small white asters have ended their season. One goldenrod, broken off early in the fall, is blooming now, but the chicory has closed for the year, and the Jerusalem artichoke plants are withering. Don's burning bush is still bright, but Lil's has lost most of its foliage. Not a single Asian lady beetle seen this year. In the yard, three pink rose buds remain, two Shasta daisies. Louis the cat caught a vole in the greenhouse last night.

This afternoon, Jeanie and I planted daffodils, tulips, anemones, and allium. The sun was shining, and the high reached near 70 degrees for the first time in what seemed like weeks.

2008: The hardest freeze of the season this morning, the elephant ears finally burned badly. In the alley, the one apple still held to its branch. Burl's maple is yellow, Don's is almost gone, Lil's is pale gold, the Danielsons' sheds orange, Mrs. Timberlake's beginning. The big ginkgo on Xenia Avenue is just starting to yellow. Along the road to Wilmington, many of the woodlots are almost bare. Maples are still bright in town. At the junction of Highway 35, the high wires were filled with starlings. At around four o'clock this evening a skunk in the yard sprayed Bella.

2009: Last blackbirds in Goshen, reported by Judy.

2010: Standing at the end of October, I hold fast to remnants and to positions, the frames and the emotions that stick to them, feelings that reflect the things I see, spun from the tilting of the Earth toward solstice.

From the alley: the last two apples still hanging from apple tree, the wilting of the final purple fall crocus, the blackening of the tall goldenrod behind Mateos's house. In the field by the Antioch School: a handful of milkweed plants, pods splayed, silky seeds shining in the low sun. In South Glen: the path suddenly becoming clear as the wood nettle leaves come down.

In the yard: the blushing of the oak leaf hydrangea, the withering of Japanese knotweed leaves, yellowing of the Jerusalem artichoke leaves, the hosta leaves and the wild asparagus stalks, the blackening of the dahlia stems and the impatiens burned by frost, the resilience of the last maroon viburnum, two autumn violets hidden among the sweet Williams, the stubborn last pink roses and golden coneflowers, the steady feeding of chickadees, titmice, nuthatches, sparrows, cardinals, finches. The very last raspberry is ripening. One of Jeanie's clematis vines on the trellis has a single purple blossom, and an orb-weaver spider still waits in his web on the screen of the southeast bedroom window.

Down High Street: a disheveled magnolia, a gilded ginkgo, the emptiness of the Danielsons' maple tree and Mrs. Timberlake's maple tree, the scarlet of Lil's burning bush, black privet berries appearing as their foliage thins, the changes gathering momentum piece by piece, the ground covered by leaves from the corner sugar maples, grass by the pavement still glowing in the low October sun, crab apples firm and fat, soft honeysuckle berries all along the street. And a great flock of robins, starlings and grackles traveling with them, circling and pausing and flying on from the northeast over the bare locusts and hackberries, chirping and chortling for hours in the morning.

2011: Crows at 6:55 a.m. in the crisp morning, and the peeping, chortling and even spring-like singsong from robins all around in the honeysuckles. One very substantial camelback cricket in the bathtub this morning when I went in to take a shower. New York digging out from under record snowfall (Denver having received its own blizzard a few days ago).

2012: Hurricane Sandy moves north through Pennsylvania, devastating much of the Northeastern shore. Light snow here in Yellow Springs, but the East is flooded and without power in many areas. In our back yard, the white mulberry leaves came down heavily through the night, maybe a third to a half left on the tree. I found two more rust-brown woolly-bear caterpillars in the woodpile this evening.

2013: Soft, misty morning, starlings whistling, robins peeping their migration calls. Lil's maple is turning now, lightly bronzed. Leaf-fall accelerating, some yards covered. At Ellis Pond with Bella: The sugar maple grove was gold and orange, starting to shed. Along Fairfield Road, hickories deep ochre. Anne's burning bush is bright red, her bush daisies finished for the year, her birch yellow and thinning. T.K.'s fledgling maple matches Mrs. Timberlake's ancient maple, full butter yellow. The ginkgoes on Xenia Avenue are becoming pale. In the greenhouse, the Christmas cacti that were put outside during the summer are in full bloom.

2014: Large flock of starlings across Dayton Street near Alice's house, filling the trees, coming and going. At Bob's Halloween get-together, Casey and Bob both talked about being overrun by Asian lady beetles this October. I saw only one in town.

2016: Breezy and mild then cooling: Lil's maple turned overnight, Mrs.Timberlake's not far behind. The neighborhood burning bushes deep red. The secret maple, all grown up, shines orange-gold through the lot behind my property. At Ellis Pond, the maple grove holds, but the cypress trees have started to rust. All around town, the color seems to be peaking. From Italy, Neysa calls to tell about the earthquakes that are occurring all around her.

2017: Hurricane Jose disrupts the East this morning, but with none of the major damage of Sandy five years ago.

2018: A soft and sunny day. I walk surrounded by the summer that has collapsed from frost, scattering so much new color and new angles and shapes. At the shop, the Kentucky coffee trees are pale yellow and half shed; the Zelcovas are well rusted, but not fully turned. At Ellis Pond, the ash and the sugar maple groves have thinned. The oaks and sycamores are still rusty green, silver maples summer gray-green. As we left, we saw a great flock of starlings swooping over the north field, the branches of several trees black with birds.

2020: Another day in the 40s, but at least with some sun. Hurricane Zeta moves across the Southeast into the Georgia mountains. Winter Storm Billy blankets the central states. Here, Middle Fall becomes tattered, remaining leaves sometimes seeming like flowers. The ginkgo trees along Xenia Avenue have been shedding for days. One burning bush on High Street is losing leaves. At Ellis Pond, the largest gathering of geese yet: about 150 all on the water this afternoon.

2022: Mild, cloudy, rain, robins peeping, blue jay calling, Lil's tree two-thirds gone, all the asters finally to seed, more quince leaves fallen to the pond, solid gold. The large hostas have collapsed now, disintegrating from age, still mostly caramel colored. My north viburnum has lost almost all its foliage. The view from my north window shows the mottled green and rust and pale yellow of the hedge that hides Moya's house (now Basim's house).

2023: Full moon time. The last peach leaves fall today, the last maroon viburnum hold on. Lil's tree is down to maybe a tenth of its leaves. The weather is cold, and everything is coming apart.

Notebook

I find it impossible to keep track of all the losses in the trees I see now, to pay attetntion which tree where falls when and how. I rely on my old journals, paying attention to Lil's maple and the Danielsons' maple and Mrs. Timberlake's, Moya's and T.K.'s maples.\

I collect the notes within the parentheses of October and November. My pretense is to use them to make time real, to make the autumn actually appear salvageable, virtually permanent because it happens to specific trees, not just to trees in general.

Trees in specificity are almost like agents whom I accompany when I watch them or stand next to them and call them by name, the trees that have been recognized decade after decade as though the dates of their turning and full color and collapse had some ulterior meaning, were a measure or affect of their personalities.

Too, I connect them to parallel events that complement and fulfill the dramatic end of the world's year in this place, counting absences, listing memories, making inventories of goldenrods and asters and bittersweet berries and on and on.

There is no amount of enumeration that suffices. Every day, I pass by so much; I cannot pause to look at every particle, nor understand how one blends into another and is related to another and is reminiscent of another and depends on another and is prophetic of another, no matter how much minding and repeating and retelling and reminiscing I do.

It is the very kernel of the universe that absence and presence are complementary, that they are two aspects of the same thing. Death or ending is the mirror of life or beginning. Each dimension is the key to other, and I cannot understand them if I view them as separate or out of balance. Through the awareness of sensations lost, absences flesh out past events and fill up the present's hollow and deceptive pod, create wholeness from the part that seems so transitory or so broken, but is only incomplete.

Leon Quel

October 31st
The 304th Day of the Year

When the Pleiades are strong, then remember to plough in season:
and so the completed year will fitly pass beneath the earth.

Hesiod

Sunrise/set: 7:03/5:34
Day's Length: 10 hours 31 minutes
Average High/Low: 58/39
Average Temperature: 49
Record High: 80 – 1950
Record Low: 20 – 1909

Weather

The 31st is typically a pleasant day, with temperatures in the 70s thirty-five percent of the time, highs in the 60s another 35 percent, 50s coming 20 percent, 40s ten percent. Rain or snow falls one year in four. Skies are mostly sunny 80 percent of the days, and frost occurs on only 25 percent of the mornings.

The Natural Calendar

Sometimes the maple and white mulberry leaves that survived October drop all at once. The ginkgoes too may shatter overnight into a shining circle below their limbs. Willows, though, are only half turned. Bradford pears are still green, prolonging an illusion of September. Silver maples can be untouched by the radical shift in the season, holding until the nights go into the teens. Dogwoods will be pink, magnolias gold, oaks red-orange for a few days longer. Beneath them, privet and spicebush will remain strong throughout November. Above them in the night, the Pleiades are rising, just like they did at the time of Hesiod almost three millennia ago.

Daybook

1982: Some new ragweed has grown three feet tall. Some goldenrod is still golden along High and King Streets, still a few asters, some chicory blooming. Willows hold on, grape leaves red and purple at the end of their color peak.

1983: One red quince has flowered at the northeast corner of the yard; the foliage around it: shades of mustard, forest green, blood red, specks of black. Rose of Sharon graying, thinning, oaks full color, rust and burnt sienna, white mulberry still untouched, mock orange still green, Chinese maple deep scarlet, holding all its leaves, apple, locust, peach gradually disappearing. Magnolia on Dayton Street almost bare.

1984: Full second-spring parsnip blossoming. Queen Anne's lace seems to be getting stronger in places. Chicory continues. Clovers, sow thistles common. Many forsythia bushes flowering, jimson weed and burdock blooming in a late pasture, hemlock and sweet rocket growing back by the Covered Bridge. White mulberry starts to turn. At Brush Row, two ginkgoes have lost all their leaves, a third is mostly green. All peach and cherry foliage gone.

1986: A cardinal sang at 7:51 a.m. Lil's leaves half down. Buzzards still circling. A few crickets at night. At Sycamore Hole, chubs bite fiercely. Right after the peak leaf drop, there is another phase for the later maples, sugar gum, and oaks; that period seems more durable, maybe because I expect the last leaves to fall at any minute – they persist another week or two.

1987: Robins peeping in the yard this afternoon.

1991: Cardinal at 6:55 a.m. Lil's tree gone. Bradford pear leaves falling, maybe a fourth down. Christmas cactus blooms, earliest ever.

1992: Most red mulberry leaves, twisted, dark gray, have fallen in the last couple of days with rain and temperatures in the 40s. The southern boundary to the yard is open. Quince at the southeast corner of the house is thinning, leaves a yellow dun. Magnolias are finally bare at Wilberforce.

1993: Gray and cold, the ground mottled with snow, the chilliest Halloween since we've been in Ohio.

1999: In this most golden of late middle autumns, the poplars and birches are turning a rich ochre, and the late maples hold. The beech is coming in with the ginkgoes now, and the Bradford pears are tinged with red.

2000: Some red oak down, a third of the English oak, a third of the ginkgoes at school.

2001: On the way to Columbus, I watch the mottled landscape of Late Fall. Now, like at the end of September when leafturn is just starting, the exceptions become the focus. In Early Fall, it is the Judas maples that stand out. At the end of October, it is the occasional tree that holds its leaves. As I drive towards Washington Courthouse late in the afternoon, the grass and winter wheat shine in the low sun, glow against the dark tree line.

2003: A flock of robins loud along the river in South Glen this morning. Crows chasing turkey vultures above me. One cabbage butterfly seen in the garden this afternoon.

2005: Plenty of clucking from robins and starlings in the mornings, crows pass by east of town. Lil's maple and the secret maple are full gold, Danielsons' full and falling. Tree of heaven branches were hurt by the recent frosts, are drooping, ready to fall. Throughout the countryside, middle autumn persists. Along north garden and in the woods, euonymus berries are white. In the alley, dogwood berries are white. Climbing bittersweet is open at the Antioch School; Jeanie brought some home for our front door wreath yesterday. More Asian lady beetles seen today. Talked to Mateo, just returned from Tuscany: The vines are turning, he said.

2007: Peak color continues throughout the countryside. In town, many maples are shedding (the alley maple is almost all gone), but the Secret Maple and Moya's maple hold with at least half their foliage. Lil's maple is just becoming tinted with rust, the Danielsons' maple is reaching full color, while Mrs. Timberlake's is still August green. Many ashes continue to be strong maroon and gold. On the way to Beavercreek, I saw a huge flock of blackbirds feeding in the soybean fields. Large flocks of starlings and blackbirds throughout my drive.

2008: The last apple fell from the alley tree last night. Robins were chirping and twittering in the neighborhood when I walked Bella about 8:30 this morning. In the yard, I noticed that our box elder leaves came down all at once, probably from the frost two nights ago. The Korean lilac foliage dropped too last night. Hackberry leaves are about two-thirds gone. Burl's maple is more than half gone. The star magnolia across the street is yellowing. Danielsons' tree is half down, Lil's full gold, Mrs. Timberlake's full yellow.

2009: Beaufort, South Carolina to Fancy Gap, Virginia: Only a little turning in Beaufort, then gradually the sweet gums show more red up the coast, then color appears in the hickories and sycamores but still very minor until Charleston. Full color in the landscape from Columbia to a little north of Charlotte. North of Statesville, suddenly entry into the last week of Middle Fall, then in Virginia and Fancy Gap, no leaves at all when we climb 2,500 feet, and we have traveled into November and full Late Fall.

2010: Crows heard at 6:47 a.m. Frost for the second day in a row, then cumulus then stratus clouds. A camel cricket has taken up residence underneath the legs of the wood stove, came out last night after supper and again this morning as I was doing katas. Lil's maple holds full gold as the Mrs. Timberlake's comes down quickly. Rachel's ginkgo has turned, as has the Hermon Street ginkgo. The Dayton Street beech has blotches of orange. At the Mill Dam walk, I found robins moving through the honeysuckles, some zooming across the river, appearing in full migration. Above the empty canopy, a small flock of buzzards circled. High wispy cirrus, but no rain in the forecast. Judy called from Goshen this evening, said her back yard had been full of robins earlier in the week, and today she thought she heard red-winged blackbirds calling. No crickets in the cold tonight.

2011: Distant crows and the migratory chirping and peeping of robins in the pre-dawn morning. Three frosts have ended the season of annuals. The last two days spent pulling zinnias, digging beds for daffodils and tulips, removing dahlia and elephant ear bulbs.

2012: To the Sanctuary Reserve with Jeff: Robins migrating through the wetlands.

2013: Storm moving up from Texas, hard winds for tonight. This morning, I walked Bella before dawn, just enough light to see that Lil's maple was full gold, had turned color completely in the past twenty-four hours. On the way to Wilmington, it seemed the maples had followed Lil's, the remaining trees deep and glowing, countering the trees that were bare.

2014: The gingko at the corner of Herman Street and Xenia Avenue has lost most of its leaves, a great skirt around its trunk. At Ellis, the oaks are red and brown and thinning. Throughout the town and countryside, the peak is well past, many more bare trees than trees with foliage.

2015: At Ellis Pond, no geese today. The cypress trees are fully rusty orange now, and the tulip trees are almost bare. The oak grove is still dark brown.

2016: Moya's maple and the Danielsons' are about gone, but the rest of High Street is deep and fragile, following the lead of the Secret Maple behind Gerard's property, gilding the sky behind it. Jeanie's river birch delicate leaves mottled, shedding, Robins peeping along Limestone Street at sunrise, crows off toward Xenia Avenue.

2018: Hostas yellowing. Moya's maple and the Danielsons' maple and the rest of the leaves mentioned in 2016 are the same as they were two years ago. Two small blossoms on the north-side viburnum. The violet autumn crocus are still open, tall and lanky. The whites have fallen over. A cardinal sang at about 8:00, as he has for the past several days. Wind and storms moving in, leaves coming undone.

2019: The first snow of the year today with wind gusts above 30 miles an hour. The month ended several degrees above normal (the seventh year in a row above average), with slightly higher precipitation.

2020: Sun and brisk, but one violet autumn crocus pushed up and flowered in the coldest night so far this fall. Walking through the southeast corner of town, bright sun and blue sky, the remaining colors of maples, sweet gums, oaks, redbuds vibrant. I surprised a monarch butterfly along Livermore Street. Statistics for the end of the month: October 2020 was just .9 degrees above normal, 54.8, but rainfall was 4.53 inches, 1.60 inches above average, making up some for last month's shortfall.

2021: After three days of rain, mostly sunny: Lil's tree is gilding in the sunlight. Full color all around. This month's average temperature was 62.4, six degrees above normal.

2022: Mild, misty, gentle, peeping robins, ginkgoes with golden skirts and still shedding, burning bush shrub foliage collapsing as the ginkgoes go, white mulberries and Osage full yellow, redbuds browning, light rain blending all the shades of the day. And Emily writes: "Around 30 juncos were in my backyard this morning. And last week the white throated sparrows came back and started singing again." Casey mentioned bluebirds in his yard a few days ago, and John has seen another bald eagle. Average temperature for the month was 54.7, close to normal, but rainfall was less than an inch. Traces of snow were reported on October 17, 18 and 19.

2023: Chris Walker reported seeing a small flock of sandhill cranes this past week, the earliest so far in my local history. First hard frost, temperature to 26 degrees. All the Paulownia leaves came down in the course of an hour after dawn. The castor bean plants are finished now for the year. The quince tree by the pond is full bright yellow, the brightest in the neighborhood. Average temperature for the month: 57.0 degree, precipitation 2.47 inches after a very dry start to the mo th.

Some Notes on Peak Leaf Color

Even though "peak color" occurs in the eye of the beholder and depends on which kinds of trees are observed where, the following list represents an attempt to place October's best coloration in perspective.

October 3, 1987 and 2013: First phase of early peak leaf color began today.

October 4, 1991: Peak leaf color began yesterday, coinciding with a number of opossums killed on the highway overnight. Is there a connection between the opossums and the leaves? Why wouldn't there be a connection?

October 5, 2012: Peak leaf color spreading so quickly.

October 9, 1994: Peak leaf color from Yellow Springs to Columbus, the late ashes blending with the best of the maples.

October 12, 1989: Now it seems to be early peak leaf color just before the real decadence of full Middle Fall.

October 13, 1999: Peak leaf color throughout the area now, many of the first and second foliage tiers holding as the maples turn.

October 14, 2022: Peak leaf color estimate near today.

October 15, 1984: Peak leaf color ended today, the maples shedding quickly.

October 16, 1983: Peak leaf color is starting.
            2020: Peak leaf color well underway.
            2023: Peak leaf color began suddenly.

October 18, 1979, 1987, 1988 and 1992: Peak leaf color throughout the county.

October 20. 1995: Peak leaf color in the maples now.

October 19, 1998: Peak leaf color all the way west through Indiana.

October 22, 1980, 2014, 2015, 2017, 2019 2020: Peak leaf color time.

October 28, 2018: Peak leaf color in the rain.

October 29, 1983: Where maples dominate, peak color holds.

October 31, 2021: Peak leaf color from northern counties has gradually overwhelmed the reluctant changes in and around Yellow Springs. Halloween full color.

All heart's ease be your days; no leaf of rue
Darken the nosegay Time shall cull for you!

James Russell Lowell

Bill Felker has been writing nature columns and almanacs for newspapers and magazines since 1984. The radio version of his commentary can be heard weekly on WYSO, a National Public Radio station, and it is available on podcast at **www.wyso.org.** His collections of essays, *Home is the Prime Meridian: Essays in Search of Time and Place and Spirit, Deep Time Is in the Garden: New Essays in Search of Time and Place and Spirit,* and *The Virgin Point: Meditations in Nature,* along with the entire twelve volumes of *A Daybook for the Year in Yellow Springs* are available on Amazon.

For more information, visit **www.poorwillsalmanack.com.**